The Juicy Parts

The Juicy Parts

Things Your History Teacher
Never Told You
About the 20th Century's
Most Famous People

JACK MINGO

A PERIGEE BOOK

A Perigee Book
Published by The Berkley Publishing Group
200 Madison Avenue
New York, NY 10016

Copyright © 1996 by Jack Mingo
Book design by Irving Perkins Associates
Cover design by Dale Fiorillo

First edition: August 1996

Published simultaneously in Canada.

The Putnam Berkley World Wide Web site address is
http://www.berkley.com

Library of Congress Cataloging-in-Publication Data

Mingo, Jack.
    The juicy parts : things your history teacher never told you about
  the 20th century's most famous people / Jack Mingo.
      p. cm.
    "A Perigee book."
    Includes bibliographical references.
    ISBN 0-7394-0267-6
    1. Celebrities—Biography.   2. Biography—20th century.
  I. Title.
  CT120.M56   1996
  920.073—dc20
    [B]   95-52132
                                                              CIP

Printed in the United States of America

10 9 8 7 6 5 4 3 2 1

Contents

Contributors

When I decided it would be interesting to recruit help for researching and writing this book, I put out a call for volunteers in writers' hangouts on America Online and on the Usenet "misc.writing" newsgroup. I found some remarkable, persistent, and talented assistance. This research and writing team kept in contact by the magic of E-mail and the U.S. Postal Service.

To the people who helped research, fact-check, write, and edit, I feel a great sense of gratitude, friendship, and affection, despite having met only one of you face-to-face. I thank you for your contributions.

Far Beyond the Call of Duty

Kathy Vincent, Winston-Salem, NC

Very Special Contributors

Chris Koloske, Fremont, CA
Marja Moyer, Fremont, CA

Writers and Researchers

Scott Berkun, Redmond, WA
Earl Blanchard, Fort Pierce, FL
Connie Brown, Sterling Heights, MI
Jon Campbell, Chandler, AZ
Annette Couch-Jareb, Charlottesville, VA
D. L. Crockford, Seattle, WA

Linda Cunningham, Falls Church, VA
Tyrone D'Souza, Mississauga, Ontario
Donna Diehl, Dallas, TX
James A. Gardner, Fowler, IN
Valerie Gaston, St. Louis, MO
Kelli L. Hendrickson, Watertown, MA
Mike Huber, Milwaukee, WI
P. R. Kingston, Oakhurst, NJ
Kate Kruley, Newark, CA
Maureen Moran, Menlo Park, CA
Kathy Naugle, Cleveland, OH
Verla Negus, Pocatello, ID
Nancy Newcomer, Fountain Hills, AZ
Linda Noble, Akron, OH
Kelli O'Connell, Trent University, Ontario
John Olsen, Orem, UT
Ben Ostrowsky, Miami Springs, FL
Eva Solano, Dallas, TX
Radhika Sivaramakrishna, Winnipeg, Manitoba
Steven Tidd, Cocoa, FL
Marisa Trevino, Dallas, TX

Special Thanks for Other Contributions

John Javna
Nuna and Elana Mingo
Roger Mingo
Jim Trupin
Heather Jackson
Jennifer Lata
Pierre Bourque
John Dollison
Lenna Lebovich
Sarah Cahill
And the amusing folks on misc.writing

Foreword

Biographies: People love to read them. And why not? We can learn a lot from studying the lives of the famous and infamous.

I used to especially like to borrow biographies from certain friends and acquaintances who had the habit of marking the good parts: the strange coincidences, unusual friendships, furtive affairs, drugs, strange philosophies, ironies, contradictions, lies, loves, hates, and passions of famous and accomplished people. Sometimes I could find out as much as I wanted to know simply by reading the sections that my friends had marked.

I enjoyed my friends' notations because standard, six-hundred-page biographical tomes required wading through a whole lot of extraneous and boring information, useful only if you're working on your doctorate: the subjects' family histories, their babyhood, how many times they moved when they were kids, where they went to school, and on and on. Absolutely essential to a full biography, but not always so interesting.

Admittedly, there are times when I, as a reader, want to know every step someone took from conception to death. But not that often. Usually, I just want to know some fascinating and unusual details that'll amaze me and impress my friends.

I think most casual readers go through biographies with some of the same impulses in mind, looking for the "juicy parts"—the interesting details that they never knew before. That's the idea behind this book: to extract the facts that were never covered in the required reading at school, the parts you might mention during a conversation to astonish and amuse your friends and colleagues. Did you know that Harpo Marx was a member of the Algonquin Round Table and best buddies with George Bernard Shaw? Did you know that Henry Ford, Walt Disney, Charles Lindbergh, and Winston Churchill were notorious anti-Semites? Have you heard about Howard Hughes's longtime affair . . . with Cary Grant? Do you know what Michael Jackson reputedly has tattooed next to his genitals, or why Muhammad Ali only kissed "ugly" women?

Think of me as your friend, going through the books and marking the really good parts for you, separating the wheat from the chaff, the gold from the ore . . . or the "juicy parts" from the pulp. This little collection of fascinating facts is not what you would read if you wanted to pass a history exam—but it might be just the thing you need if you want to pass an evening with your friends.

Jack Mingo
Alameda, California

The Marx Brothers

The Marx Brothers—Groucho, Chico, Harpo, and sometimes Gummo or Zeppo—started in vaudeville and rapidly became the premier comedy troupe of the 1930s and 1940s. Their movies are considered classics of slapstick and surrealism.

• When the Marx brothers were growing up in Brooklyn in the 1890s, magician Harry Houdini lived across the street.

• Who was the oldest brother? Most people guess fast-talking Groucho, but he's not. First was Manfred, who died without a nickname at age one, then Leonard (Chico), Adolph (Harpo), Julius (Groucho), Milton (Gummo), and Herbert (Zeppo).

• The brothers' nicknames were given to them in 1914 from monologist Art Fisher during a backstage poker game in Galesburg, Illinois. As Fisher dealt the cards, he also began dealing nicknames: "Harpo" for the harp-playing brother, "Groucho" for the gloomy brother (or, some say, because he carried the "grouchsack" that held the brothers' money), "Chicko" for the notorious womanizer (a printer's error changed the spelling somewhere along the line, although the pronunciation stayed the same), and "Gummo" for the gumshoes that hypochondriac Milton wore constantly to ward off colds. When Herbert joined the group, his older brothers named him "Zippo" after a famous trained monkey. "Please, it's *Zep*po," he would retort in a mock snob voice.

- Groucho came to hate his adopted name. "It's terrible," he told an interviewer. "It sounds like I'm the kind of guy who goes around whipping little children."

- Harpo dropped out of school in the second grade because two of his classmates kept throwing him out the window every time the teacher left the room. Chico, a math whiz, quit school when he was twelve to become a full-time pool hustler and gambler. Chico had begun gambling compulsively at age nine. During his lifetime, he lost about two million dollars. Harpo had to come out of retirement and perform with him in comeback tours during his later years so Chico wouldn't die broke.

- As kids, Harpo and Chico both played piano in a whorehouse. Chico did fine, but Harpo was at a disadvantage: he knew only two songs and played them over and over again at different tempos.

- The first time the young brothers ever saw a urinal was during their cousin Polly's wedding reception. They jumped on top of it, breaking it off the wall, unleashing a flood. The bridegroom had to pay for damages before the reception could continue.

- When he was ten, Groucho was caught stealing a $1.98 toy printing press from Bloomingdale's. The floorwalker let him go, but told him to never set foot in the store again. He took the warning to heart and didn't go into the store until seventy years later.

- Chico was exceptionally "well endowed," according to Groucho. He also was a notorious philanderer, cheating on his wife even during their honeymoon. Said Groucho, "Chico was a character. By the time any show opened he'd already have had sex with half the chorus. Women were crazy about him. He'd walk up to a girl and say, 'Do you fuck?' And many times they said yes."

- Groucho wasn't so lucky. He had sex for the first time when he was sixteen. It was with a prostitute in Ottawa while he was traveling the vaudeville circuit with his brothers. He immediately came down with syphilis. He was also afflicted with an extreme case of premature ejaculation all his life. When he was dating Eden Hartford, the woman who would become his third wife, he gave her money after every date. "Since I'm a very bad lay," he told her lawyer Marvin Mitchelson in a deposition, "she was entitled to this."

● Chico would pass girls down to his brothers, and often all four would share one girlfriend. In at least one case, a woman got pregnant and the four decided the fairest thing to do was to split the abortionist's bill among themselves.

● Harpo's first near-sexual experience came at age thirteen: "At the top of the stairs, a fat woman smoking a cigarette gave me a towel, took my fifty cents, and told me to go to room number two," he wrote. "The open doorway of room number two was as close as I ever got to the promised land. Inside, a naked woman lay on an iron bed, her knees raised and her legs spread apart. I never saw her face. She said 'Next? Come *on*, for Christ's sake!' I took one look and dropped the towel and ran down the stairs and out the back door."

● Years later, while doing the run of the play *A Day at the Races* in Chicago, Harpo bought a full-sized teakwood penis from a novelty dealer. Backstage, he convinced a chorus girl to engage in a quick go-round and surreptitiously employed the wooden penis instead of his own. After several thrusts, he stopped and said, "Gee, it's drafty in here. I think I'll close the window." He jumped up without removing the wooden dildo, and the woman fainted.

● In Harpo's professional debut with the Marx Brothers, he looked out at the audience . . . and immediately wet his pants.

● Gummo hated the stage. For one thing, he had a terrible stammer which got worse in performance. He read dictionaries constantly and developed a huge vocabulary so that he could pull a synonym out of the air for any word that might make him stutter.

He retired from the act as soon as Zeppo was old enough to take his place, and started a company to manufacture ladies' dresses.

• Zeppo also retired after a few years. He started a company that became the world's largest manufacturer of coupling devices. It made the clamps that secured the atomic bombs for their flights to Hiroshima and Nagasaki.

• It's been reported that Harpo never spoke in performance from 1914 until he announced his retirement from the stage fifty years later. But that's not technically true. He and Chico looked and sounded so much alike that they decided once to exchange characters during the long Broadway run of *The Cocoanuts*. Harpo got dressed like Chico and talked in an Italian accent all night. Chico ran around with a red wig and horn. Nobody noticed the difference.

• Zeppo, despite his image as a not-too-bright straight man, was equally flexible. During the stage run of *Animal Crackers*, Groucho was rushed to the hospital for an emergency appendectomy. Zeppo put on Groucho's makeup and played his wisecracking role, complete with ad-libs. Again, nobody was the wiser.

• It's surprising that Harpo was able to make such beautiful music. Self-taught, he had come up with an idiosyncratic way of holding his harp, and most of its strings were tuned completely wrong.

• Margaret Dumont, the butt of the brothers' jokes on-screen, was never told what was going to happen to her—her script showed only her lines, not the action. That was because they wanted her surprise, distress, and dignified fury to be absolutely genuine when, for instance, they dropped her unexpectedly into water during a boat scene.

• Dumont's distress was real offscreen as well. The Marxes would pull cruel practical jokes on her that would leave her in tears. In one fancy hotel, the brothers almost got the straitlaced lady arrested for prostitution. Another time on a train, they stripped the pants off a hapless railroad conductor and threw him on top of Dumont who was sleeping soundly in her berth. She became hysterical. Dumont quit a number of times, but allowed herself to be wooed back because she needed the work and because the studio kept falsely promising that in her next movie she would get to play a serious character part.

● The jokes in the Marx Brothers' movies were subjected to sophisticated market research. The brothers would take the movie out on the road as a live show before shooting began and test gags on live audiences. Their reaction would determine which jokes would be used when the movie was finally shot. They would even try different variations of the same joke: "I'd rather have it rusted than *missing*," for instance, was found to get more laughs than "I'd rather have it rusted than *gone*."

● The only Marx Brothers' movies Groucho could stand to watch, he said, were *A Night at the Opera* and, to a lesser degree, *A Day at the Races*.

● *Love Happy* was so badly underfinanced that the producer invented what is now known as "product placement." He devised a rooftop chase scene from one neon sign to another—the whole thing was one long commercial that corporations paid money to be a part of.

● Groucho had once been excluded from a resort because he was Jewish, leading to his famous quip: "Since my children are only half-Jewish, can they go into the water up to their knees?" When he joined an all-Jewish country club, he and Harpo led a successful drive to include gentile members. One of the first to join was Danny Thomas.

● Groucho ate his first bagel at age eighty-one.

● Groucho was great at ad-libbing, but not as good as he looked on his TV quiz show *You Bet Your Life*. He had several writers who carefully crafted his spontaneous quips and projected them by overhead projector onto a screen right behind the contestants.

Also, the show was filmed long and then heavily edited down to its best parts.

● Groucho's favorite songwriters: Gilbert and Sullivan. Vegetable: lima beans. Book: *Charlotte's Web*. He was a prolific letter-writer, and one of his pen pals was poet T. S. Eliot.

● Harpo once went to the fourteenth tee of the golf course near his house with a golf club and dozens of balls. He stripped off his clothes and began shooting balls toward the hole, attempting, he said, to become the first naked man to hit a hole in one.

● When Harpo first met George Bernard Shaw, Harpo was wrapped in a towel, having just emerged from a nude swim. Shaw held out his hand as if to shake Harpo's, but at the last second jerked Harpo's towel off him. "And this," the seventy-four-year-old playwright said, a twinkle in his eye, "is Mrs. Shaw." Harpo and the Shaws became fast friends.

● It probably served Harpo right. He and his brothers often pulled a similar trick, suddenly ripping the clothes off male acquaintances and leaving them standing in their underwear or less.

● Visiting the French Riviera, Harpo found he was being excluded from restaurants and casinos because he wasn't wearing a dinner jacket. He went to a tailor and had one made . . . out of green pool-table felt.

● Harpo was a member of the famous "Algonquin Round Table" along with Dorothy Parker and the rest. It was about this time that fellow members Moss Hart and George Kaufman wrote *The Man Who Came to Dinner* with thinly disguised characters Sheridan Whiteside, based on Alexander Woollcott, and the illiterate practical joker, Banjo, based on Harpo. According to Groucho, Woollcott's attraction to Harpo was more than friendship: "Woollcott was in love with Harpo."

● Author and publisher of the *Realist*, Paul Krassner, wrote that he once dropped LSD with Groucho in the mid-1960s.

• About that same time, the Nixon administration looked into prosecuting Groucho for making threats against the president. He was quoted in an interview in an underground newspaper as saying, "I think the only hope this country has is in Nixon's assassination." Groucho disavowed the quote, saying, "I deny everything, because I never tell the truth." Nonetheless, Marx's name went into a file numbered CO1297009205 as a potential threat. Actual prosecution for the felony offense was stopped by cooler heads in the administration, who realized that it would be a public relations disaster to take the popular elderly comedian to court.

Fidel Castro

Fidel Castro led a successful revolution in Cuba in 1958 and has ruled there for more than three and a half decades, despite repeated U.S. efforts to overthrow or kill him.

• Fidel Castro grew up in an affluent family, one of seven children. His father, Angel Castro y Argiz, worked for the United Fruit Company (which Castro eventually had thrown out of Cuba). For decades, United Fruit executives who knew Angel couldn't help but shake their heads and wonder how his quiet, polite son could have gone so bad.

• Besides the seven children, the Castro house had a flock of chickens living inside it.

• When Castro was a child, other children called him "Judio" (the Jew) because he wasn't baptized until he was six.

• At age ten, Castro got appendicitis and spent three months in the hospital. After that, he wanted to work in medicine: "Some people thought I might make a good doctor, because I used to play with lizards and a Gillette razor blade," he told an interviewer. "I had been impressed by the operations like the one I'd been through and after that I would 'operate' on lizards—lizards that usually died, of course. Then I would enjoy watching how the ants carried them off, how hundreds of ants working together could carry the lizard and move it to their heap."

• Known as "El Loco Fidel," he was so competitive in basketball games that he would forget which side he was playing for, switching sides and making baskets for the other team.

• Castro organized a baseball team and was its pitcher, even though he had an out-of-control fastball. When his team wasn't winning, Castro would simply halt the game and go home. He claimed years later that a scout had tried to recruit him for the American major leagues.

• In 1940, as a teenager, Castro wrote a letter to Franklin D. Roosevelt. "My good friend Roosevelt: I don't know very English, but I know as much as I write to you. I like to hear the radio, and I am very happy, because I heard in it that you will be president of a new era. I am a boy but I think very much but I do not think that I am writing to the President of the United States. If you like, give me a ten dollars bill green american, in the letter, because never, I have not seen a ten dollars bill green american and I would like to have one of them." He received a letter back thanking him for his "letter of support and congratulations," but no ten-dollar bill.

• For his honeymoon, Castro and his new wife, Mirta, traveled to New York City for three months, courtesy of his new father-in-law. A friend of both families gave the couple one thousand dollars for spending money. His name? Fulgencio Batista, who would later become Cuban president and be overthrown by Castro's revolutionaries. In New York, Castro used part of the money to buy a huge white Lincoln Continental.

• The Castros' first son, Fidelito, was a healthy baby, but then he suddenly became gravely ill. Doctors were mystified until Mirta discovered that Fidel was force-feeding his son three times the recommended concentration of formula so that his son would grow bigger and stronger than other children. She stopped the overfeeding then—and again, a few months later, when Fidel began doing it again.

• On Castro's first revolutionary attack on a military post, he forgot his glasses. As a result, he could barely drive to the post, much less aim his gun accurately.

• He was jailed after the attack. His marriage began breaking up when he failed to follow a cardinal rule of prison: Don't write to your wife and your mistress on the same day. The prison censor switched the two letters when he put them back in their envelopes.

• While training his revolutionaries in mountain camps, he confiscated all shaving supplies, toothpaste and brushes, and soap, saying true revolutionaries don't concern themselves with personal hygiene.

• Castro, knowing the power of the American press to mold opinions, once tricked Herbert Matthews, a *New York Times* reporter, into thinking he had hundreds of soldiers when he had only twenty by having them march into a clearing by ones and twos, and then march in again and again. One man had a shirt without a back, so he had to march sideways. Che Guevara then had a man come running into the clearing, feigning exhaustion, to report on a completely fictitious Army Number 2. Matthews wrote an article saying that Castro's band was so large that "General Batista cannot hope to suppress Castro's revolt."

• The Cuban Communist Party opposed Castro's rebellion, saying armed struggle was futile. On the other hand, it was supported by the Havana Lions and Rotary Club.

• In those tense, prerevolutionary times, Johnny Weissmuller, taking a break from playing Tarzan in the movies, was participating in a Cuban golf tournament. Suddenly, he was surrounded by a group of Castro's soldiers who had emerged from the rough near the fourteenth hole. Weissmuller pulled himself up to full height, beat his chest, and let out a Tarzan yell. After a shocked pause, the rebels shouted in delight, "Tarzan! Tarzan! *Bienvenido!* Welcome!"

• After Batista fled Cuba, mobs went around breaking up casinos, which they saw as symbols of the American Mafia that had run Cuba for so long. Tough-guy actor George Raft owned the Capri Hotel. When an angry mob began storming the front steps, he snarled at them in his famous gangster voice, "Yer not comin' in my casino!" The people stopped at the well-known voice and retreated.

• After the revolution, Castro came again to New York where he was wined and dined by members of American high society—so much so that his brother Raul called from Cuba to ask if he were selling Cuba out to the Americans. His entourage went down in New York history as the ones who plucked chickens in the city's hotels. At the time, it was assumed that the chickens were for eating—in fact, some of them were sacrificed in *Santería* rituals. Like many Cubans, Castro dabbles in the *Santería* religion. He has a mystical attachment to the number 26, picking the twenty-sixth day of a month for major speeches, decisions, and actions.

• The Bay of Pigs invasion by the United States was such a talked-about "secret" in Miami's Little Havana that Cuban intelligence agents assumed it was some sort of disinformation campaign. On the morning before the invasion, Castro aide Carlos Franqui received a call from a *New York Times* reporter asking if he had any news about "an invasion of the island," but the security breach didn't do much harm—Castro had already stationed troops at the landing site.

• Castro fancies himself quite a lady's man. In fact, there are dozens of children in Cuba who claim him as father. But his technique? One purported lover, a dancer at the Tropicana Hotel, said he read while he made love. A French actress complained that he smoked his damned cigar during the act. An American woman said he never took his boots off. Other women said he took them to romantic spots and then only talked for hours on end about things like agricultural reform.

Marilyn Monroe

Marilyn Monroe was more than a movie star. She shook up the sexually repressed 1950s and became an archetype for a series of blonde bombshell imitators who followed her.

- On June 1, 1926, a star was born, with the unlikely name of Norma Jean Mortenson. Her mother, Gladys Pearl Monroe Baker Mortenson, was a film-negative cutter in Hollywood. Her father could have been any of several men that her mother was sleeping with at the time. Gladys gave her daughter the last name of her second husband, who she was in the process of divorcing, and a first name from film star Norma Talmadge. (Ironically, Talmadge's husband, producer Joseph Schenck, would be the first to initiate Marilyn Monroe into the ways of the casting couch.)

- Two weeks after Norma Jean's birth, she was placed with a foster family with whom she'd live for the next seven years. Albert and Ida Bolender were strictly religious, teaching Norma Jean that even going to the movies was a sin. They were admirers of the charismatic evangelist Aimee Semple McPherson, and took Norma Jean to see her. (Coincidentally, up-and-coming comedian Milton Berle was having an affair with McPherson at about that time; years later, he would do the same with Monroe.)

- Norma Jean's closest playmate was a stray dog she adopted and named Tippy. Just after her seventh birthday, a neighbor became angry at the dog's barking and killed him with a shotgun. That same day her mother suddenly came back into Norma Jean's life, helped her bury her dog, and took her back to live with her.

● Gladys, still working as a film cutter, used movie houses as a form of day care for her daughter during the summer, knowing that Norma Jean would stay cool and safe there while she worked. Her mom's relaxed, amoral life shocked Norma Jean. The devout seven-year-old spent hours praying that her mother and friends wouldn't be condemned to hell.

● In early 1934 Gladys went into a deep depression and was institutionalized in Los Angeles General Hospital. Norma Jean stayed with Grace McKee, her mom's friend and roommate, until McKee married Ervin Goddard. Because neither newlywed was working, Goddard insisted that Norma Jean be put into an orphanage. She stayed there for two years before going back to live with them.

● After seeing several Jean Harlow pictures, McKee encouraged ten-year-old Norma Jean to emulate the actress, buying her white clothes only and dyeing her hair platinum blond.

● Shortly after Norma Jean returned to McKee's house, Goddard, drunk one night, groped her and tried to force himself on her. She escaped from the house. When she told McKee, she was shipped off to live with an aunt and uncle. The uncle not long after went out to buy a newspaper . . . and never came back. Norma Jean vowed at that point that she would never get married—that she was going to become a schoolteacher and have lots of dogs, instead. It was about this time, too, that she came up with the idea that Clark Gable was her biological father.

● According to Monroe, a cousin raped her when she was eleven. (Her first husband, on the other hand, claimed that she was a virgin at the time of their wedding.)

- In high school Norma Jean wrote news features for the school paper, concluding in one that "53% of the gentlemen prefer blondes as their dream girl."

- Norma Jean left school at age sixteen to marry twenty-one-year-old Jim Dougherty. She tried unsuccessfully to negotiate that they marry but not have sex.

- In April 1944 Norma Jean took a wartime job spraying varnish on fuselage fabric. She became a parachute inspector. Soon after, she was discovered by an army camera crew doing a "girls of the war effort" photo spread for GI morale.

- In August 1945 she applied for representation by the Blue Book Modeling Agency, which catalogued her height (5'5"), weight (118 lbs), measurements (36-24-34), size (12), hair color (medium blond), eyes (blue), and teeth ("perfect"). The agency's owner saw potential but thought that Norma Jean was "too plump" and that she "smiled too high on her face."

- By the spring of 1946 she had appeared on thirty-three magazine covers, including *Parade*, *Glamorous Models*, and *Personal Romances*—so many that she couldn't get work for a while because she was considered "overexposed." She had an affair with at least one photographer, and in September was granted a divorce from Dougherty.

- She was signed by Fox Studio that year. Executive Ben Lyon demanded that she change her name. She decided on her mother's maiden name, Monroe. Lyon suggested "Marilyn" after an old girlfriend, actress Marilyn Miller. (In 1956 Monroe legally changed her name.)

- Fox declined to renew her contract. Monroe spent all of her small income on acting classes, rent, and car maintenance. She filled the gaps by providing quick in-car sex off Hollywood Boulevard in exchange for restaurant meals.

• In 1948 she got a movie part at Columbia, arranged by Joseph Schenck after she performed oral sex on him for the first time. The relationship continued, the seventy-year-old man fondling her breasts, talking about the good old days of moviemaking. He was the first of a string of movie executives and other well-connected men with whom she had sex, including Johnny Hyde, executive vice president of the William Morris Agency. Finally, after signing her first big contract, Monroe reportedly exclaimed to friends, "That's the last cock I'll have to suck!"

• With roommate Shelley Winters, Monroe began compiling a list of men she wanted to have sex with. At the top of the list was genius mathematician Albert Einstein. (Whether it happened, nobody knows for sure, but later Winters came across an autographed photo of Einstein inscribed, "With respect and love and thanks.") Celebrities she successfully pursued include Marlon Brando, a Kennedy or two, Yves Montand, Frank Sinatra, Joe DiMaggio, and Arthur Miller.

• At Columbia her hairline was permanently heightened by electrolysis, and she became a blonde. Drama coach Natasha Lytess taught her an overexaggerated, breathy emphasis on each syllable which became so habitual that later she would have to go to another coach to get rid of it. Her music arranger, vocal coach, and lover Fred Karger paid for the correction of an overbite and to have her teeth bleached. Johnny Hyde arranged plastic surgery to remove a small lump of cartilage from the tip of her nose and insert a crescent-shaped silicone implant into her jaw to give it a softer line. She lifted weights to improve her bust line, and jogged through the alleys of Beverly Hills each morning—neither activity commonly undertaken by anyone, much less a woman, in 1950.

• She had a succession of dogs given to her by lovers. One she named Josefa after Joseph Schenck. Another, given to her by Frank Sinatra, she named "Maf," short for "Mafia." She was never very good at house-training them, trying the patience of her housekeepers and friends.

• Monroe was so anxious about acting that she would vomit before she went on the set. But she could be tough as well. While filming a movie in 1952, she was diagnosed with acute appendicitis. She asked to be given antibiotics and delay the operation until after the movie was finished. She returned to work and didn't have her appendix removed until nearly two months later.

• She learned her seductive "swivel" while filming a movie in which she had to walk down a cobblestone street in high heels. After she saw the reaction from onlookers, she used that walk from that day on. When asked if her walk was natural, she quipped, "I've been walking since I was six months old." The Tokyo press dubbed Monroe "Honorable Buttocks-Swinging Actress."

• She didn't wear any underwear, a custom very rare in 1952. The dress she wore in *Gentlemen Prefer Blondes* was so tight that she had to be sewn into it.

• She met Joe DiMaggio after he had retired from baseball. She was twenty-five, he was thirty-seven. DiMaggio had sought her out after he saw a cheesecake photo of her batting in a short-skirted baseball outfit. Because of the photo, he thought—erroneously it turns out—that she was a big baseball fan.

• At their wedding Monroe turned to DiMaggio and asked him if she died before him, would he place flowers at her grave every week—just as William Powell had done at the grave of Jean Harlow. DiMaggio promised, and even though they parted after a messy divorce he continued to do so.

• Their first night of married life was spent in a six dollar motel room with a double bed and (upon DiMaggio's insistence) a television set. Their second night was spent near Palm Springs, where DiMaggio demanded that their room be changed when he discovered that its TV reception was lousy.

• After returning from her honeymoon with DiMaggio, Monroe told a friend that she was going to marry Arthur Miller next.

• Monroe said DiMaggio's reaction to her work was that "he didn't like the women I played—he thought they were sluts. He didn't like the actors kissing me, and he didn't like my costumes. He didn't like anything about my movies, and he hated all my clothes." The famous "blowing skirt" scene brought matters to a head in September 1954 and DiMaggio reportedly got violent, causing bruises on her shoulders that had to be covered up with makeup. Two weeks later, Monroe filed for divorce.

• In 1955 the FBI opened a file on her because of her association with playwright Arthur Miller, whose play *The Crucible* was meant as an allegory for the McCarthy witch-hunts.

• Monroe married Miller in June 1956. At the last minute, Monroe told friends that she didn't want to marry Miller, but would go through with it because she didn't want to disappoint the wedding guests.

• Miller had second thoughts as well, writing in his journal that he feared his writing would be threatened by her continuous emotional demands. Sure enough, he immediately sunk into a bad case of writer's block. Finally, Monroe convinced him to write a script for *The Misfits* for her. As their relationship deteriorated, he continually rewrote the script, making her character more and more unsympathetic.

• After *Some Like It Hot*, Tony Curtis said that kissing her was like "kissing Hitler."

• In 1961 Monroe signed herself into the Payne Whitney Clinic for detoxification. To her horror she was locked into a padded room, stripped of her clothes and purse, and threatened with a straitjacket when she objected. She was there for two days and nights, until DiMaggio came to get her out.

• According to biographer Donald Spoto, based on the best evidence available and her conversations with friends, Monroe had only one sexual encounter with John F. Kennedy, and she never slept with Bobby Kennedy because she didn't find him physically appealing. However, she found him to be a sympathetic listener, and so began calling his office switchboard repeatedly to talk, to the point that the attorney general started avoiding the calls.

- On May 19, 1962, when she was scheduled to sing "Happy Birthday" to the president, she was over an hour tardy. As a joke, Peter Lawford announced her as "the late Marilyn Monroe."

- Monroe had several therapy sessions with Sigmund Freud's daughter, Anna.

- She started seeing a psychotherapist named Ralph Greenson, who relied heavily on drug therapy, routinely prescribing barbiturates and tranquilizers. He told her to visit him at his house instead of his office, and convinced her that she needed to see him every day. Right before her death, Greenson was injecting her with drugs at least once a day, and gave her prescriptions for Nembutal.

- DiMaggio and Monroe were scheduled to be remarried when she died.

- Monroe's last known words were to Peter Lawford, in a voice slurred and almost inaudible. "Say good-bye to Pat, say good-bye to the president, and say good-bye to yourself, because you're a nice guy."

- Was Monroe murdered because she "knew too much"? Although there are a number of unlikely conspiracy theories about her death, the most credible evidence, according to biographer Spoto, suggests that Greenson administered barbiturates or chloral hydrate as an enema (evidenced by the coroner's report that her colon bore "marked congestion and purplish discoloration") which, combined with the Nembutal she had taken earlier, killed her. Greenson and the housekeeper he had hired to keep an eye on her then tried to cover up his error, says Spoto, resulting in various contradictory accounts that have fed the conspiracy theories.

• At her funeral, the organist played "Over the Rainbow."

• When Monroe's estate was finally appraised in 1963, it was valued at a comparatively modest $92,781 (or about $390,000 in 1996 dollars).

Steven Jobs and Stephen Wozniak

Steve Jobs and Steve Wozniak set off the personal computer revolution when they started the Apple Computer company while still in their early twenties. Their Apple II introduced the first computer designed for home use; the Macintosh created a revolution in creative applications like desktop publishing, computer graphics, and computerized music-making.

● The Apple Computer was not the first time the two Steves teamed up in business. The first time was to commit a felony. While Wozniak was living in a dorm at the University of California, he built a "blue box" that allowed one to use AT&T's equipment to make free phone calls. Jobs supplied the parts, Wozniak supplied the labor, and the two sold hundreds of the devices for $150 each in UC's male dorms and through a friend in Beverly Hills. Although they were never caught, some of their customers were, including swindler Bernie Cornfeld and musician Ike Turner.

● Meanwhile, Jobs went off to an avant-garde college in Oregon where he adopted a diet from the writings of Arnold Ehret, a nineteenth-century Prussian who taught that the key to health, happiness and mental stability was the systematic elimination of mucus, excrement and gas from the body. It didn't take long before Jobs left college and moved back in with his parents.

● Jobs talked his way into a five-dollar-an-hour technician's job at Atari, maker of the first successful video game, Pong. Within days, he managed to alienate nearly all of his coworkers by poking his nose into their work and telling them what "dumb shits" they were. Jobs—unkempt and sloppy, even by computer programmer standards—figured his fruity, "no-mucus" diet eliminated his need for bathing. His supervisor, Al Alcorn, moved him to a (one-man) night shift, noting that "the engineers didn't like him, and he smelled funny."

● Night work meant that nobody was looking over his shoulder. Good thing, too, since Jobs wasn't a particularly brilliant worker. He was assigned to work on engineering a game called Breakout, which was a Ponglike handball game with a wall of bricks, each brick disappearing when hit by the "ball." Jobs tried to do the work himself, but discovering that he was in over his head, he appealed to Wozniak for help. Ever-trusting Wozniak agreed to do the job. Jobs agreed to split the fee, which he said would be $700. "Steve wasn't able to design anything that complex," said Wozniak later. "I designed the game thinking that he was going to sell it to Atari for $700 and that I would receive $350. It wasn't until years later that I learned that he had actually sold the game for $7,000." Jobs also soaked up the credit for the game, never telling anybody at Atari about Wozniak's work.

● Wozniak dropped out of college and moved back in with his parents. He started hanging around with a bunch of computer hobbyists at the Homebrew Computer Club and decided to build a computer to impress them. It was the forerunner of the Apple I, but it didn't impress them all that much.

● Jobs, back from an Oregon farm commune, suggested that they start their own computer company. He wanted a name that would appear before Atari in the phone book. Remembering his happy days picking apples at the commune, he suggested Apple Computer.

● Wozniak wanted something more technical, like "Execuitek" or "Matrix Electronics." He was afraid that the Beatles might take them to court because of their Apple Corps trademark. (His fears were well founded. Twelve years later, in 1988, Apple Corps did indeed sue, claiming that the musical capabilities of the Macintosh broke a secret 1981 trademark agreement that Apple Computer would stay out of its music/entertainment turf). But Wozniak eventually agreed that he couldn't come up with anything any better than Apple, so that was the name they put on the paper when they signed an agreement on April Fools' Day 1976.

● The partners needed money for their first one hundred Apple I computer boards. Wozniak sold his prized HP-65 calculator for five hundred dollars; Jobs, not wanting to let on that he still had five thousand dollars in the bank from Atari, sold his VW van to raise his half.

● The Apple Computer company set up shop in the Jobs family garage and paid Steve's pregnant younger sister one dollar a board to insert capacitors and resistors into the boards. (She found she could do four boards an hour while watching soap operas and *The Gong Show*.)

● Wozniak met his wife through a Dial-a-Polish Joke phone line he set up in his office. She called and he got on the line and bantered with her. After a few minutes he blurted out, "I bet I can hang up faster than you can" . . . and did. A few days later she called back and they started going out on dates. Later, he flipped a coin to decide whether to ask her to marry him. He kept flipping until the coin indicated yes.

● Meanwhile, Wozniak started working on the Apple II. This time he was going to make a computer so impressive it would knock the socks off the blasé Homebrew members. It would have a keyboard and built-in BASIC software. It would have sound and color so he could play his Breakout game. And it would have a lot of slots to slide new boards in so it could be expanded and updated and customized. Jobs's contribution? The molded plastic case. It was a huge success.

• The problem was that, like many entrepreneurs, the two Steves were not able to handle success. Jobs seemed especially good at creating chaos and hard feelings. He was eventually forced out in a power play by new president John Sculley, to the relief of Apple's investors and most of its employees.

Agatha Christie

Agatha Christie is one of the most popular detective-fiction writers of all time, selling over two billion copies of her books in 104 languages. Still, nearly twenty years after her death, her own private mystery remains.

• Considered the "slow one" in her family, Agatha Christie was painfully shy and tongue-tied as a child. This persisted even after she became famous. At the tenth-anniversary celebration of her play *The Mousetrap*, Christie arrived early and alone. Not knowing who she was, the doorman refused to let her in. Instead of arguing, she just meekly turned away.

• When Christie was young she had a recurring nightmare of a figure carrying a gun and dressed as a soldier. In her autobiography, she stated that the "dream would be quite ordinary—a tea party, or a walk with various people, usually a mild festivity of some kind. Then suddenly a feeling of uneasiness would come. There was someone—someone who ought not to be there—a horrid feeling of fear: and then I would see him—sitting at the tea table, walking along the beach, joining in the game. His pale blue eyes would meet mine, and I would wake up shrieking: 'The Gunman, the Gunman!' "

• Writing started out as a lark for Christie. What she really wanted was to become a professional musician.

• Agatha started writing detective stories as a child to show up her sister, Madge. They were discussing Sherlock Holmes and other detectives one day when Agatha said that she would like to try her hand at writing a detective story. "I don't think you could do it," said Madge. "They are very difficult to do. I've thought about it."

• Christie wrote scores of successful books, creating memorable detectives like Hercule Poirot and Miss Jane Marple. She also wrote the popular play *The Mousetrap*, which has been seen by over 7.5 million people since it opened in November 1952. Royalties from the play, still running more than four decades later, go to Christie's grandson, Mathew, making him a multimillionaire.

• One of the most sensational and mysterious events in Christie's life was her eleven-day disappearance in December 1926, an incident still shrouded in mystery.

• Here's what happened: Shortly before Agatha's disappearance, her husband, Colonel Archibald Christie, told her that he had been having an affair for some time and that he wanted to divorce Agatha to marry the woman he really loved, Nancy Neele.

• Although her defenders believe that Agatha was suffering from some kind of mysterious amnesia, all available evidence suggests that she decided to use her expertise as a mystery writer to set up a scenario in which her husband would end up as the prime suspect in a murder case—with Agatha herself as the supposed victim. Then she could reappear, after he was convicted and executed, feigning amnesia.

• On a December night, Agatha's car was found at the bottom of a chalk pit in Newlands Corner, England. It was cold, and yet her fur coat had been left in the car. No driver was in sight, and the car's ignition was turned off, indicating that someone had pushed the car into the pit. The police suspected foul play.

• Agatha's husband was contacted by the police and later brought in for questioning. Where had he been that night? At a dinner party. What was the occasion? The colonel, abashed, admitted that it was a party to announce his engagement to his new love. And the dinner party had been held just a few miles from where his wife's car had been found. Had he and his wife been getting along? No, actually they had had a screaming battle about his infidelity the morning before Agatha's disappearance, a battle witnessed by several people.

• The detectives' questioning took a harder edge. Was he at the party all evening? No, he admitted. While at the party, he had received a call from his wife, who had found out what was going on. Agatha had threatened to come and make a scene. As the party continued, the colonel had made the hour-long drive home to try to placate his estranged wife. When he arrived, no one was there, so he went back to the party.

• The detectives let the colonel go, with the firm warning that he not leave town. Even he could see that things looked pretty damned suspicious. There was evidence of foul play, he had no alibi for a crucial period of time, and he appeared to have a clear motive.

• A massive search began for the missing Agatha. Two thousand people searched forty square miles of countryside and the police dragged nearby bodies of water, looking for Agatha's body.

• Agatha, meanwhile, had fled to the far side of England where she hid out in a hotel in Harrogate under the name of Mrs. Neele (the name of her husband's new love).

• She successfully hid there for eleven days. However, because of extensive front-page newspaper coverage and an offer of a reward, hotel employees recognized her and eagerly called the police. They contacted Colonel Christie, who rushed to Harrogate.

• The next day, the Christies left by the hotel's back door to escape the press. Reporters hotly pursued them to Cheshire, where they escaped to Agatha's sister's home.

• Two physicians were called in to examine Agatha. Shortly afterward, Archibald Christie stated that his wife had suffered from amnesia and remembered nothing of the events of the previous eleven days. She had no idea, he said, how the car got in the pit, why it was miles away from her home, how she got from one end of England to the other, or where she got the large sum of money that she used to rent her hotel room and buy an expensive new wardrobe.

• A skeptical press accused Agatha of playing an elaborate hoax that had cost the taxpayer thousands of pounds and the police and volunteers hours of needless labor. The novelist's extreme dislike of publicity throughout the rest of her life can perhaps be traced back not just to her natural shyness, but to the overdose of press attention she received at the time of her disappearance.

• That very unusual case of "amnesia" continued to hide the complete truth of those eleven days from her for the rest of her life, Agatha claimed. Her authorized biography said that, under psychotherapy, she regained *some* of her memories of staying in the hotel. But she never publicly spoke about the incident, even in an autobiography that she wrote intended for publication after her death.

Albert Einstein

Brilliant, absentminded, and wispy-haired, Albert Einstein became the archetype for the brainy, somewhat daft scientist.

- As a child, Albert Einstein was slow in learning to talk and walk. As he got older, his large feet made him waddle like a duck. He was extremely introspective, spending long hours watching ant colonies or trying to befriend the family's chickens. Most children in Ulm, Germany, found him a dull companion.

- At school, he was equally inattentive. He excelled at literature and mathematics but was dismal in all other subjects. Teachers called him "Herr Langweil," which roughly translates as "Mister Dullard." One teacher threatened to have him expelled, saying Einstein's "dreamy ho-hum attitude" was undermining his attempt to create a respectful class. Einstein hated the rigid school curriculum and refused to "pretend to learn."

- Although Einstein was Jewish, his family neither attended synagogue nor observed any of the dietary laws. Einstein attended a Catholic school. One traumatic year during Lent, his teacher held up three large rusty nails and told the students, "These were the nails the Jews used to crucify Jesus."

- As he grew up, Einstein was a lousy student who rarely took notes and often cut classes. He also had an attitude problem, preferring to work solutions out for himself instead of accepting the teacher's answer. "The problem is you don't think anyone has anything to tell you," scolded one teacher.

• When his father asked his headmaster what profession Albert should adopt, he got the answer, "It doesn't matter, he'll never make a success of anything."

• Einstein applied to the Federal Polytechnic Academy in Zurich, but flunked the entrance exam. One of the examiners noticed his brilliance in mathematics and recommended he go to a small liberal arts school; if he did well he could return to the Polytechnic in a year. Easy enough. A year later Einstein began a four-year course in physics.

• At college, he met Mileva Marić, who became his first wife. She was a bright and independent women who was studying to become a mathematics teacher. She and Einstein's best friend, Marcel Grossman, made sure that Einstein, perpetually lost in the world of physics, remembered to take care of basics like eating and going to classes.

• After Einstein graduated in 1900, he couldn't find a teaching job, so while he continued to work on his theories at night, he was employed in the Swiss patent office by day. Finally, in 1905 he published five papers that shook the physics world. The first paper, on molecular dimensions, earned him his doctorate; the other four explained Brownian motion, photons, and relativity. He began teaching theoretical physics in Zurich in 1909.

• Einstein and Marić had two sons, the younger of whom was schizophrenic and spent most of his life living either with his mother or in an institution.

• Einstein's second wife, Elsa, also had to protect him from his absentmindedness. Once when Einstein was sick and confined to his bed, Elsa banned paper and pencils from his room to keep him from working. She allowed a small group of students to visit him on the condition that they not talk about physics or math.

But after the students left, Elsa found equations scrawled all over Einstein's bedsheets.

● Einstein gave his eldest son the fatherly advice, "Don't get married." When his son married shortly after, Einstein warned him, "At least don't have children." His son ignored his father's advice and had several children in a happy marriage. Einstein grumbled, "I don't understand it. I don't think you're my son."

● Einstein's image in the public had more to do with the budding movie-newsreel industry and its incessant search for "news" than it did with his work in physics. He was a visually captivating man. With his white hair, whiskers, and an old, ratty suit, he was the perfect image of the eccentric scientist. As groundbreaking as his work was, the vast majority of people did not understand what his theories were all about. Charlie Chaplin joked, "I'm famous because everyone can relate to what I do, but you are famous even though no one understands what you do."

● Einstein charged people a dollar for his autograph, turning the proceeds over to charity. He made an exception when he met Charlie Chaplin, giving him an autographed photo for free.

● For many years Einstein thought of his work in physics as something of a hobby. He regarded himself as a failure because what he really wanted to do was play concert violin. Einstein was uncharacteristically intense when he played his violin, cussing a blue streak whenever he made a mistake. One evening, while playing violin duets with Queen Elizabeth, Einstein suddenly stopped in the middle of the piece and unceremoniously told her she was playing too loudly.

● His most cherished possession after his violin was a leaky boat he named the *Lisa*. She leaked so badly that his friends called her the *Drunken Lisa*. After he became famous, he received from a wealthy admirer a beautiful mahogany yacht complete with a "head." Einstein had never seen a toilet in a boat before and was delighted to show it off.

● He was already living abroad when Hitler rose to power. Einstein was reluctant to give up his rarely used home in Germany until a friend convinced him that he would be dragged through the streets by his famous hair if he returned. As the Nazi regime intensified its anti-Semitic campaigns, Einstein renounced his German citizenship and abandoned the country of his childhood forever.

● After the war, Einstein used his fame to support political ideas he favored like Zionism and pacifism. He also remained an iconoclast in other areas as well: for example, he gave up wearing socks as an unnecessary complication. Meanwhile, he continued on with his work.

● In 1950, at the age of seventy-one, he presented his generalized theory of gravitation, the product of half a lifetime's work. Unfortunately, he had not yet been able to work out all the mathematical proofs. His health was failing and he knew he wouldn't live long enough to prove the theory either true or false.

● When asked about the proofs he'd joke weakly, "Come back in twenty years." Five years later, he was dead. Since then, his theory of a "unified field" in physics remains unsubstantiated.

Muhammad Ali

Muhammad Ali, born Cassius Clay, Jr., in 1942, was a remarkable boxer. He fought through the terms of seven presidents, holding center ring for twenty years. As an ambassador of goodwill, Ali has been a source of inspiration to many people around the world.

- For some reason, as a child, Cassius Clay always walked on his tiptoes. When he got older, he played touch football but wouldn't play tackle football because he thought it was too rough.

- Cassius often asked his brother to throw rocks at him. His brother thought he was crazy, but Cassius was trying to develop his dodging speed. No matter how many rocks his brother threw, he apparently never managed to hit Cassius.

- He started boxing early and was confident in his own abilities. In school he would pretend they were announcing over the loudspeaker "Cassius Clay, heavyweight champion of the world." As a youngster he trained six days a week, and never drank alcohol or smoked a cigarette. He did, however, try sniffing gasoline a few times to get high.

- In high school, Clay ranked 376 out of a graduating class of 391. His best grade was in metal work. He was embarrassed as an adult when his less than superlative high school academic records were leaked to the public: "I said I was the greatest, not the smartest."

• Upon seeing the Atlantic Ocean for the first time, at age seventeen, he said, "Man, that's the biggest damn lake I've ever seen."

• By the time Clay was eighteen he had fought 108 amateur bouts and had won six Kentucky Golden Gloves championships, two National Golden Gloves tournaments, and two National Amateur Athletic Union titles.

• Because he was afraid to fly, Clay almost didn't go to the 1960 Rome Olympics, where he won a gold medal in heavyweight boxing.

• The boxer eventually overcame his fear. On one flight, a stewardess asked him to fasten his seat belt before takeoff. "Superman don't need no seat belt," he replied. The stewardess responded sweetly, "Superman don't need no plane."

• Clay may have been the first rap performer. He ended training sessions in the 1960s by talking to the crowd and reciting his bragging, "I am the greatest" poetry. In 1963 he recorded an album of monologues and poems devoted to extolling his own abilities for Columbia Records.

• When he found out that photographer Flip Schulke did a lot of underwater photography, Clay told him that he trained underwater. He made up a story about how fighting against the resistance of the water made him the fastest heavyweight in the world. *Life* magazine ran five pages of Clay up to his neck in a swimming pool, throwing punches. In reality, Clay couldn't even swim.

• Sonny Liston genuinely scared him, and there was no love lost between the two fighters. Once, while Liston was trying to play craps, Clay began taunting him. Liston threw down the dice, walked over to Clay, and said, "Listen, you nigger faggot. If you don't get out of here in ten seconds, I'm gonna pull that big tongue out of your mouth and stick it up your ass." Clay left.

• When the Beatles came to the gym to see him in late 1963, Clay didn't know who they were. While he was talking with them, he used one of his favorite lines, "You guys ain't as dumb as you look." John Lennon looked him right in the eye and told him, "No, but you are."

• He was actively recruited by the Black Muslims and became their first "big name" convert. In January 1964, when he left training camp and traveled from Miami Beach to New York, Malcolm X went with him. His fight promoter threatened to cancel a bout unless he publicly disavowed the Muslims. He refused, and the promoter backed down.

• After becoming a Muslim, he signed his name "Cassius X Clay" for several months, incorporating the "X" as symbolic of his lost African identity. Eventually he changed his name to Muhammad Ali, but it took several months to convince newspaper reporters and broadcasters to stop using his old name.

• Malcolm X called Ali his "little brother." On February 21, 1965, the night Malcolm X was assassinated, a mysterious fire broke out in Ali's apartment.

• Ali met Sonji Roi on July 3, 1964. He proposed to her that same night and they were married forty-two days later. He told his wife that they couldn't buy a house because the men from the "mother ship" would come in three years to take them away. Less than a year later, Ali filed a complaint in Dade County Circuit Court to annul his marriage because his wife wouldn't follow Muslim law.

• In 1964 Ali was ruled ineligible for the draft, based on his scores on the army's mental aptitude test. But in 1966 the military, in the middle of a massive buildup in Vietnam, lowered its standards and decided Ali was eligible for the draft after all.

• On March 17, 1966, Ali appeared before his draft board requesting exemption from the draft as a conscientious objector. His request was denied.

• The FBI kept Ali under constant surveillance for this "disloyalty." Even an appearance on *The Tonight Show* with Johnny Carson was monitored by an FBI agent and summarized in a memo to J. Edgar Hoover.

• On March 6, 1967, the National Selective Service Presidential Appeal Board voted unanimously to maintain Ali's 1-A classification, making him liable for immediate service, and he was ordered to report to Houston, Texas. But, citing his religious beliefs, he refused induction. One hour later—before he'd been charged with any crime—the New York State Athletic Commission suspended Ali's boxing license and withdrew recognition of him as world champion. All other jurisdictions in the United States quickly followed suit, and the title Ali had worked for all his life was gone. It would take him seven years to get it back.

• On May 8, 1967, Ali was indicted by a federal grand jury in Houston. He was released on five thousand dollars bail on the condition that he not leave the continental United States. His trial took one day and the jury returned a verdict of guilty within twenty minutes. Ali requested that the judge give him his sentence immediately, instead of waiting. He imposed the maximum sentence allowable for draft evasion—five years' imprisonment and a fine of ten thousand dollars—and ordered that Ali's passport be confiscated.

• Ali appealed his case all the way to the Supreme Court, which in 1971 reversed the conviction.

• When Ali tried to return to the ring, his promoters had trouble trying to get a state license to hold a fight. They had been assured of a license in California, but then-governor Ronald Reagan announced, "That draft dodger will never fight in my state, period."

• Ali loved to do magic tricks, and one time at a press conference he did a levitation trick in front of the reporters. But because of his religion, he felt it was wrong to deceive another person. So after he performed a trick, he demonstrated how it was done, much to the chagrin of other magicians who like to keep their techniques secret.

● He once offered college students one thousand dollars to anyone who brought him his friend Howard Cosell's toupee.

● "I know celebrities don't have privacy, but at least they should be able to sleep with who they want," he once said. He practiced what he preached, having one child with mistress Veronica Porsche. He justified his infidelity by pointing out that Muslim law allows men to have two wives.

● At his peak, his name and image were licensed by DC Comics for a special edition entitled "Superman vs. Muhammad Ali: The Fight to Save Earth from Star-Warriors." He earned a $250,000 endorsement fee from Idaho potato growers. Other licensed products included an Ali candy bar, Mr. Champs Soda, and African Feeling sheets. There were supposedly even plans for a Muhammad Ali automobile but, like the proposed "Champburgers" fast-food chain, it never got off the drawing board.

● Besides potatoes, Ali has endorsed a number of Republican candidates for office.

● There was Muhammad Ali Sportswear Ltd. with the logo of a butterfly and a bee. When sales reps went to stores, the reaction was muted. Said one buyer, "For years, we've been trying to keep blacks out of our store. They shoplift; they turn off other customers. Why should we carry a product line that invites them in?"

● In 1978 he went to Moscow and met Leonid Brezhnev, who made him an unofficial ambassador for peace to the United States. Ali took his diplomatic role seriously, occasionally referring to himself as "the black Henry Kissinger." In November 1990, against all advice, he traveled to Iraq and met with Saddam Hussein in the hope that his presence would promote dialogue and forestall war. After ten days in Iraq, Ali returned to the United States with fifteen of the three hundred American hostages then being held.

● On December 11, 1981, Ali entered the ring for the last time. The fight started two hours late because the promoters couldn't find the key to the gate of the baseball field where the fight was being held.

● Today, his voice is weak, he moves slowly, and when he's tired his hands tremble. He does not have Parkinson's disease, he has parkinsonism from damage to his brain stem from the physical trauma of head punches. Some slurring of his speech was noted as early as 1978.

● He prays five times a day "to clean my mind."

● Ali once visited a women's prison in California, and all the women were lined up to shake his hand. He started going down the line, signing autographs and kissing the least attractive women. When he was asked why, he said, "The good-looking ones ain't got no problem. But them ugly ones, who's gonna kiss them? If I kiss them, they got something to talk about for the rest of their lives."

● Jimmy Swaggart visited Ali in Los Angeles and tried to convince him to accept Jesus as his lord and savior. Ali said, "Think about it. If Jimmy Swaggart can convert the best-known Muslim on Earth back to Christianity, what would that do for Jimmy Swaggart?" A few months later Jimmy Swaggart was caught up in a sex scandal. A friend told Ali, "You know what you should do? You really ought to write Jimmy Swaggart a letter, saying that God still loves him and Jimmy Swaggart should accept Allah as his only lord and savior."

Abbie Hoffman

Abbott Howard Hoffman—Abbie—was the clown prince of the 1960s New Left antiwar protesters. A founder of the fun-loving Yippies (Youth International Party), he used stunts, street theater, and verbal humor to poke fun at the "Establishment."

- Hoffman liked to say that he invented himself as a public personality "out of left-wing literature, sperm, licorice, and a little chicken fat."

- As a baby he would lie on his back and perform acrobatics, as if he were showing off. This hyperactivity was later determined to be a symptom of the manic-depressive condition that he had to deal with his entire life.

- His father didn't go to war because he was 4-F, a deferment because of physical difficulties, so Abbie's uncle Schmully became his hero because he had served in the army during World War II.

- To avoid trouble from the Irish Catholic toughs in the neighborhood, he would sometimes take his hat off and cross himself when passing the neighborhood parochial school.

- When he was a child, his parents took the family to a resort in New Hampshire. Upon discovering that the resort only accepted Christians, they turned around and went home. Abbie was furious that his parents wouldn't fight for their rights.

- Whatever sport was in season, Hoffman played it: sandlot softball, basketball, and tackle football without any helmets or pads. He later said that these football games toughened him for the beatings he received from police in Mississippi, New York, and Chicago.

- He was also a Duncan Yo-Yo Championship finalist.

- Hoffman wrote a paper for his sophomore high school English class in which he defended atheism. His teacher grabbed hold of his collar, ripped it off his shirt, and called him "a little communist bastard." In response, Hoffman overturned the teacher's desk and pummeled him. That he had gotten kicked out of school as a result became one of his favorite boasts.

- As a freshman at Brandeis, he was required to take an introductory course in psychology, and by the end of that year, Abbie decided to major in psychology. His hero was psychologist Abraham Maslow. Hoffman became a staff psychologist at Worcester State Hospital.

- Hoffman joined the Freedom Riders in Mississippi, battling local politicians to insure voting rights for nonwhite citizens. He was stopped in his car by Mississippi police for running a traffic light in a town that, according to Hoffman, didn't even *have* a traffic light.

- In the late 1960s Hoffman became a hippie and began experimenting with psychedelics. He and his merry prankster friends at one point planned to stick up a tourist bus and rob the tourists of their socks, just to "blow their minds."

- He tried to give free clothes away in a Macy's store before security police hustled him away. He and some friends rained dollar bills onto the floor of the New York Stock Exchange, stopping trading as brokers scrambled for the bucks. Noting that pentagrams are a satanic symbol of evil, he organized a circle of people around the Pentagon in Washington, D.C., to conduct a mass exorcism.

- The Yippies ran a pig for president in 1968, complete with campaign slogans and realistic-looking Secret Service agents.

- Before a demonstration, Hoffman would give the participants lessons in nonviolent protection: Don't wear pins, earrings, anything that can stick you or be grabbed. If attacked, try to relax, roll up into a fetal position, and protect your groin and the back of your head from kicks and punches.

- Hoffman was an equal opportunity prankster. He was nearly thrown out of a left-wing symposium on Communism when he displayed a Fuck Communism poster.

- For five years Hoffman was under continuous police surveillance. He would often hitch rides with the government agents who were tailing him.

- Once he wrote the word "Fuck" on his forehead to keep his picture out of the newspapers. He was arrested for obscenity and served a thirteen-day sentence, the longest he ever spent in jail throughout his political protest career.

- He had to self-publish his book *Steal This Book* because major publishers were afraid that bookstore patrons would take the title literally. The book was about how to live for free or nearly so. Much of the advice included instructions on how to carry out creatively illegal acts. Hoffman practiced what he preached, using tricks like gluing a piece of string to a nickel so that he could retrieve it after making phone calls.

- While the Who were getting ready to play at Woodstock, Hoffman walked out onto the stage, tripping on acid. Pete Townshend pushed Hoffman aside, and said that he didn't want any damned politics interfering with his music. According to Hoffman, Townshend also hit him on the head with his guitar. The incident wasn't immortalized in the official Woodstock movie, for some reason.

• Hoffman was arrested after the stormy Democratic National Convention in Chicago in 1968. During the trial of the Chicago Eight, which became the Chicago Seven, Hoffman did a handspring upon entering the courtroom every morning. One day he and fellow Yippie Jerry Rubin appeared in the courtroom wearing black judicial robes over Chicago police uniforms. Hoffman took his robe off in front of the stand and stomped all over it. Hoffman was sentenced to six days in prison for insulting the judge in Yiddish, and seven days for wearing the robe.

• When speaking on college campuses, he would puff on a joint on stage, daring campus and local police, state troopers, and the FBI special agents to arrest him, knowing that they knew that such a move would likely touch off a student riot.

• Because of his electric hair and cherubic face, he was the "cute" antiwar radical. One major toy company wanted to market a windup Abbie doll. The William Morris Agency put in a pitch to represent him in licensing matters. And on Sesame Street, Muppets who looked like him and Jerry Rubin occasionally appeared.

• With financial help from Jimi Hendrix, Hoffman bought a large quantity of marijuana and rolled it into thousands of joints in 1969. These he mailed—along with a message explaining that the recipients were now legally felons—as valentine "gifts" to news reporters, politicians, and a thousand other people whose addresses were randomly chosen from the phone book.

• Grace Slick asked Hoffman to go to her class reunion as her "beau." She had graduated with Tricia Nixon, the president's daughter, and the reunion was being held at the White House. They were turned away at the White House gates. She said later that she had hid LSD under her long fake fingernails, and had planned to mix it into the punch.

• Hoffman and his wife, Anita, named their son "america," deliberately spelling it with a small "a." Hoffman sent a birth announcement to the Nixon White House so that they could show off the personal congratulations of Dick and Pat that the White House staff routinely sent to new parents who wrote to them.

• In the early 1970s Hoffman began to use cocaine. At the time it had a bad reputation within the political "movement." Hoffman started serving as a coke broker, funneling drug money into movement projects. But then one day he set up a big cocaine deal that backfired on him and got him arrested.

• Hoffman, awaiting trial, jumped bail in February 1974. A number of radicals had gone "underground," and he thought it would be an adventure and a new challenge. He had plastic surgery on his face to alter his looks. He developed new speech patterns, a new gait, and new gestures.

• While underground, Hoffman traveled around the continent. He taught English at a girl's school in Guadalajara, Mexico. He had a kitchen job in Mexico City, where he met and fell in love with Johanna Lawrenson. They moved to Santa Fe, New Mexico, where Hoffman got a cooking job at a hotel. But the pressures of the "underground" life began getting to him. He freaked out in a hotel room, shouting at the walls that he was Abbie Hoffman. He started taking risks; for example, showing up at the funeral of a friend in New York City. He later moved to New York State, and told people that he was Barry Freed, a freelance writer.

• He was congenitally unable to keep a low profile. His most audacious act was a birthday party that he threw for himself at the Felt Forum in Madison Square Garden in 1977. As Barry Freed, he worked to save the Hudson River and spoke in front of a U.S. Senate committee in Washington, D.C., posing for photos with members of Congress. He regularly played shortstop on a local coed softball team that had U.S. Customs officers on it. He eventually emerged from hiding and charges were dropped.

• In 1980 Hoffman was finally diagnosed with manic depression, or bipolar disorder. He was glad to have a name and explanation for his episodes of mental instability. Hoffman began taking lithium. Because it upset his stomach, he would occasionally stop taking it, and fall again into a severe depression.

● Hoffman was one of the few veterans of the sixties radicalism who talked to college students about the sixties as a positive experience and continued to be politically active and socially concerned into the greedy 1980s. He also appeared as himself in the Oliver Stone movie *Born on the Fourth of July*.

● In February 1989 Hoffman started to feel that he was losing control of his mental equilibrium. His depression was deepening. He was prescribed Prozac. On the evening of April 12, 1989, Hoffman's landlord found him in bed, fully clothed under the covers, his hands folded beneath his cheek. Hoffman had taken 150 phenobarbitals, more than enough to kill anybody, and had washed them down with alcohol. His death was ruled a suicide. Hoffman, who rarely let a chance pass to get his message to the media, left no note.

Henry Ford

Henry Ford revolutionized the car industry by introducing the Model T, affectionately known as the Tin Lizzie, in 1908. But like most mechanical innovators, he seemed to have a few screws that were not quite tight.

• Ford didn't invent the automobile, he simplified it. A tinkerer since childhood, Ford built his first gasoline engine in 1896 from plans published in a magazine called the *American Machinist*. Until he came along, only the rich could afford to buy a car, but Ford hit on the idea of making a car for America's rural population. A farm boy himself, he created a rugged, all-purpose machine designed to run machinery, pump water, and still be able to take the family to church on Sunday. Best of all, farmers could fix it themselves, keeping maintenance costs down.

• The Model T was an instant success. Rural America loved the car and the man who gave it to them, quickly turning Ford into a millionaire folk hero. The *Denver Express* in 1915 told of an old-timer in Colorado who asked that he be buried with his Ford car because "the darned thing pulled me out of every hole I ever got into, and it ought to pull me out of this one."

• At the height of the Model T's popularity in the early 1920s, the Sears Roebuck catalog featured five thousand items that could be added to or run by a Model T, including plows, harvesters, butter churns, and flour grinders.

● Despite his open approach to problem solving, Ford was obstinate once his mind was made up. With the Model T, he resisted pressure to add or improve anything despite a hundred customer letters a day with suggested changes. "They can have any color they want," he was quoted as saying, "as long as it's black." He thought speedometers were an unnecessary luxury.

● Ford also disdained effete refinements like electric starters. You had to hand crank the car to get it started. But because the car would sometimes suddenly start with a powerful bang, you had to stand clear and not wrap your thumb securely around the handle for, if you did so, you risked breaking your hand or worse.

● Ford's best innovation was changing the way cars were built. He perfected the concept of mass production using a constantly moving assembly line. He bought steel and lumber mills, glass works, trains, hydroelectric plants, coal mines, ore boats, and a pine forest so that he could keep supplies running smoothly to the line. He built manufacturing plants around the world.

● It took a few attempts to get it right, however. Ford had founded two unsuccessful car companies before the Ford Motor Company. The third was the charm.

● In his early years, he was an enlightened employer. He made history by reducing the work week from six days to only five. He offered subsidized housing, stores, and a hospital. He was cursed by other industrialists when he announced that his workers would receive $5 for an eight-hour day in an era when average wages were $2.34 for a nine-hour day. For the first time auto workers could afford the cars they were working on.

● Ford hired blacks at the same pay as whites and promoted them into supervisory positions at a time when that was nearly unheard of. (Yet, their housing was centered in a town in the Detroit area that's still called Inkster, a derogatory racial term).

● He also hired people with disabilities. In 1919 nearly a quarter of his workforce, including a number of World War I veterans, had some kind of physical handicap, such as missing limbs, blindness, or deafness.

● However, despite the women's movement of the time, he treated his female workers as if they were just passing through. "I consider women only a temporary factor in industry," he told a reporter. "Their real job in life is to get married, have a home, and raise a family. I pay our women well so they can dress attractively and get married."

● Ford believed in reincarnation. Since he was born a few weeks after the battle of Gettysburg, he decided that he had been a soldier killed in that battle. Later in life, he decided that his niece was really the reincarnation of his mother.

● His only in-wedlock child, Edsel, was named after a childhood friend. It is a Germanic derivation of the name Atilla. When Edsel was a child, Henry was an ideal father. But as he grew into an adult and became nominal head of the Ford Motor Company, Henry dominated and berated him, even bribing one of Edsel's servants to spy on him. When, during Prohibition, his spy reported that Edsel had a supply of liquor in the house, teetotaler Henry went immediately to Edsel's house and smashed every bottle.

● Reports indicate that in 1923 he very likely fathered a child with Evangeline Cote, a vivacious stenographer who worked for him. By all evidence, he set up a sham marriage between her and one of his personal assistants, Ray Dahlinger, and settled them into a 150-room mansion near his home. The mansion had a secret stairway that led up to her bedroom suite, and Henry would visit her regularly—and not very discreetly—from up the river by boat.

● Ford lavished money on Cote, giving her her own personal seaplane. He treated her son well, buying him a shetland pony when he was four weeks old and insisting that the child sleep in the crib that he himself had slept in as a child.

• In experimental gardens, Ford grew marijuana, hoping he could use it to manufacture plastic. He believed the car of the future would be completely vegetable based and spent a lot of research money on finding uses for soy beans.

• When he started assembling an outdoor museum called Greenfield Village to preserve the past as he remembered it, Ford bought historic buildings like the Wright Brothers' shop and moved them to Dearborn, Michigan. During that time, he would walk into an antique store, look around, and give a discreet nod, leaving an assistant to negotiate a price for the contents of the entire store.

• The most disturbing aspect of Ford's character was his flagrant anti-Semitism, and the corrosiveness of it seemed to slowly poison his attitude toward the world and his workers. Ford was convinced a worldwide Jewish conspiracy existed against gentiles. He believed every evil in the world could be attributed one way or another to the Jewish people. In 1919 he began publishing a newspaper called the *Dearborn Independent*. Week after week its editorial page harped an anti-Semitic tune.

• As Ford stirred up a furor in the United States, he excited a führer in Germany. Ford was already greatly admired by the German people because of his industrial innovations, and, for Adolf Hitler, his anti-Semitism added to his allure. Ford is the only American praised in Hitler's *Mein Kampf*, and portions of it were lifted directly from Ford's *Dearborn Independent* articles.

• Evidence of Hitler's admiration of Ford was easy to see in his private office, which contained a large picture of Henry Ford as well as many of Ford's books. There have been persistent but unproven reports that Ford kept the Nazi Party afloat with donations during the 1920s and early 1930s.

• According to Albert Lee in his book *Henry Ford and the Jews*, "Hitler and Ford had much in common. Both felt that Jewry was not a religion but a different race. They both felt Jewry was an inferior race to the Nordic strains. And within that superior race, some would be superior to others. This view contributed to Ford's and Hitler's dislike of democracy. Ford is quoted as saying there is 'no greater absurdity and no greater disservice to humanity than to insist all men are equal.' "

● In July 1933 Ford was awarded the Nazi government's highest award—the Grand Cross of the German Eagle—which he chose to receive in a low-key ceremony.

● By 1939 anti-Semitic signs started appearing in the employee parking lots stating such propaganda as "Jews are traitors to America and should not be trusted—buy gentile."

● Ironically, when he got older he entertained children with a Jew's harp.

● With his endorsement of Nazi aims, his plants became more totalitarian as well. What had once been a progressive place to work became intolerable by the mid-1930s. Workers were fired for even small indiscretions, such as talking. As working conditions worsened, Ford's workers pressed for unionization, which Ford decided was some sort of Jewish takeover plot. He fought back by hiring a band of thugs known as the Ford Service, which patrolled the plants and eventually began spying on the workers outside the plant. Anyone caught doing "wrong," such as talking to union organizers, was beaten and fired.

● According to *Trading with the Enemy* by Charles Higham, "in 1940 Ford refused to build aircraft engines for England and instead continued building trucks used by the German army. They also arranged to ship tires to Germany despite shortages." A German Ford plant publication read, "At the beginning of this year we vowed to give our best and utmost for final victory, in unshakable faithfulness to our führer."

● At one point in the 1920s, Ford considered running for president and decided it was wise to publicly apologize for his anti-Semitism. Still, he continued to blame the world's troubles on

Jews and "bankers, munitions makers, alcoholic drink, kings and their henchmen, and schoolbooks" up to the end.

● The last reporter allowed to talk to him shortly before his death in 1947 asked if the family-owned Ford Motor Company would ever go public. The eighty-three-year-old Ford, displaying energy not seen for months, sat up in his sickbed and said, "I'll take my factory down brick by brick before I'll let any of those Jew speculators get stock in my company."

Harry Houdini

Harry Houdini was the most famous magician ever. He made it a personal crusade to expose phony mediums and psychics. Did he communicate to us after his death?

• Harry Houdini started his show-business career in the early 1890s, fronting for traveling medicine shows with his brother Theo. The pair billed themselves as "the Houdini Brothers." Houdini, who began life as Erich Weiss in 1874, took his stage name from Jean-Eugène Robert-Houdin, a popular French magician, adding the "i" suffix so that he would be "like Houdin."

• In 1894 Houdini married, and wife Bessie joined the act. Theo went his own way as "Hardeen," performing many of the same escapes that Harry did and even sometimes filling in for his famous brother, but he never enjoyed the same fame.

• In 1897, after struggling through years of poverty, Houdini and Bessie joined Dr. Hill's California Concert Company. While the troupe was in Kansas, Dr. Hill learned that a spiritualist was drawing a large crowd in the same town. Hill offered Houdini top billing if he appeared as a spirit medium.

• Houdini had learned the tricks of the medium trade from one Josef Gregorowich, a spiritualist healer in Milwaukee. In his act, Houdini had himself tied into a chair as "proof" that no hoax was being perpetrated. Using his escape tricks, he played bells, tambourines, and floating mandolins, and then he appeared from behind drawn curtains to tell the audience about the spirit world and to answer questions about dead loved ones using information gleaned from audience members before the show.

- Meanwhile, Houdini was perfecting the escapes for which he would soon gain worldwide fame. He eventually moved out of the spiritualism racket and into straight magic.

- He had learned the secret of picking locks while apprenticed to a locksmith as a teenager. To drum up publicity for the shows, he would routinely challenge the local police to provide a restraint from which he could not escape.

- In 1899 Houdini was publicly challenged by Martin Beck, a booking agent for the Orpheum vaudeville circuit, who doubted that the handcuffs Houdini used in his act were genuine. Beck purchased several pairs of his own and sent them onstage. Houdini escaped from them in seconds. Impressed, Beck offered the Houdinis bookings. After traveling in obscurity for five years, they were finally headed for the big time.

- Over the next twenty-seven years, Houdini built a reputation as a master magician and showman. Escaping from handcuffs was nothing new for magicians, but Houdini's standing challenge to police forces was a first. In 1899 Houdini was accused by a policeman of concealing keys on his person. Houdini challenged the police to "strip me naked." After being closely examined by a police doctor, he was shackled hand and foot with ten pairs of handcuffs and then locked in a closet. Houdini emerged after ten minutes. The "naked test" became a staple of Houdini's publicity campaigns.

- Houdini was able to escape from straitjackets because he could dislocate one of his shoulders. He often performed this stunt while suspended upside down.

- Houdini became famous for "bridge jumps," in which he was handcuffed and locked in a trunk, and then thrown into the water from a bridge. One persistent part of the Houdini legend insists that he miraculously escaped from a trunk dropped through the ice of the Detroit River. Newspaper accounts of the event, however, neglect to mention any ice.

● For Houdini's famous Walk Through a Brick Wall illusion, an actual brick wall was built onstage by brick masons while the audience watched. The hardest part of the trick was to keep the masons from disturbing the rug they were building the wall on top of. It hid a trapdoor that let Houdini slither under the wall like a snake.

● Houdini's first European tour in 1900 was so successful that he stayed five years. Accused of being a fraud by a German police officer, Houdini sued the man for libel and eventually extracted an official apology from Kaiser Wilhelm II after he escaped from every set of manacles the Germans tried on him.

● To make his water escapes more exciting, Houdini developed the Water-Torture Cell, a glass box filled with water, into which he was lowered upside down. The top of the cell was a set of stocks in which his feet were locked. Houdini thrilled audiences with this escape for fifteen years, and his many contemporary imitators never equaled it.

● Houdini also made a foray into the movie business. He started the Houdini Picture Corporation and starred in several features in the early 1920s. *The Man From Beyond*, about a man frozen in ice for one hundred years, was pronounced by mystery writer Sir Arthur Conan Doyle to be the very best picture he had ever seen. Critics pointed out that though the hero was supposed to have been frozen for one hundred years, he expressed no surprise whatever at the technical advances now surrounding him. Besides that, Houdini's magic did not translate well onto the silver screen, and the movie venture failed.

● An early flying enthusiast, Houdini became the first man to fly a plane in Australia while touring there in 1910. He had brought the biplane with him aboard ship. In *The Grim Game*, Houdini was inadvertently featured in the first plane crash recorded on film while attempting to change planes in midair.

• Everywhere Houdini performed, rumors sprang up that he had supernatural powers. One writer, a spiritualist, claimed that Houdini possessed the ability to dematerialize and that this was the secret of his baffling escapes. Houdini was adamant in denying that his escapes were made possible by anything other than his remarkable physical conditioning, his skill, and by other natural means. The rumors persisted anyway.

• After meeting Sir Arthur Conan Doyle in New York, Doyle invited the Houdinis to visit him at his hotel suite in Atlantic City. Doyle was a devout spiritualist and Houdini was a skeptic who could not understand how the creator of superlogical Sherlock Holmes could be taken in by simple parlor tricks.

• Doyle's wife was a practitioner of "automatic writing," whereby the medium's hands are ostensibly guided by ghostly hands to write messages from beyond. Lady Doyle produced a message she claimed was from Houdini's mother, who had died in 1913. The message was written in English, a language Houdini's Yiddish-speaking mother didn't know.

• When confronted with this information, Doyle, ever the logician, calmly replied, "Elementary, my dear Weiss—she probably learned English in heaven."

• After that, Houdini went on a personal crusade to expose fraudulent spirit mediums. A mama's boy at a time before Freud's theories made extreme devotion to one's mother suspect, Houdini had sought out genuine mediums all over the country to reach Mama Weiss on the other side. He was first disgusted, and then outraged, at the fact that every medium he visited used easy magic trickery to play upon people's grief for profit. In challenge after challenge, he exposed all comers. Demonstrations of spiritualist methods, accompanied by detailed explanations, became a prominent feature of Houdini's stage act.

• Confronted with counterclaims by die-hard spiritualists that Houdini's act also fooled people, Houdini reminded his critics that he claimed no supernatural abilities.

• Houdini posted a standing reward of ten thousand dollars to any medium whose methods he could not uncover and duplicate. He was hoping, he said, to find one that was genuine. Many applied for the reward but none collected.

• In October 1926, while on tour in Montreal, Houdini agreed to a backstage interview with two students from McGill University. One of the young men wanted to test Houdini's claim that he could withstand any blow to the midsection. Houdini agreed, but through some misunderstanding, the young man delivered a punch to Houdini's abdomen before he could prepare himself. Unknown to Houdini, his appendix was ruptured by the blow. Two days later he collapsed after a show in Detroit and was rushed to the hospital. Houdini fought the infection for a week, but in those days before antibiotics he had little chance of survival.

• Houdini died on Halloween. On his deathbed, he promised his wife that he would return from the great beyond if at all possible, using an agreed-upon code word in any communication, to help sort the real mediums from the fake ones.

• Three years later Dr. Arthur Ford of the First Spiritualist Church of Manhattan claimed to have channeled a word in their stage code. It was "Believe." There was more: "Tell the world, sweetheart, that Harry Houdini lives and will prove it a thousand times over." The headlines flashed around the world.

• Two days later the "Houdini message" was exposed as a fake. Bessie admitted she had known Dr. Ford for nearly a year, even though she had stated that at the time of the message he was a stranger. It was further learned that the code the Houdinis had used had been published in a Houdini biography two years earlier, and that anyone could have learned it, including Ford.

● Bessie repudiated her belief that the message had really been from Houdini. Though many mediums continued to contact her with alleged messages from him, she never again professed a belief in any of them.

● Still, the vigil kept up. Each October 31—the anniversary of Houdini's death—Bessie would sit by a large portrait of Houdini in her living room where she burned an "eternal light." On the tenth anniversary of his death, a séance was conducted at the Knickerbocker Hotel in Hollywood with Bessie in attendance. Nothing happened. Bessie said sadly that she did not believe that Houdini would be back.

● Returning home, she blew out the light by his portrait.

● In the nearly seventy years since his death, Houdini has remained an enigma. Many who wonder at his enduring fame puzzle over the reason for it. This question was perhaps answered best by Bessie in a letter to Doyle in December 1926. "He buried no secrets," she wrote. "Every conjurer knows how his tricks were done—you, Sir Arthur could do the same tricks—it was Houdini himself that was the secret."

Michael Jackson

Michael Jackson has had phenomenal success in the fields of rock and soul. His Thriller *album is the highest-selling album of all time. Yet the bizarre and sometimes horrifying accounts about the man-child have often dwarfed his musical accomplishments.*

- The first line of Jackson's favorite book, *Peter Pan*, reads, "All children, except one, grow up." He was born Michael Joseph Jackson on August 29, 1958, in the grimy midwestern town of Gary, Indiana. Forced to grow up fast because of his father's determination to have a hit music group, Jackson—even as he approaches middle age—seems determined to stay stuck in the childhood he never had.

- Both of Jackson's parents were musical. His father, Joe, played blues guitar. His mother played clarinet and, surprisingly, country and western piano. The Jackson 5 began when Michael's older brothers started sneaking Joe's guitar out and playing it. When he discovered them, Joe whipped them . . . and then decided to encourage their playing and singing as a way out of poverty.

- Jackson started singing in the family group when he was five years old. That meant constant drilling after school and at night when other kids were playing. At their first gig, the brothers made seven dollars. As an eight-year-old, Jackson worked with his brothers in nightclubs and dives until four or five in the morning, and then had to be up for school by eight. He remembers, "People would throw all this money on the floor. . . . Tons of dollars, tens, twenties, lots of change. I remember my pockets being so full of money that I couldn't keep my pants up."

• The Jackson 5's first album with Motown was called *Diana Ross Presents the Jackson 5*, initiating the myth that she was the one who "discovered" them. She didn't, but the publicity folks at Motown decided it would make a good story and Ross was happy to go along with it. (Motown also decided to lop two years off ten-year-old Michael's age.) Motown head Berry Gordy convinced Diana Ross, his lover at the time, to let Michael move in with her until the Jackson family got settled in Los Angeles.

• Ross and Jackson eventually became good friends. One completely unsubstantiated rumor has it that she initiated him into manhood. Actually, though, all the women that Jackson has been linked with "romantically"—Ross, Tatum O'Neal, and Brooke Shields—have denied that anything vaguely resembling sex ever took place in their relationship with Jackson. (O'Neal said, "Sex was something Michael neither knew nor cared about.") Presumably, that may have changed with his marriage to Lisa Presley—or maybe not.

• In *Michael Jackson: The Magic and the Madness*, author J. Randy Taraborrelli quotes an anonymous Jackson associate quoting Michael's oldest sister, Maureen "Rebbie" Jackson: "She happened to say to me, 'Michael doesn't have time for girls.' I asked her, 'What kind of guy doesn't have time for girls?' . . . She told me a truly horrible story. When Michael was fifteen years old, a certain member of his family, someone he trusted—I won't say who, even though Rebbie did—decided he was old enough to have sex. So this person arranged the services of two hookers for Michael, told them to work him over, and then locked Michael up in a room with them. Rebbie said that this incident absolutely traumatized her brother. I don't know whether or not Michael actually had sex with the hookers. Rebbie wouldn't say."

• Jackson's mom, Katherine, a fervent Jehovah's Witness, also drummed the message into him from I Corinthians 6:9: "Neither fornicators, nor idolaters, nor adulterers, nor effeminate men" would enter the kingdom of heaven. For many years, Jackson was a believer, going to meetings four times a week, knocking on doors and evangelizing, as Witnesses are required to do. (Jackson wore a hat, glasses, sweater, and tie, and a phony beard and mustache.) Later, after the church elders thought that his "Thriller" video was a satanic sacrilege and hassled him about that biblical passage about "effeminate men," Jackson and the Witnesses parted ways.

● In 1979 Jackson's surgery-enhanced appearance inspired rumors that he was intending to have a sex-change operation in order to marry songwriter and television actor Clifton Davis. "No, I'm not gay," he angrily told an interviewer at the time. "I am not homo. Not at all. People make up stories about me being gay because they have nothing else to do. I'm not going to let it get to me. I'm not going to have a nervous breakdown because people think I like having sex with men. I don't and that's that. If I let this get to me, it will only show how cheap I am. I'm sure I must have a lot of fans who are gay, and I don't mind that. That's their life and this is mine . . . What is it about me that makes people think I'm gay? Is it my soft voice? All of us in the family have soft voices. Or is it because I don't have a lot of girlfriends? I just don't understand. . . ."

● Jackson's first hit without his brothers was "Ben," a song from the movie of the same name, about a lonely boy whose only friends were rats. Jackson put some real-life passion into the song: As a lonely child, Jackson loved rats. His mom was horrified one day to discover that he had thirty of them in a cage in his room. The love affair went sour, however, when Jackson discovered firsthand that rats often eat each other.

● In 1974 the Jackson 5 toured Africa and were genuinely awed by seeing the lands of their ancestors. Accustomed by now to luxury, however, they were appalled by the general poverty and the relatively primitive accommodations in the hotels where they stayed. Sixteen-year-old Michael turned to the group's lawyer, Richard Arens, and said, "Richard, I'm sure glad you white people brought us to America."

● The Jackson family had signed a standard "sucker's" contract with Motown, without hiring legal representation or even taking the time to read it. They lived to regret the decision: its royalty rate was pretty low, it gave Motown the right to dictate what songs they'd record, and it held the Jacksons liable for all recording expenses such as studio time and salaries of musicians and technicians, even for songs that were never released. Motown kept the Jacksons busy, recording 469 songs in six years. Of these, however, Berry Gordy decided that only 174 were worthy of release. When the Jacksons left Motown, they were chagrined to discover that they owed more than five hundred thousand dollars in production costs.

● When Jackson was a young teen, his older brothers could tease him to tears by calling him "liver lips" and "big nose." He reportedly hated the fact that he was growing up looking like his father, and so he started getting plastic surgery. His nose got thinner with each of four separate operations. His cheeks became better defined. His chin grew a cleft. Furthermore, Jackson's skin became lighter and lighter.

● Jackson denied that he was consciously trying to look like Diana Ross. Still, the rumors persisted. Ross's reaction, when an associate repeated the rumor, was a dismayed wail: "I look like *that*?" It's worse than that, if you believe Nancy Reagan. When she met Jackson, she observed that Ross didn't look *half* as pretty as he did.

● During the seven months of filming *The Wiz*, in which he played the Scarecrow, Jackson became so involved with his role that he refused to take off his makeup at the end of the day.

● "I don't know much about politics. Nothing, I guess. Someone told me recently that Gerald Ford was president," Jackson said in August 1978, nearly two years after Ford was defeated by Jimmy Carter.

● Jackson once met Andy Warhol and Alfred Hitchcock and thought, for some reason, that they were brothers. He has also been reported as saying that he believes that human beings can fly.

● Jackson can't play an instrument or read music. Most of the songs he has recorded have been written by other people; when he comes up with a song of his own, he sings it into a tape recorder and hires a musician to transcribe it.

● Jackson is an inventive dancer, but did he originate the step most associated with him, the "moon walk," with which he mesmerized the country during Motown's twenty-fifth-anniversary broadcast in March 1983? No. Three years before, he had seen sixteen-year-old Geron Candidate performing the peculiar backward-dancing step on *Soul Train* and had contacted him through the show's producers. Candidate taught Jackson a few steps for a fee of one thousand dollars. After a few hours, Jackson had it down, more or less. However, he got the name wrong—the step was called the backslide. The moon walk employs a backslide in a circular pattern.

● *Thriller* sold an unprecedented 38.5 million copies worldwide, and spawned seven Top 10 singles, but Jackson still had trouble getting his videos onto MTV. (Of the sixty videos in rotation in February 1983, only two featured nonwhites: one by Tina Turner and another by the English Beat, a multiracial group.) After MTV turned down "Billie Jean," founder Robert Pittman explained that Jackson's "rhythm and blues" had no more place on MTV than country music. With the release of "Beat It" CBS reportedly issued an ultimatum: Play Jackson's "Beat It" or kiss all future CBS videos good-bye. MTV played the video, and the song became a big hit.

● "One of my favorite pastimes is being with children—talking to them, playing with them in the grass," Jackson has been quoted as saying. "They know so many secrets, but it's hard for them to get it out. I can recognize that and learn from it. They say some things that just astound you. They go through a brilliant, genius stage. But then, when they get to a certain age, they lose it."

● To the great discomfort of his own family and those of the children involved, Jackson began befriending preteen boys. The first was actor Emmanuel Lewis, TV's "Webster," who he carried around as if he were a toddler. Jackson, twenty-five years old, would wrestle and chase the twelve-year-old Lewis around his estate and buy him expensive presents. Lewis's mother finally put the brakes on the relationship after the two registered in a nearby hotel as father and son.

● Other parents had similar reactions. Jackson was sued and threatened with prosecution over another such relationship, reportedly settling for millions of dollars to keep the case out of court.

● According to writer Christopher Andersen in *Michael Jackson, Unauthorized*, the thirteen-year-old boy who had accused Jackson of molesting him said that Jackson has a tattoo of Winnie the Pooh near his genitals. When he first saw Jackson naked, he pointed at his brown-and-white skin blotches—the reason Jackson wears so much makeup—and said, "You look like a cow! You look like a cow!"

● Jackson thought so much of Jane Fonda's insights that he tape-recorded many of the conversations they had together. During the filming of *On Golden Pond*, Jackson lived in a cabin on the location, and became good buddies with Henry Fonda. In a case of life imitating the art of the movie, Henry taught Jackson how to fish. His first meeting with his longtime idol Katharine Hepburn didn't go as well, however. She shook his hand quickly and walked away. "What is it with him?" she asked somebody. "First of all, why is he here? That's what I don't understand. And why does he talk like that, with that whisper? What is he trying to pull?" Jane interceded, acting as interpreter, and Hepburn and Jackson eventually became friends.

● On Sundays, in his own personal rite of purification, he fasts, ingesting nothing but liquids.

● Getting ready to film the first in a series of Pepsi commercials, the crew of the shoot heard a muffled but bloodcurdling scream coming from a bathroom. A sheepish Jackson explained that somehow he had dropped his trademark spangled glove into the toilet. The glove was fished out, washed carefully, blown dry with a hair dryer, and returned to Jackson. Later, he had the ultimate "bad hair day," when a Roman candle caught his mane on fire and sent him to the hospital. He was okay; he spent much of his stay cheering other patients.

● Jackson squeezed another $1.5 million out of Pepsi because of the accident. He donated it to charity, establishing the Michael Jackson Burn Center at Brotman Memorial Hospital in Culver City. (Unfortunately, three years later the center closed its doors permanently because of financial difficulties.)

● After his accident, Jackson became obsessed with medical procedures. He arranged to watch operations in the UCLA Medical Center surgical ward. He reportedly best liked cosmetic surgeries such as liposuctions and tummy tucks, but also watched brain surgery at least once.

● Jackson's favorite song? He told a group of reporters that it was "My Favorite Things," performed by Julie Andrews.

● Jackson prefers to talk to even his best friends over the phone rather than in person because "I'm much deeper in conversation on the phone than I am in person."

● Jackson fears driving. When he has to drive himself, like most people in mall-heavy southern California, he doesn't know how to parallel park. Unlike most, however, he avoids freeways ("I can't get on 'em and I can't get off 'em, either"), driving elaborate detours to avoid them.

● Doubleday paid him a three hundred thousand dollar advance for his autobiography, *Moon Walk*. His editor was Jackie Onassis. Jackson wrote a small part of the book with a string of ghostwriters, but soon gave up; the bulk of it was written by Doubleday editor Shaye Areheart.

● Paul McCartney cowrote "The Girl Is Mine" with Jackson while they watched Saturday morning cartoons. Jackson used it on his *Thriller* album. During a break, McCartney happened to mention that he had bought publishing rights to hundreds of favorite old songs, and got a royalty every time anybody performed a song like "Stormy Weather" or "The Sweetheart of Sigma Chi." Inspired by this in 1984, Jackson bought the rights to most of the Beatles' songs for $41 million, outbidding McCartney himself. He promptly inspired the outrage of Beatles fans by licensing them for use in TV commercials, and after that, whenever McCartney performed any of the songs he wrote between 1964 and 1971, he had to pay a fee to Jackson.

● Most people know that some of the rumors about Jackson are false. What is not generally known is that many of them were started by Jackson himself. He learned early, when he was told as a ten-year-old to lie about his age, how little truth means when seeking publicity. Later in life, he began reading biographies of hokum-master P. T. Barnum for ideas. At the Grammy Awards in 1986, he hired a teenage girl to run onto the stage screaming and then jump all over him. (It didn't work—the girl got stuck behind a mob of people and couldn't get through in time).

● Remembering the volume of publicity that the burning-hair accident garnered him, Jackson decided to do something similar to publicize his work on Disneyland's *Captain E-O* extravaganza. He pretended that he badly sprained his wrist and was rushed to the hospital where press photographers were already waiting.

● At the Brotman Memorial Hospital he became curious about an oxygen chamber and had his photo taken inside it. Later, he sent copies of the photo to newspapers with the anonymous story that he had bought one and was sleeping in it so that he could live to be 150 years old.

● Later, Jackson made up the widely reported hoax that he had offered $500,000 for the skeleton of the "Elephant Man," John Merrick. (In response, *Playboy* magazine jokingly reported, "Descendants of the Elephant Man have offered ten thousand dollars for the remains of Michael Jackson's nose.")

● Jackson's office also created the rumor that he was so obsessed with his chimp, Bubbles, that he was learning "monkey language" in order to communicate with him.

● Jackson, like many superstars, has often felt that others are overrated in comparison to his own talents. In recent years, he demanded that the media refer to him as "The King of Pop" if they wanted an interview.

● His opinion of other singers: Paul McCartney? Okay writer, not much of an entertainer. "I do better box office than he does." Frank Sinatra? "I don't know what people see in the guy. He's a legend, but he isn't much of a singer. He doesn't even have hits any more." Mick Jagger? "He sings flat. How did *he* ever get to be a star? I just don't get it. He doesn't sell as many records as I do." Madonna? "She just isn't that good. Let's face it. She can't sing. She's just an okay dancer. What does she do best? She knows how to market herself. That's about it."

● Says Jackson, "People think they know me, but they don't. Not really. Actually I am one of the loneliest people on this planet. I cry sometimes, because it hurts. It does. To be honest, I guess you could say that it hurts to be me."

Virginia Woolf

Virginia Woolf was an early feminist and, with Joyce and Proust, an innovative pioneer of the stream-of-consciousness novel, in which the plot unravels from the main character's interior monologues. Did her periodic insanity hurt her ability to write—or did the voices she heard actually help?

- The third of four children, Adeline Virginia Stephen was born on January 25, 1882, in London. Virginia's parents had intended to stop at two children, but contraception was still more of an art than a science at the time.

- Virginia also lived with four older half siblings, three from her mother's first marriage, and one half sister (Laura, who was mentally ill and eventually moved into an asylum) from her father's.

- Nine-year-old Virginia and her twelve-year-old sister Vanessa began publishing their own neighborhood weekly newspaper. They faithfully kept it up for four years. Virginia also caught and killed butterflies for display, and was considered a "demon bowler" (an excellent pitcher) at cricket. Her nickname, which she kept for the rest of her life, was "Goat."

- But not all was completely innocent on the home front. According to Virginia's later accounts, her eighteen-year-old half brother Gerald Duckworth once stood her on a ledge and explored her genitals with his hand. In her adolescence, Virginia's other half brother, George, moved from friendly fraternal hugs to visiting her bed at night to kiss, fondle, and caress her. This went on until she was twenty-two. Virginia wrote later that she felt George had spoiled her life before it began.

- George would later became her first publisher.

- Virginia's mother died when she was thirteen. Virginia experienced the first of a series of mental breakdowns. Her pulse raced uncontrollably, she suffered delusions, and heard voices. According to Thomas Caramagno in *Flight of the Mind*, Virginia inherited a manic-depressive disorder from both branches of her family, the symptoms of which were triggered in times of great stress. In her manic phase, she was known to talk incessantly for as much as two days and nights.

- When Virginia began writing seriously in her teens, she did so while standing at a tall, sloping desk. "Her principle motive," according to her nephew and biographer Quentin Bell, "was the fact that Vanessa, like many painters, stood to work. . . . This led Virginia to feel that her own pursuit might appear less arduous than that of her sister unless she stood as well." Virginia finally began sitting while writing at age thirty.

- At age sixteen Virginia experienced her first crush. It was on Madge Symonds Wyamar, married to one of her cousins.

- At age twenty Virginia fell in love with Violet Dickinson, nearly twice her age at thirty-seven. The two had a passionate ten-year relationship, largely carried out in correspondence. Each signed their letters "Your lover" and were full of sentiments like this from Violet: "When you wake in the night I suppose you feel my arms around you"; however, most biographers believe that the relationship stopped just short of sex, like most of Virginia's relationships.

- Virginia tried her hand at teaching in 1907, but stopped after she found the experience too flustering. She wrote ruefully to Violet after the first night, "I can tell you the first sentence of my lecture: 'The poet Keats died when he was 25; and he wrote all his work before that.' "

● At age twenty-three Virginia moved into an apartment with her brother Adrian, who was younger by eighteen months ("fifteen years," she claimed jokingly). Their dining room walls and ceiling became scarred from little round pats of butter, which they sometimes shot at each other during meals.

● Virginia and some friends twice perpetrated elaborate hoaxes to convince local authorities that they were visiting royalty from far-off lands. The first time they were supposedly from Zanzibar; the second time, they successfully boarded a top-secret navy vessel by claiming to be the Emperor of Abyssinia and his entourage. Virginia wore a beard, and the well-educated hoaxers simulated speaking Swahili by quoting from Virgil's *Aeneid* in Greek.

● In 1908 Vanessa had a baby and became completely absorbed in mothering. Clive Bell, her husband of eighteen months, entered into a long and passionate relationship with Virginia; whether it was physically sexual is still debated. The baby in question, Quentin Bell, who would become Virginia's biographer, not surprisingly preferred to believe it was a "flirtation" because "I doubt whether the business would have lasted for so long if Virginia had given him what he wanted . . . a delightful little infidelity ending up in bed."

● Virginia, twenty-seven, began looking for a husband of her own, but was stymied by the fact that most of the men she was attracted to were gay. One, Lytton Strachey, was such a good friend that he proposed anyway one day in 1909; Virginia immediately accepted even though Vanessa warned, "I should like Lytton as a brother-in-law better than anyone I know, but the only way I can perceive of bringing that to pass would be if he were to fall in love with Adrian." Strachey quickly came to his senses and the two canceled the engagement, with a relieved Strachey explaining to friends, "I was in terror lest she kiss me."

• Another somewhat promising suitor fell out of the running when he sat Virginia down and told her that, as a practicing sadist, he enjoyed hurting his lovers, and asked if she would mind. She did.

• At about the time that Clive and Virginia's relationship was cooling down in 1911, Vanessa had an affair with painter Roger Fry. Within the "Bloomsbury group" of friends and associates, she initiated a new licentiousness, dancing at one time with such enthusiasm that she shook off all her clothes from the waist up. She and Virginia scandalized a Postimpressionists' Ball by arriving with naked legs and shoulders as "Gauguin girls." And there were rumors that Vanessa had copulated in the middle of a crowded drawing room with not-so-dismal economist Maynard Keynes.

• In that spirit, Virginia went to stay with poet Rupert Brooke at Grantchester, where they bathed naked by moonlight. But again, there is some doubt as to whether a sexual relationship was ever consummated. Shortly thereafter she shared a house with Adrian and two other men. Many of her friends and family were shocked at this outrageous arrangement, including, ironically, George. "Oh, it's quite all right, George," Vanessa quipped, "you see, it's so near the Foundling Hospital."

• One of the other men was Leonard Woolf, who shortly afterward left to become a British colonial administrator in Ceylon. When he returned in early 1912, he began actively wooing Virginia. Soon after she took to her bed with another breakdown, but eventually he proposed, and she accepted. They married on August 10 and, after briefly considering an Icelandic honeymoon, traveled instead to Spain.

• Perhaps Iceland would have been more appropriate. Despite Spain's warm weather, their relationship in bed was as cold as the fjords. Virginia wrote in a letter from Saragossa to a friend, "Why do you think people make such a fuss about marriage & copulation? . . . Certainly I find the climax immensely exaggerated. Except for a sustained good humour due to the fact that every twinge of anger is at once visited upon my husband, I might still be Miss S."

• After the honeymoon they consulted with Vanessa, who wrote afterward, using Virginia's childhood nickname, "They seemed very happy, but are evidently both a little exercised in their minds on the subject of the Goat's coldness. I think . . . she never understood or sympathised with sexual passion in men. Apparently she still gets no pleasure at all from the act, which I think is curious. They were very anxious to know when I first had an orgasm." The three decided it was all the fault of her abusive half brothers. The couple's sexual relations stopped permanently shortly after their honeymoon ended, but otherwise they would remain reasonably content for the next twenty-eight years.

• After an elaborate round-robin game in which a circle of her friends took roles of fictitious characters and created a "novel" through correspondence, Virginia wrote, "Life is certainly very exciting . . . Oh how I wish I could write a novel!"

• However, writing novels was more exciting than she bargained for. When coming to the end of what would become the first draft of *The Voyage Out*, Virginia began suffering headaches, insomnia, nervous irritation, delusions, depression, and the inability to eat. Later, when the book, her first, was accepted for publication, she became immobilized while reading the proofs— she couldn't eat, sleep, or go out, thinking people would jeer at her in the street because her writing was so bad. She had to be rushed to the hospital after taking a lethal dose of veronal. She slowly recovered her sanity, thanks in part to rave reviews for the book. Mental breakdown near the end of each book became a pattern she would continue for the rest of her life.

• To distract Virginia from the pressures of her novels, Leonard suggested that they start their own small publishing house, The Hogarth Press. Virginia agreed, hoping that it would draw Leonard away from his involvement in Fabian socialist politics.

They bought a small tabletop press and learned to set type. Their first booklet, containing a short story from each of them, sold 135 of the 150 copies printed, actually making a small profit.

• The Hogarth Press expanded from the kitchen table into the rest of the house and began publishing twenty-five to thirty books a year, including the first edition of T. S. Eliot's *The Wasteland* (Eliot had worked as their assistant editor at one point), the complete works of Sigmund Freud, and books by Dostoevsky, Tolstoy, Gertrude Stein, and dozens of major British authors of the day. The Woolfs did, however, reject James Joyce's *Ulysses* based on Virginia's appraisal after reading the first two hundred pages: "I was stimulated, charmed, interested, then puzzled, bored, irritated, and disillusioned, as by a queasy undergraduate scratching his pimples. . . . It seems to be the book of a self-taught working man."

• In 1923 the Woolfs met Harold Nicolson and his wife, Vita Sackville-West, and the two couples became fast friends. The two women quickly became more than that—their affair lasted five years, making it Virginia's longest-lasting sexual relationship. The two husbands took it in remarkable good spirits, remaining calm and not seeing it as a threat to either their marriages or to the four-way friendship.

• In 1926, with the success of Virginia's novels *Mrs. Dalloway* and *The Common Reader*, the Woolfs splurged and invested in indoor plumbing, giving them the luxury of flush toilets, hot water, and a full-size bathtub. Still, the scale of publishing in Britain at the time was small—a best-seller might sell fewer than ten thousand copies. It wasn't until *The Years* became a best-seller in the United States in 1938 that the Woolfs actually became wealthy.

• Virginia could finally relax a little. She took up simple pleasures like baking bread, canning marmalade, and working needlepoint to interrupt the strains of writing. She also had a bowling green built and took up the sport with a passion, playing twelve hundred games in five years.

- But Hitler's gains in Europe were causing her great distress. After bombs damaged her house and destroyed her sister's studio, Virginia was convinced that it was just a matter of time before the Germans conquered England. She made a suicide pact with her husband, who was Jewish.

- "The only way I keep afloat is by working," she said—ironically, considering how she died. On November 23, 1940, she finished her last novel, *Between the Acts*, and spent the next several months writing in her diary what's been called "the longest suicide note in the English language."

- On March 28, 1941, she wrote a loving note to her husband. "Dearest, I feel I am going mad again. I feel we can't go through another of those terrible times. And I shant recover this time. I begin to hear voices, and I can't concentrate. So I am doing what seems the best thing to do. . . . You have been incredibly patient with me and incredibly good. . . . If anybody could have saved me it would have been you. Everything has gone from me but the certainty of your goodness. . . . I don't think two people could have been happier than we have been. V." She placed her note on the mantelpiece at 11:30 A.M. and walked to the Ouse River in Sussex. After forcing large stones into the pocket of her coat, Virginia stepped into the water to meet what she had called "the one experience I shall never describe."

Thomas Alva Edison

Thomas Edison is famous for inventing the electric light, the phonograph, and the movie projector. But did you also know that he invented the mimeograph machine and a "rat paralyzer"? Or that he tried to sabotage the development of AC power?

- Thomas Alva Edison's head was so abnormally large when he was born, the village doctor thought that he might have brain fever.

- As a child he was called "Al." A scientist from the start, he burned his father's barn down when he set a small fire inside it "just to see what it would do."

- At age eight he was enrolled as a student in a one-room school run by one Reverend Alva Engle and his wife. The reverend liked to implant his lessons in his pupils' minds with the help of a leather strap. After he had been at school for three months, he heard the schoolmaster saying that his mind was "backward." Edison stormed out of the school and ran home, refusing to return. His mother taught him at home from then on.

- Decades later, the same schoolmaster wrote Edison a letter. He told him that he had not pushed his father to pay Al's school bill, but he was retired now and "as you now have a large income, I thought perhaps you would be glad to render me a little aid." Edison responded by sending him a check for twenty-five dollars, liberal enough in view of his unhappy memories of school and teacher.

● He never learned how to spell, and as an adult his grammar and syntax were appalling.

● At age nine he read R. G. Parker's *School of Natural Philosophy.* It described and illustrated various scientific experiments that could be performed at home. All his pocket money began to be used for chemicals and supplies for science experiments. Sometimes his parents would hear muffled explosions and worry that he would blow up the house.

● After reading about Benjamin Franklin's discoveries in static electricity, he tried rubbing vigorously together the fur of two big tomcats whose tails he had attached to wires. The result of his experiment? He was unmercifully clawed.

● He knew that balloons would go up because of the volatile gas in them. He gave a large quantity of Seidlitz powders, an upset stomach remedy, to a trusting but simpleminded playmate, reasoning that the gas produced might send the boy flying through the air. The boy became terribly sick to his stomach, and Edison was soundly spanked by his mother.

● His deafness was the result of a bout with scarlet fever, and was helped along through periodic infections of the middle ear that went unattended. By age thirteen he already had a substantial hearing loss. He was totally deaf in his left ear and had limited hearing in the right when he ran the Edison Record Company, but he insisted on making the final decisions on what music got recorded and released.

● As an itinerant telegrapher he often lived in vermin-infested rented rooms. He invented what he called a "rat paralyzer." When the rat stepped on the metal plates just right, "it would render up it's soul and depart this earthly sphere."

● He invented the stock ticker, the mimeograph machine, and a rock crusher for separating metals from ore.

• But not all of Edison's inventions were winners. He invented an electronic vote-counting machine which never got produced. And he came up with something called "Polyform," a bottled concoction "guaranteed to cure sick headaches, neuralgia, and other nervous diseases."

• He made the fluoroscope, the first x-ray machine. He came to realize that its rays were harmful when an assistant by the name of Clarence Dally became poisonously affected: his flesh became ulcerated, and his hair fell out. Several years later, after numerous amputations, Dally died.

• When trying to find the best filament for the electric light bulb, he sat at a microscope while he had his assistants gather up mountainous piles of rubbish—bark, rags, old carpets, wild grasses, horses' hooves, hides, cornstalks, and more than six thousand other samples—so that he could examine and dissect them.

• In order to keep his associates from taking his prized cigars, Edison bought a box of trick cigars made of old paper and hair. Two months later, the man who had sold him the cigars came by to see how the hoax had worked. "Hoax?" said the always pre-occupied Edison. "Oh . . ." He had smoked them all himself without noticing any difference.

• He and his second wife, Mina, talked to each other privately even when they were in a room full of people by tapping messages out in Morse code on the palm of the other's hand. In fact, that's how he proposed to her.

• He was disdainful about the idea of using the phonograph to reproduce music, thinking that its best use was to record dictation for busy businessmen. "I don't want the phonograph sold for amusement purposes. It is not a toy," Edison thundered. "It is for business purposes only."

• "Everybody steals in commerce and industry," Edison once said. "I've stolen a lot myself. But at least I know how to steal well."

● When a huge fire erupted in his factory, in the area where the chemicals and motion picture film was located, Edison watched it with folded arms, and finally told his son to go get Mina and his siblings, because "they'll never see a fire like this again."

● One distasteful episode in Edison's professional life: In 1888, he electrocuted dozens of cats and dogs by getting them to walk onto a sheet of tin which was supplied with one thousand volts of electricity. He bought the animals from schoolboys, no questions asked, for twenty-five cents each—resulting in fewer pets in West Orange, New Jersey. It was part of Edison's scare campaign against alternating current—whereby electricity wiggles back and forth instead of moving in a direct line—which was being championed by a rival, George Westinghouse. In most ways AC was superior. Edison owned all the patents for direct current technology. He decided the only way to fight back was to show that AC was deadly dangerous.

● He printed up an eighty-three-page pamphlet written in the most inflammatory way to scare people from letting AC into their houses. He conducted "experiments" for the press one night at midnight to avoid being stopped by the ASPCA. In one, he wrapped wet bandages and copper wires around the paws of a fox terrier and increased the AC voltage until it died. He killed over fifty former household pets in this way.

● The press was gratifyingly morbid in their accounts of the animals' deaths by "killer AC." Edison decided to play his trump card. Although personally opposed to the death penalty, he endorsed an idea by the state of New York to kill condemned criminals by electricity which would, he wrote, "perform its work in the shortest space of time, and inflict the least amount of suffering upon its victim. Especially," he added wickedly, "alternating machines, manufactured principally in this country by Geo. Westinghouse. . . . The passage of the current from these machines through the human body, even by the slightest contacts, produces instantaneous death."

● Edison's lab helpfully volunteered to research how much current was needed to cause death in a human. He began zapping calves and horses to death. He testified to the humaneness and painlessness of the process. He even tried to popularize a new term to describe killing someone with electricity: Turning down "ampermort," "electromort," and "electricide," he suggested the coinage "westinghoused, or to use the noun, we could say that . . . a man was condemned to the westinghouse."

● Despite Edison's tireless research, however, the electric chair that it inspired was anything but painless and humane. When the authorities tried to "westinghouse" Charles McElvaine in 1892, he wouldn't die. He writhed in pain as they jolted him first for twenty-two seconds, finally for seventy-two seconds, until smoke came from his head and body and he finally died. The *New York Times* called it "an awful spectacle, far worse than hanging."

● Yet, in spite of Edison's propaganda and grisly "experiments," AC won the current battle, primarily because it was easier to transmit over long distances. It is the system we still use today.

● When Edison turned seventy-five, Mina demanded that he cut his working hours down to "only" sixteen a day.

● Thomas Alva Edison died on October 18, 1931. President Hoover asked that people voluntarily dim their lights for a few minutes at 10:00 P.M. on October 21, the day of Edison's funeral.

Pablo Picasso

Probably the greatest artist of the twentieth century, and most certainly the greatest innovator, Pablo Picasso was in the forefront of art for over fifty years.

- Born not breathing, Pablo Picasso was set aside by the midwife, who thought he was dead. An uncle, who was also a doctor, saved him by breathing cigar smoke into his nose.

- Picasso could draw before he could talk, and, according to his mother, his first word was the Spanish word for pencil.

- Picasso's father was a professor of art. An artist himself, he specialized in "dining room" art and often let young Pablo finish his paintings as practice. One day he was so stunned by the quality of his son's work that he handed his brushes, palette, and colors to Pablo, vowing never to paint again. Pablo was only thirteen.

- When only fourteen, Picasso took an exam so that he could take the advanced course at the School of Fine Arts in Barcelona. The examiners told him that he had a month to finish the exam; instead, he brought it back the next day, exhibiting more talent than students several years older. Picasso pulled a similar stunt when he was sixteen, producing drawings in one day to enter the Royal Academy of San Fernando in Madrid.

• Prolific creator of at least fifteen thousand titles during his ninety years, Picasso was painting as many as three canvasses a day by the time he was in his late teens. By his early twenties, he had already produced over one thousand paintings, drawings, and engravings.

• Picasso's visual memory and line placement were extraordinary. He often drew complete figures and animals—even a whole bullfight scene once—with a single, unbroken line. But his great talent did not make him an immediate success. To keep warm in the winter of 1902, he was forced to burn a large number of his drawings.

• Gertrude Stein sat for her famous 1906 portrait some eighty to ninety times. Picasso was criticized for not creating a better likeness. "Never mind," said Picasso, "she will manage to look like it in the end." Stein was satisfied with her portrait: "For me, it is I." She kept it with her until she died.

• Picasso's 1907 painting *Les Demoiselles d'Avignon* is now considered the beginning of cubism and of twentieth-century art. But when Picasso showed it to friends as a work in progress, almost all of them hated it, so he stopped working on it. The painting was shown once in 1916 and then rolled up and stored on the floor of his studio until 1920, when it was purchased by a collector, sight unseen. It wasn't given its name until 1925, and wasn't widely exhibited until 1937, thirty years after it had been painted.

• Picasso did not like to exhibit his work or haggle with dealers. He was often miserable when his paintings were sold. Much of his work he kept, unable to part with it, including a painting he completed at age fourteen of a little girl with bare feet.

• Picasso and Georges Braque collaborated so closely during their cubist period, they often did not even sign their paintings, and after a while even they could not remember who painted what. Braque said their relationship at the time was like being "roped mountaineers." Picasso referred to Braque as his "wife" during their collaboration and as his "ex-wife" afterward.

● Cubism, unlike abstract art, used real images as its point of departure, but not everyone could tell. The first owner of *The Accordionist* (1911), an American, believed it was a landscape. Perhaps it took a certain way of seeing: When art dealer Ambroise Vollard exhibited Picasso's 1910 portrait of him, most people complained that they did not "see" Vollard in the portrait. However, a four-year-old son of a friend saw the painting and immediately announced, "Look! That's Vollard!"

● Stein and Picasso were out walking in Paris one night in 1914 when a camouflaged army truck passed. They had heard of camouflage but had never seen it, and Picasso was amazed. "Yes, we did that!" he shouted. "That is cubism!"

● In his early years of obscurity, Picasso joked that someday his art would be valuable enough that burglars would break in and steal it. By 1914 Picasso was becoming well known. One day he came home to find that his house had been burglarized. To Picasso's surprise the only things missing were his bed and table linens.

● For Picasso, the newly whitewashed walls of rented rooms were a temptation too great to resist. In 1900 he painted the walls of his small apartment in Barcelona with lavish decorations. The landlord insisted that Picasso pay to repaint the apartment. "What a fool," Picasso said years later, "he could have sold the whole wall for a fortune if he had only had the sense to leave it."

● In 1912, in Les Clochettes for the summer, he liked one of his wall paintings so much that he had the wall dismantled and sent to him in Paris.

● Picasso painted *Guernica*, his mural-sized painting depicting the horrors of war, in a month. The canvas was too tall for Picasso's studio, so he mounted the canvas at an angle and moved a ladder along as he worked. For the parts of the canvas that were out of reach, he used special long-handled brushes. During the Nazi occupation of France in World War II, a German officer, seeing a reproduction in Picasso's studio, reportedly said to the artist, "So you did that!" To which Picasso replied, "No, you did."

● The Germans confiscated metals, especially bronze, for the war effort, but friends "diverted" some of the metal for Picasso's statues. Under the eyes of Nazi guards, Picasso's friends slipped his models into the foundry in carts full of garbage and brought the finished casts out the same way.

● Art supplies were scarce during the war, so Picasso often created art from things that he found lying around. One friend, filmmaker Jean Cocteau, called Picasso "King of the Ragpickers" for his art from scrap materials, one of the most famous of which is the 1943 *Bull's Head*, created from the handlebars and seat of a bicycle.

● Picasso enjoyed the company of movie stars, including one of his favorites, Gary Cooper. Cooper once visited Picasso, bringing a Colt .45 revolver along as a present. The two men spent the afternoon happily shooting away at a tin can. Neither hit it once.

● Picasso took four days in January 1941 to write his first play, *Desire Caught by the Tail*, in which all of the play's characters die in the end, suffocated by fumes from fried potatoes.

● He had over the years not only an assortment of dogs and cats, but also a pet goat, a tortoise, a monkey, and an owl. Pigeons were allowed to fly through the studio, and became a recurring subject in his paintings. Picasso used the head of his Airedale as the model for a minotaur.

● After World War II, Matisse gave Picasso a Milanese pigeon. When the French Communist Party asked Picasso to design a poster for the Second Communist Peace Congress (Paris 1949), he let them use a lithograph that he had made of it. The pigeon became a "dove of peace" for the conference and the image was afterward distributed throughout the world. During the congress,

Françoise Gilot, Picasso's mistress at the time, gave birth to the daughter they named Paloma, Spanish for "dove."

● Early in his life, Picasso and his friends experimented with opium and other drugs. But Picasso stopped his experiments primarily because he found that, though the drugs enhanced his vision and imagination, they lessened his drive to paint.

● The cities of Chicago and Marseilles were the first cities to ask Picasso to design monuments for them. When the delegation from Chicago visited him in his studio, Picasso told them he was delighted that the first two cities to approach him were cities famous for their gangsters.

James Dean

James Dean played a disaffected youth in the 1950s and then he died tragically—a perfect way to become a role model for crazy mixed-up teens. Dean has been a perpetually young icon for four decades now.

• In how many movies did movie legend James Dean appear? Because he's such a famous icon, most people guess many more than the real answer: three.

• James Byron Dean, born February 8, 1931, killed in an auto accident on September 30, 1955, led a contradictory life. Co-workers like Elizabeth Taylor and Dennis Hopper described him as alternately generous and mean-spirited, solitary and social, wise and adolescent. Directors found his mood swings—from soft-spoken to impossible—difficult to work around.

• After his mother died of uterine cancer when he was nine, Jimmy Dean went to live with his aunt and uncle in Marion, Indiana. In high school, Jimmy participated in theatrical productions and played on the basketball team.

• There are a lot of stories suggesting Dean's pansexuality. During his high school years, he supposedly became the gay lover of a Wesleyan minister appropriately named Dr. James DeWeerd. However, Dean himself was vague when questioned about his preferences. Self-identified former lovers have described him as practically everything—heterosexual, homosexual, asexual, bisexual. Of course, in the 1950s it was virtually deadly to admit to an alternative lifestyle, especially when one's livelihood was based in part on attracting young women and girls. Some biographers claim that Dean dodged the draft by claiming homosexuality; others say it was because of poor eyesight.

• When Dean started Santa Monica City College, he moved in with his father, who had remarried. But father and son didn't get along, so James moved into a fraternity. When he was asked to leave the fraternity after assaulting another member for referring to him as a "fruit," Dean and friend Bill Bass moved in together. Bass had difficulty handling the future icon's mood swings, and he eventually moved out.

• Dean's first professional acting job was in a Pepsi commercial. After also appearing in a TV play, a group of Los Angeles girls formed the first James Dean fan club. In 1951 Dean moved to New York to act in the theaters there and was accepted by the Actors Studio, which is considered a great honor. However, after experiencing some harsh criticism, Dean moved back to California.

• Dean answered a cattle call and director Elia Kazan cast him as Cal in *East of Eden*. Kazan, who became a close friend, gave him the nickname "Creep." During the filming of *Eden*, Dean had a serious affair with Italian actress Pier Angeli. The relationship ended in heartache for the heartthrob when she abruptly married singer Vic Damone at the urging of her family, who wanted her to marry a Roman Catholic.

• Although he was called Jimmy, he used the name James Dean because "Jimmy Dean" was already being used by the country singer and future sausage maker.

• As a result of his acting in *East of Eden*, Dean was offered lots of work. He starred in two more big-screen movies, *Rebel Without a Cause* and *Giant*, which was released after his death. He also acted in several T.V. movies, including "The Dark, Dark Hours," a melodrama with Ronald Reagan.

● Because Dean was a "method" actor, he often left fellow actors and actresses at a loss for how to treat him. Method acting encourages the actor to fully "become" his character, both onstage and off. For instance, if a character is supposed to be tired and nervous, an actor might not sleep for a day or two (or more) and drink a lot of coffee before shooting that scene. He agreed with the assessment of many of his costars: "If I were them, I know I couldn't tolerate myself."

● Still, Elizabeth Taylor, Julie Harris, and several other women he worked with were fond of him. Taylor, in fact, gave him a cat, Marcus, and a rather eccentric recipe for its food which included Karo syrup, evaporated milk, egg yolks, and distilled water. His male costars, however, often had difficulty accepting his odd behavior. Raymond Massey, who played his father in *East of Eden*, for instance, felt deep antagonism from Dean and did not understand the actor; director Kazan exploited this difficult relationship to enhance the on-screen father-and-son conflicts.

● As Dean's stature in Hollywood grew, he was able to meet several of his idols, including Humphrey Bogart, Gary Cooper, and Alec Guinness. Unfortunately, the seasoned actors rarely had a positive word for him, perhaps partly because of his brash attitude and statements such as, "I'm not disturbed by the comparison to Brando—nor am I flattered." He claimed to have a great desire to play Hamlet, contending, "Only a young man can play him as he was—with naïveté. Laurence Olivier played it safe. Something is lost when the older men play him."

● During the filming of *Giant*, Dean became extremely nervous during a scene with Elizabeth Taylor. Finally, Dean walked from the set, unzipped his pants, and calmly urinated in front of the astonished crowd. He then proclaimed that he was ready to do the scene. His reasoning was "If you're nervous your senses can't reach your subconscious, and that's that—you can't work. So I figured if I could piss in front of all those people, and be cool about it, I could go in front of the camera and do just about anything at all."

● "He really wanted to look uptight. So to get himself really uncomfortable, he told me he didn't pee all day until ready to do the shot," said Dennis Hopper, costarring in the film.

● Despite the difficulties Dean caused for directors, he had aspirations of becoming one himself, believing that he would be better at directing than acting. He kept a notebook of set designs, camera angles, and other directions from the movies he worked on.

● If there was anything that Dean loved as much as acting, it was fast cars and motorcycles. During the filming of *East of Eden*, Dean traded his Triumph T-110 sports car for a more powerful model, the Triumph 500. Of course, studio execs weren't pleased with this, and future contracts forbade him to race cars while filming a movie.

● Ironically, a few days before his tragic auto accident, Dean had filmed a road-safety message, ad-libbing, "Take it easy driving. The life you save may be mine."

● The day before his fatal accident, Dean drove his Porsche 550 Spyder at high speed through fog and darkness on Highway 101 near Santa Barbara and attracted the attention of a highway patrol officer, who pursued him. Dean's car easily outran the police cruiser, and he returned home at 3 A.M., tired but unticketed.

● On September 30, 1955, Dean and his mechanic, Rolf Weutherich, started on a long trip north for a race in Salinas, California. On the way, Dean was pulled over by a highway patrol officer and ticketed for going 65 mph in a 55 mph zone. After passing through Bakersfield, Dean turned west onto Highway 466, a straight road running through flat land, and pushed the car up past 100 mph. Dusk began falling and the grey Spyder blended in with the color of the road.

- Donald Turnipseed, a year younger than Dean, was driving for a weekend jaunt from college in his father's black and white 1950 Ford Tudor. In the town of Cholame, the highway split in a Y shape at a dangerous intersection. Turnipseed stopped, saw nothing coming, and began the left turn onto Highway 41. Dean and Weutherich, rapidly approaching the intersection from the other direction, saw Turnipseed's Ford edging out.

- Turnipseed heard squealing tires and realized there was something wrong. He slammed on his brakes and jerked the steering wheel to the right, but continued skidding forward. The cars collided with a deafening crash. Turnipseed, smashed against the windshield, saw a fist over his head and then a body as Dean flew over his car, holding his arm out in a futile attempt to protect his head. Next, he saw the Spyder for the first time, flying upside down above him.

- Dean ended up facedown on the pavement with arms and legs twisted into a contorted pose. The car landed near him, practically unrecognizable. Weutherich, trapped in the ball of metal, was freed and rushed to the hospital. Both he and Turnipseed survived, but Dean was dead before emergency crews arrived.

- Dean's last words were: "The guy's got to stop! He's seen us. . . ."

Joseph Stalin

In 1879, Yekaterian and Vissarion Dzhugashvili became parents to a son who would become one of the world's most-feared personalities; his name was Iosif, nicknamed Soso. To the world, he would be known as Joseph Stalin—the post-Lenin leader of the USSR.

- For one who would have such a profound effect on his country and the world, Joseph Stalin had a rather humble and uneventful childhood in the Georgian village of Gori.

- Joseph's two brothers, Mikhail and Georgii, died before reaching the age of one. Joseph's father, Vissarion, a shoemaker, was an alcoholic who abused his wife and child. His mother was supportive, ensuring that he was educated first in a theological school and later in a seminary in Tiflis. As he progressed in the Russian Communist Party, however, Joseph evidently did not feel a strong bond with her; when she died in 1937, he had not visited her for two years.

- Stalin was expelled from the seminary in 1899 and became politically active shortly before Lenin and Martov began their revolutionaries' newspaper *Iskra* (*The Spark*). In 1901 Stalin became an elected member of the Tiflis Social Democratic Committee. This began his "career" as a political activist.

- Tsarist officials kept an eye on him between the times when he was either imprisoned or exiled. This physical description was circulated among the police at that time:

—5'4" male
—sunken hazel eyes
—soft voice
—birthmark on left ear
—pockmarked face
—thick black hair and mustache (but no beard)
—withered left arm
—second and third toes of left foot grown together

• Stalin escaped the Tsarist prisons a record five times. The prisons weren't as bad as you would imagine—they were thought of as universities of sorts because the prisoners generally spent a lot of time reading, with access to vast libraries. Stalin, it's said, vowed that "his" prison system would neither allow escapes nor become an educational system. It would, he said, become a grim exercise in survival.

• In June 1904 Stalin, still known as Soso Dzhugashvili, married Yekatarina "Kato" Svanidze at St. David's Church, with fellow seminarian Khristofor Tkhinvoleli officiating. Stalin had no real career and they were forced to live "on the run." He became known as a "Robin Hood" of sorts, taking part in robberies to assist the Party, although he was actually once expelled for these "expropriations." His son, Yakov, was born in 1905. In 1907 his wife died of typhoid.

• In 1912 he changed his name to Stalin, meaning "man of steel," and made an aggressive entrance into Bolshevik politics. After escaping from deportation in western Siberia, Stalin visited with Lenin in Cracow and proceeded to Vienna, where he met Trotsky and began writing political tracts. Stalin was selected for the Bolshevik Central Committee at a Party conference in Prague.

• Stalin avoided being drafted into World War I service of Russia because of his withered arm and deformed foot. During the war, he was exiled for four years to Turukhansk.

• When the Bolsheviks seized power from the temporary revolutionary government after the assassination of the tsar, Stalin was named commissar for nationalities. Following this revolution, unrest continued in Russia and neighboring states; all those still resisting would later be defeated by the Red Army, ultimately leading to the formation of the Union of Soviet Socialist Republics. In 1922 Stalin was elected secretary general of the Party's Central Committee, positioning himself to take over once Lenin's health failed.

• In 1924 Lenin died and Stalin seized power. The only real opposition to Stalin's power grab came from Leon Trotsky, whom Lenin had trusted and valued. However, Trotsky was more of a revolutionary thinker and philosopher, and he did not pay close attention to politics, allowing Stalin to easily gain the support and power needed to lead the Party from the secretary general's position. Trotsky was expelled from the Party, later permanently exiled from the USSR, and eventually assassinated in Mexico.

• Stalin pretty much lived to rule. Although he remarried and was the father of more children, his personal life hardly existed as he rose into power. Nadezhda, Stalin's second wife and mother of two of his children, committed suicide on November 8, 1932. Stalin did not appear to blame himself for her death (as most others around him secretly did); instead, he viewed her action as treachery on her part. He did not attend the funeral.

• His relationship with his children was so distant as to be virtually nonexistent, and his children did not lead happy lives. Stalin's eldest son, Yakov, attempted to shoot himself, but the bullet missed vital organs and he survived after a long recuperation. Shortly after this suicide attempt, Stalin reportedly greeted his son with "Ha! You missed!" Yakov later joined the army and became a commander; he was killed while attempting to escape from a prison camp during World War II. Stalin's other son, Vasili, was also in the army, but he finished life an invalid, the result of alcoholism.

● Stalin did appear to have a closer relationship with his daughter, Svetlana, but that faded quickly as she grew older and he grew more paranoid. The relationship became seriously strained when he had her first boyfriend, Alexander Yakovlevich Kapler, sentenced, on a trumped-up charge, to ten years in a prison camp.

● Meanwhile, Stalin focused on ferreting out or "unmasking enemies of the people." He made accusations against friends and even family members who were previously regarded as allies, and he did nothing to assist those who might have been unjustly accused. Instead, he grew more intensely suspicious.

● By the time Stalin began his infamous five-year plans, he was far removed from the people, and he had little regard for the human difficulties associated with collectivization. The kulaks (the farming peasant class) became desperate as their properties were confiscated. The agricultural life of the USSR was in turmoil: half to two-thirds of all livestock were slaughtered by 1933 to feed hungry people, the amount of cultivated land fell sharply, and families torn from their land became homeless. Hunger and desperation led to petty thievery of food and basic supplies, which was punishable by an unconditional ten-year imprisonment. By 1933 more than fifty thousand people had been sentenced to concentration camps.

● During this time, Stalin trusted aides and colleagues less and less, preferring to direct Soviet life personally. He purged anyone that seemed to threaten his power. The relationship between Stalin and the rest of the Party became so strained in the early 1930s that almost a quarter of the Party delegates voted against Stalin in a leadership vote. After that, Stalin no longer took the chance of putting himself up for reelection. He directed that Party and state documents stop listing him as secretary general, an elected position, and he continued ruling without an official title.

● Toward the end of the 1930s Stalin became more hard-lined and paranoid. Officials and workers alike could be accused of

"Trotskyism" and sentenced to death. In a two-year period, 30,514 people were sentenced to be shot for disloyalty to the state. The NKVD, Stalin's police force, rounded up thousands of people suspected of capital crimes; Stalin and the chief of NKVD signed orders for their executions after reading only the total number of crimes for each category of criminals, regardless of circumstance or proof.

● By the end of the 1930s the purges began tapering off. Party membership had understandably declined, so Stalin seemed less inclined to purge and more inclined to work on filling the ranks with properly dogmatized young Stalinists.

● The USSR entered World War II eventually, joining the Allies against Germany. After the war ended, the wary Allies quickly split again. Stalin continued his hard-line tactics through the last years of his reign, and there was continual unrest within the Party. He focused on military development and a show of world power while living standards within his country suffered.

● Stalin died in 1953. The posthumous inventory revealed his possessions to be very simple. Apart from a government-issue piano, there were no valuable furnishings of any kind. Stalin's clothes were largely inexpensive suits and a marshal's uniform, and his linens consisted of army-issued blankets. The only original art he owned was a photo of himself and Lenin together in a friendly pose at Gorky Park. This was later determined to be a carefully constructed photo montage—a fake rendition of a scene that never happened.

Janis Joplin

San Francisco rock star Janis Joplin combined a whiskey voice, a high-energy blues style, and a "Just say yes" lifestyle to become a heroine of the 1960s counterculture.

● Janis Lyn Joplin was born the oldest of three children in Port Arthur, Texas, on January 19, 1943. A pudgy, acne-scarred kid, she was an outcast with a terrible reputation, in part because she let boys play with her breasts in the choir loft at church when she was fourteen. "They laughed me out of class, out of town, and out of the state," she said of her hometown. The city didn't have much reason for self-righteousness, since a good part of its tax revenue in Joplin's time came from more than thirty whorehouses that were more or less out in the open and which catered primarily to sailors.

● Her hometown continued to snub her after her death. Although the only major celebrity to come out of Port Arthur, the city council refused for decades afterward to name a street or park after her because (as one council member put it), "How could we set her up as someone for young people to emulate?" Biographer Ellis Amburn, in his book *Pearl*, writes, "While Memphis rakes in millions from Graceland, home of a bigger junkie than Janis, Port Arthur would rather sit and rot than collect one penny from fans wanting to visit the birthplace of Janis Joplin."

• Joplin was a reporter on her junior high school newspaper. She wanted to be an artist and a beatnik, but joined the Future Nurses of America to have something to fall back on. If nothing else, the experience made her handy with a hypodermic needle.

• After borrowing some Bessie Smith records, Joplin decided she wanted to become a blues singer. Years later, upon hearing that Smith was buried in an unmarked grave, Joplin bought her a headstone.

• Joplin was a voraciously sexual being with males and females alike. Her first homosexual experience occurred in high school: She was a senior and her lover was a freshman.

• At age eighteen Joplin moved to Los Angeles to live with her aunt Barbara, where she got a job first with the phone company and then Bank of America. She decided to move back to Texas later that year, where she made her singing debut in a small club and got a job serving sandwiches in a bowling alley.

• Joplin moved to Austin and enrolled at the University of Texas. She started singing on open-mike nights at a local folk club. One night she insulted some frat boys. They retaliated by nominating her for an ugliest man on campus contest, which she nearly won.

• While a student, she went to the Mardi Gras in New Orleans with a girlfriend. After a drunken fight, she was thrown out of a car without even her purse. "How did you get home?" she was asked. "I did what any girl would do," she replied, "I turned two tricks."

• And speaking of prostitution, Joplin began singing commercials for local businesses. One was a bank commercial, sung to the tune of "This Land Is Your Land": "This bank is your bank/ This bank is my bank/From Nacogdoches to the Gulf Coast waters/Sixty years of savings/Sixty years of earnings/This bank was made for you and me."

● In 1963 Joplin hitchhiked back to California, this time to San Francisco, where she began making a name for herself in the folk scene. In quick succession, she began shooting methampheta- mine, found an African-American girlfriend, and got arrested for shoplifting in Berkeley. She began drinking heavily, waking up from alcoholic blackouts in Memphis or New York, wondering how she got there and with whom.

● By 1965 she was down to eighty-eight pounds and in terrible shape. Her friends threw a party and passed the hat to buy her a bus ticket home to Port Arthur. A fiancé from San Francisco fol- lowed her home but, as wedding plans unfolded, he suddenly disappeared and didn't return. Her mom nursed her back to health, convinced her to get a Texas-fashionable beehive hairdo, and enrolled her in secretarial school where she got A's. Joplin gave up alcohol, even though friends complained that she was boring when she was sober. She also gave up singing for a while, believing that her singing and her drug use were directly related. Painfully shy and afraid of rejection, she felt compelled to use booze and other drugs to give her courage during a performance.

● She went to a therapist in Port Arthur, and the only advice he gave was that she should move to a more interesting place like Austin or San Francisco that would accept her eccentricities.

● After a few months friends convinced her that she could start singing again without doing damage, and she began performing again in folk-music cafés. Meanwhile, back in San Francisco, a group of friends and acquaintances put together a band. Narrow- ing a long list of names, they got stuck trying to decide between the two favorites. One was "Big Brother," and the other was "The Holding Company." Finally, as a compromise, they de- cided to use both. They also decided that they needed a lead singer. Their manager suggested Joplin, but the response was "No, she's good, but she's weird. She'll give too strange an aura to the band." Finally, though, after auditioning fifty to sixty vo- calists, they decided to ask Joplin to join them. She hitchhiked with a friend, carrying a light pack of clothes and necessities, and two books, *The Ten Commandments* and Billie Holliday's *Lady Sings the Blues.*

● At the band's audition in a reconditioned firehouse, Joplin was tentative and scared, straining to be heard in her folk voice. Losing that battle against the screaming guitars behind her, she began shrieking the songs as loud as she could. Poster artist Stanley Mouse came down from his studio upstairs to watch. He thought the band was better off without her. After the audition, one of the band members was asked what he thought. "She's either great or really awful." A few minutes later two police officers showed up to investigate a report of a woman screaming. "Oh no," said Mouse, "that was no woman. That was Janis Joplin."

● Many of Big Brother's fans were equally unimpressed at her debut. Before she joined, the hallmark of the band had been endless free-form improvisations—after, they had to actually play structured songs. Guitarist Sam Andrew, the only member who could actually read music and chart chords, wrote some songs, but had to struggle to teach his unwilling band mates how to play them. Joplin didn't help band morale either. She quickly became the centerpiece of it. She became lovers with James Gurley, Big Brother's married lead guitarist, while constantly berating him for being a "lousy fuckin' guitarist." Before Joplin, tapes of performances showed why he was considered the equal of Jimi Hendrix; after Joplin arrived, his playing got worse and worse, finally fulfilling her appraisal.

● When Gurley's wife found out about the affair, she was upset, but got over it when she discovered that she and Joplin had a mutual affection for shooting drugs. They also sought out Boris Karloff movies, claiming they were loaded with secret heroin messages and symbolism.

● At about the same time, Joplin fell into a complicated but good-natured love triangle with a lesbian couple, one of whom had previously been Joan Baez's girlfriend. The other, Peggy Caserta, wrote *Going Down with Janis*, a so-so book with a great first line: "I was stark naked, stoned out of my mind on heroin, and the girl lying between my legs giving me head was Janis Joplin."

● On the cusp of stardom, strung out on heavy drugs, hanging out with Hell's Angels, Joplin wrote to her parents and asked them to send her one present for Christmas 1965: "a *Betty Crocker* or *Better Homes & Gardens* cookbook."

● Joplin's musical lovers included Jimi Hendrix and Jim Morrison, both of whom died within a few months of her. She was also reportedly linked with Eric Clapton, Country Joe MacDonald, all or nearly all of her band, and Kris Kristofferson, who wrote her biggest hit, "Me and Bobby McGee." In addition, she bedded Joe Namath and once went on a blind date with Bill Bennett, who was apparently so traumatized that he eventually became drug czar under Reagan and a conservative Republican "family values" scold.

● The relationship with Morrison was a stormy one. What they had in common—heavy drinking and monstrous egos—led to monstrous brawling. In a New York club, Morrison unzipped Jimi's fly while Hendrix was performing and started sucking him. Already annoyed because a drunken Morrison spilled drinks on her, Joplin tackled him and each landed several punches before other people intervened. The band played on.

● A few months later the two had a rematch at a party at pretty-boy crooner John Davidson's house. They argued, and Morrison grabbed her hair and slammed her head against a coffee table. As Morrison left the party, she ran up behind him and, in front of barbecue guests of next-door neighbor Don Drysdale, bonked him on the head with her Wild Turkey bottle. She let out a manic cackle over his prostrate body, returned to the party, and carried on as if nothing had happened.

● Joplin got the nickname "Pearl" in a health-food store when a friend noticed a bin of pearl barley and suggested that as a good takeoff on the name of singer Pearl Bailey.

● All the members of Big Brother became heroin users. Said their road manager, Richard Hungden, "At the Avalon Ballroom, fans thought Janis and Big Brother were always running backstage to adjust the amplifiers, but they were vomiting. They had a bucket back there especially to puke in. When you do heroin, you vomit a lot."

● Joplin discovered she was pregnant around Christmas 1967 while she was visiting her parents in Texas. She celebrated her twenty-fifth birthday in January by going to Mexico to get an abortion.

● Between July 1968 and December 1969 Joplin suffered six serious heroin overdoses, nearly dying several times. Her reaction when a girlfriend died of a heroin overdose was to go out and buy a bag for herself. Some of her friends steeled themselves for Joplin's apparently inevitable final overdose. Her manager, making sure he'd profit either way, plunked down $3,500 for a $200,000 insurance policy on her.

● She smoked dope with Dick Cavett after appearing on his talk show.

● Joplin's favorite song out of all her recordings was "Little Girl Blue," a Rodgers and Hart ballad first introduced in the circus musical *Jumbo* in 1935. Joplin heard it first in the 1962 movie version, sung by none other than blues shouter Doris Day. While Benny Goodman was a Joplin fan (in fact, in one concert the band tried to get him up on stage to do a solo on the Gershwin tune "Summertime"), songwriter Richard Rodgers was not. When Columbia Records' president played him a tape of Joplin's version of his song, he sputtered, "If I am expected to undergo this kind of humiliation, I don't see how I can ever again cut another record at Columbia."

● The melodic guitar counterpoint in "Summertime" was a piece by Johann Sebastian Bach played at half speed.

• Joplin appeared at Woodstock, but her performance was not particularly good, so her manager refused to allow her footage to appear in the movie. The food supply at the festival grounds was running low in the face of the unexpectedly large crowd, but Joplin didn't suffer from that or the cold of the rain—she was back at the Holiday Inn eating a seven-course steak and champagne dinner with Grace Slick. Right before going on, she monopolized a portable toilet with a long line behind it to cook and shoot her heroin while people in line pounded on the door telling her to hurry up. She almost blacked out and revived herself by alternately swigging from a bottle of vodka in her right hand and a bottle of tequila in her left. Three people helped her to the stage and literally shoved her up to the microphone. Still, she was given credit for helping to wake the spirit of Woodstock with her announcement between songs: "If you have some food left, share it with your brother and sister—the person on your left and the person on your right."

• Joplin left Big Brother later that year, going solo with her own band. In New York she visited a tawdry gay bathhouse and came back talking about a singer she saw there, Bette Midler, saying, "That's my next competition." That never quite happened before Joplin died in 1970, but a few years later Midler played a thinly disguised Joplin figure in *The Rose*.

• In the summer of 1970 Joplin joined a traveling festival called the Festival Express, which traveled by train and gave concerts across Canada. Over the five-day trip, Joplin calculated that she had sex with sixty-five people—but complained that the other three hundred people on the train had given her the brush-off.

• Jack Nicholson wanted her to appear in *Five Easy Pieces*, but the offer never got to her from her management's office, so he found someone else.

• Joplin's heroin dealer wasn't a user himself, so he had a "taster" who helped him add the customary level of inert fillers to the "smack." On the weekend that Joplin died, his taster was gone, but he sold the batch anyway. It was apparently way too strong—about ten times stronger than expected—and eight people reportedly died from overdoses because of it. One was Joplin. On a Saturday night, October 3, 1970, she shot up in the Landmark Hotel in Los Angeles and went down to the lobby for Marlboros. She got to her room, stripped down to her underclothes, and died. Her body was found eighteen hours later, still clutching her change from the cigarettes.

• *Rolling Stone* publisher Jann Wenner had feuded with Joplin in his pages for years. When he heard of her death, his first words were "Cancel her subscription."

• In her will Joplin left two thousand five hundred dollars for a wake for her friends. She had been recording the album that was later released as *Pearl*. She had recorded the vocals for every track but one. The song, "Buried Alive in the Blues," written by her friend Nick Gravenites, was released on the album as an instrumental cut.

Walt Disney

Innovative and brilliant, Walt Disney created dozens of amazing cartoons and animated features, and revolutionized amusement parks. But, of course, geniuses are often impossible to work with.

- Walter Elias Disney was born in Chicago, Illinois, on December 5, 1901, the fourth son of Elias and Flora Disney. Elias was a hard man. Never particularly successful at any of his endeavors, he used his sons as laborers, offering room, board, and beatings with a strap as payment.

- While in their teens, Walt's older brothers ran away from home, leaving him to take the brunt of their father's temper. Walt retreated into fantasy, pretending that he was adopted because he figured his real father would never treat him as this man did. Walt's mother fed his fantasy life by reading fairy tales to him, but otherwise did little to intervene on his behalf against her husband.

- When Walt was fourteen, he decided he had had enough of his father's beatings. When his father raised a hammer to strike him, he grabbed the hammer away and held his father's wrists. Elias broke down and cried and never again tried to physically discipline Walt.

- When the United States entered World War I, seventeen-year-old Walt was eager to enlist. When he was asked to present his birth certificate, he was surprised to discover that his parents didn't have a copy and that the local registry had no record of his birth. His childhood fantasies that Elias was not his real father suddenly began to seem more plausible.

● Unable to enlist in the military because he couldn't prove his age or identity, Walt was accepted as a volunteer in the American Red Cross. His mother gave permission, forging the signature of Elias, since he would not sign.

● Leaving behind a childhood sweetheart, Disney was stationed at Saint Cyr, France, to take care of sick American soldiers. In celebration of his eighteenth birthday, Disney's comrades threw him a surprise party where he drank, smoked, and had sex for the first time. When it came time to pay the tab, however, his friends slipped away. Disney, not having any money, had to sell his extra pair of boots.

● Returning home after his stint with the Red Cross, Disney was eager to renew his relationship with his sweetheart, with whom he had continued to exchange letters. What he didn't know was that she had gotten married three months earlier.

● Disney turned his attention to drawing, which he had dabbled at throughout his childhood. Wanting to become a commercial artist, Disney submitted samples of his work all around Kansas City. He got one job, but was quickly let go because his work was not good enough. Teaming up with a friend, Ub Iwerks, Disney began a short-lived commercial art business that resulted in bankruptcy. He headed out to California to live with his brother Roy.

● The brothers decided to set up a small cartoon studio and make short subjects for the burgeoning film industry. Disney convinced Iwerks to move west and join them. Iwerks was the quieter, more talented of the two. Disney loved to play practical jokes on him because he embarrassed easily and didn't retaliate.

● Walt and Roy stayed close throughout their lives even though they disagreed constantly. Walt was the one who was always willing to bet the company and their entire fortunes on the next new idea; Roy, the one who provided an anchor. Roy thought making a feature-length cartoon was just too risky; Walt plowed into making *Snow White* anyway. Roy refused to let Walt spend company money on the harebrained idea of starting an amusement park, and even initially threatened to sue Walt if he used the family name on it. Walt took out a new mortgage, cashed in his life-insurance policy, and worked out a deal with ABC-TV so he could start work on Disneyland. In nearly every case, Walt's "impractical new idea that will ruin us all" became a huge success.

● During this time, Roy married his longtime fiancée. Walt, feeling abandoned by Roy and deciding that he (as he put it) "needed a new roommate," took a bride himself three months later. His new wife was Lillian Bounds, who worked at the studio. Spending their honeymoon night on a train from Idaho to California, Walt developed a toothache and spent the night shining shoes in the porter's car to keep his mind off the pain . . . and out of the bed.

● Disney's studio came up with an animated character named Oswald the Rabbit that became very popular. However, when it was time to renegotiate the contract in New York, Disney found that his distributor had not only claimed all legal rights to Oswald, but had hired away much of his animation staff and offered to hire him as well. Disney threw an Oswald Rabbit badge down on the distributor's desk and shouted, "Here, you can have the little bastard! He's all yours."

● On the train ride back to California, Disney came up with a vague idea for a mouse character who he wanted to call Mortimer. Discussing it with Iwerks, the two put all their ideas down on character sheets. Using his own face as a model, Disney sketched a figure. When Iwerks saw the mouse, he rejected it because it looked so much like Disney. Redrawing it, Iwerks, who had always been a better artist than Disney, came up with the character who came to be known as Mickey.

• The Disney organization made two Mickey Mouse cartoons that flopped. The problem was that they were silent movies. Sound in movies was a popular new fad, and so Disney decided to use it in his third Mickey Mouse cartoon, *Steamboat Willie*. It found a wildly enthusiastic audience, and the studio got the funding to create better and longer cartoons. This led to a series of successful short cartoons, and eventually to the masterpiece *Snow White and the Seven Dwarfs*.

• Despite the studio's success, not everybody was happy to be there. Disney was not easy to work for, and Iwerks, for one, decided that he had had enough of it. After years of silently fuming about humiliations, underappreciation, and Disney's moodiness, he left the Disney studio to start his own.

• The stress at the studio, his friend Iwerks's defection, and an inability to impregnate Lillian were factors that drove Disney to a near-suicidal nervous breakdown in 1931.

• To appease Lillian in her quest for a child, Disney submitted to injections of liver extract directly into his thyroid gland and to having his genitals packed in ice for hours at a time. Eventually, Lilly gave birth to a daughter. Several years later, not wanting to go through that ordeal again, the couple adopted a second daughter and let the public assume she was also their natural child.

• Yet everything was not completely pleasant back at the studio. Disney was still a harsh employer and demanded the utmost from his employees, all the while refusing to give proper credit to those who deserved it. It galled a number of the animators that their work was not even acknowledged publicly in the credits of the cartoons, leading the public to believe that Disney did everything himself.

• When Roy urged employees to give Walt a surprise thirty-fifth birthday party, a couple of the animators decided that a good joke on the boss would be a short movie of Mickey and Minnie consummating their relationship with animation, as it were. When they premiered it at the party, Walt feigned amusement and asked who was responsible. When the two confessed, Walt fired them on the spot. Employee morale hit a new low.

• Disney had no idea that his employees were unhappy. He considered them to be like members of his family and couldn't fathom that they could be unhappy with his management style and the studio's low pay structure. When his animators joined a union and went out on strike in 1936, Disney was shocked. He decided that Communists had infiltrated his studio and were attempting to take over the industry.

• He didn't trust Jews or blacks, equating both groups with Communism. He contributed to a number of extreme right-wing causes. "Roosevelt called this the Century of the Common Man," he told associates. "Balls! It's the century of the Communist cutthroat, the fag, and the whore! And FDR and his National Labor Relations Board made it so!"

• Disney's anti-Communist fervor became known to J. Edgar Hoover through his network of informers. Hoover recruited him to become an FBI informant himself. In exchange for Disney's help in identifying Hollywood leftists, Hoover offered to check into Disney's background and have his agents investigate Walt's suspicions that Elias and Flora Disney were not really his parents.

• Hoover kept his part of the bargain, but didn't turn up any completely satisfactory alternatives. He thought he might have traced Disney's beginnings to a small village in the south of Spain called Mojacar. In the village lived a beautiful woman who became impregnated by the married doctor of the town. Soon after the birth, the doctor died and the young mother decided to travel to America. Disney believed that while in America her path *might* have crossed that of Elias Disney who *might* have taken the boy as his own. However, the dates didn't really match up, and the strong family resemblance to Roy belied that theory.

• Meanwhile, Disney kept his part of the bargain as well. He took photos of those who marched in the picket line in front of his studio and turned the photos over to the FBI and the House Un-American Activities Committee. The turmoil at the studio triggered a second nervous breakdown.

• President Roosevelt feared that Nazi influence was spreading across South America and asked that Disney travel there to collect information and spread goodwill. While he was gone, Roy, always pragmatic, settled the strike. One of the concessions he made was that animators would begin getting their names in the credits.

• Bitter and suspicious after the strike, Disney regularly wandered the corridors of his studio after hours, rifling through the work and trash bins of his animators to see what they were doing. He became distrustful of everyone except his maintenance crew, whom he considered to be his only loyal employees.

• In 1947 Disney was spiraling down into a third breakdown, depending heavily on sleeping pills and booze. Actress Dolores Del Rio became his frequent dinner, dancing, and drinking companion. Rumors of an affair circulated through Hollywood.

• Disney enforced a stringent dress code at his studio and anyone breaking it was subject to immediate dismissal. In the 1950s he asked Annette Funicello, one of his biggest stars, to wear a bosom-flattening bra and to refrain from wearing low-cut bathing suits in beach movies in order to preserve the modesty of her image—and his.

• Disney's successes did little to relieve his bad temper. Because of it and a hacking cough from smoking three packs of cigarettes a day, his employees privately nicknamed him "Wounded Bear" in his last years. He died of emphysema on December 15, 1966.

William Randolph Hearst

William Randolph Hearst was the prototype for the hard-driving media baron, willing to trumpet scandals on the front page, pander to the lowest common denominator . . . or even start a war, if it helped circulation.

———————————

- William Randolph Hearst's father, George, struck it rich during the California gold rush. George was nearly illiterate and when he tried to enter California politics, his opponents joked that he spelled bird "b-u-r-d." He responded, "If b-u-r-d doesn't spell bird, then what the hell *does* it spell?" Still, his lack of literacy didn't prevent him from buying the *San Francisco Examiner* newspaper in 1880 in the hope that it would help sway public support toward his candidacy for governor in 1882.

- It didn't. George wasn't nominated, and he thought of selling the paper. However, his son William, now in Harvard, begged his father to let him run the paper when he graduated. "Good God," his father said, "haven't I spent enough money on that paper already? It's a sure loser. Instead of holding it for my own son, I've been saving it up to give to an enemy."

- While attending Harvard, Hearst kept a small alligator, named Champagne Charlie after a popular song of the time, giving it wine to drink. Oftentimes the alligator would wander around campus drunk. In his second year, Hearst became the business manager of the *Lampoon*, the college's humor magazine. The position was usually a liability because losses that the magazine incurred had to come out of the business manager's own pocket. Hearst used his energy and inventiveness to raise circulation. The magazine soon went into the black and the staff was forced to have frequent parties to keep the surplus down. This success sparked in Hearst a whole new interest in taking over the *Examiner*.

● Hearst got himself expelled at the end of 1885 because of a lack of attention to his studies, but not before "inheriting" a mistress from a classmate whose allowance had been cut off. The young woman, a former waitress named Tessie Powers, traveled west with Hearst and remained his mistress for several years.

● In 1887 Hearst, only twenty-three years old, took over the *Examiner*. Trying to overtake its rival, the *San Francisco Chronicle*, he starting putting sports, sex, sleaze, and sensationalism on the front page, a shocking and déclassé departure from journalistic codes of the time.

● In 1889 George Hearst cut off the money pipeline to William, fearing an increase in losses by the *Examiner* (although the paper had made great financial strides), as well as disapproving of his relationship with Tessie Powers. William neatly circumvented his father's action by having the California Democratic Party committeeman, Michael Francis Tarpey, ask George Hearst for a contribution of one hundred thousand dollars. George complied quickly, and Tarpey, wanting a strong Democratic newspaper in San Francisco, turned over half the money to William. He used it to capitalize his paper, and also to buy a house for Tessie in Sausalito, a short boat ride from San Francisco.

● Hearst decided his paper needed an eye-catching story on page one every day. The problem was that mind-boggling events didn't occur every day. Hearst began demanding that his reporters not just go out and cover news but—when necessary—make it. For instance, when actress Sarah Bernhardt came to town, she was commandeered by a group of *Examiner* reporters who took her to an opium den in Chinatown and then reported the shocking details. Another time, Hearst's reporters solved a sensational love-triangle murder that had stymied the police.

● An *Examiner* reporter once got himself committed to an insane asylum for a month and wrote bloodcurdling stories of what went on there. Another reporter, dressed in grungy clothes, pretended to collapse on the street in downtown San Francisco. After being ignored for some time, she was finally taken to the City Receiving Hospital where, she wrote, she "was insulted and pawed by vulgar interns, given an emetic of hot water and mustard, and turned loose." The story caused a great deal of public uproar and a shake-up at the hospital.

● There's nothing like a war to increase the public appetite for news, so Hearst agitated for a war in the Spanish colony of Cuba. The last colonial power in Latin America, Spain impeded the United States's hemispheric influence. Tensions were already high between the two countries, and Hearst did his best to aggravate them into full warfare. He sent artist Frederick Remington to Cuba to cover the "war" which had not yet begun. Remington telegraphed, "Everything is quiet. There is no trouble here. There will be no war. I wish to return." Hearst replied, "Please remain. You furnish the pictures and I'll furnish the war."

● Eventually, Hearst got what he wanted. Through "coverage" of battles, insults, and atrocities that never happened, he and other warmongering publishers swayed American public opinion to the point of making war nearly inevitable. When the battleship *Maine* blew up in a Cuban harbor, the American people were ready to erroneously assume that it was because of hostile Spanish action instead of a defective boiler. The Spanish-American War began.

● Hearst's circulation stunts worked. He made enough money to begin buying up other newspapers around the country. At age thirty-four he moved to a new headquarters in New York City. Hearst began squiring Millicent and Anita Willson, members of the Merry Maidens dance troupe, around New York. He was interested in Millicent, who was only sixteen; her older sister acted as chaperone. Six years later, in 1903, Hearst married Millicent, but his mother, Phoebe, not at all pleased with his selection, did not attend the wedding.

• William was never 100 percent faithful to Millicent, and in 1917 he went from discrete little affairs to living openly with chorus girl Marion Davies (who, according to various sources, was either seventeen or twenty at the time).

• Hearst was a collector of art and antiquities even before he got independently rich. He had a five-ton well shipped from Italy to San Francisco because it caught his fancy. He also bought a crateful of mummies in Egypt to decorate his office at the *Examiner*. Later, his collecting became nearly pathological as he indiscriminately snatched up antique pieces of the Old World. For example, he bought an ancient monastery in Spain and had it shipped to the United States in pieces packed in protective straw. Upon arrival, the straw was found to be infected with hoof-and-mouth disease. During repacking and sterilization, the instructions on how to put the monastery together again somehow got lost. What had once been a historic building eventually became fill rocks for San Francisco's Golden Gate Park.

• When architect Julia Morgan designed San Simeon castle for Hearst, she was prevailed upon to include bits and pieces of antique buildings, wood engravings, trim, and stonework into it in a crazy patchwork of styles, nationalities, and eras. Still, there was plenty of material left over. When Hearst ran into a cash-flow shortage in 1941, he took over the entire fifth floor of Gimbel's in New York City—one hundred thousand square feet—and filled it floor to ceiling with castoffs from his collection. It was the world's largest garage sale of art objects from Italy, Spain, France, and Germany, yet it was only a fraction of the crated materials that Hearst had gathered over four decades in a Bronx warehouse.

● Hearst spent more than $40 million on dwellings for Davies and himself, and his wife and children. These included San Simeon; St. Donat's, a castle in Wales; a beach house in Santa Monica; Davies's southern California bungalow; a mansion on Long Island; and a plot of land near the Grand Canyon. "He spent more for housing and decoration that any man in history, king or commoner," wrote one biographer.

● When word leaked out from Hollywood that twenty-five-year-old Orson Welles was working on a thinly fictionalized movie of Hearst's life to be called *Citizen Kane*, Hearst mobilized his organization to stop it, putting pressure—including blackmail—on anybody he could think of who could stop the project. Rumors spread through Hollywood that the Hearst newspaper chain was going to retaliate with an editorial barrage or embarrassing disclosures about the private lives of certain film moguls. Hearst's friend, Louis Mayer of MGM, offered to buy the movie from RKO so he could destroy the negatives. RKO refused to sell.

● For a while, Hearst's papers were able to convince theater chains to refuse the movie, and retaliated against RKO by refusing to review, publicize, or even acknowledge its movies. Still, *Citizen Kane* eventually got out to the public and was nominated for an Academy Award for Best Picture of 1941.

● In 1947, sixty years after taking over the *San Francisco Examiner*, Hearst suffered a painful seizure from a heart condition. He and Davies moved from remote San Simeon to Beverly Hills to be closer to decent medical care. He continued to follow his newspapers and call editors day or night complaining, making demands, and offering advice.

● Marion Davies was with him to the end, loyally sitting by his side on bad nights. On his behalf, she started making calls to his newspapers (leading to uneasiness and confusion there about whether the orders were coming from Hearst, or whether Davies herself was taking over).

● Finally, death seemed imminent. Davies stayed with him day and night. Hearst's doctor finally suggested she nap and gave her a sedative; while she slept, Hearst died, alone, on August 14, 1951, at age eighty-eight.

● The Hearst relatives, long hostile to Davies, took over the moment Hearst died. The body was whisked away even before Davies awoke; within a few hours her friends and allies on the Hearst newspapers were fired, and her free subscriptions were canceled. She flew to San Simeon to find the gates had been locked by family order to "outsiders." Millicent, estranged for decades but legally Hearst's widow, flew in from New York for the funeral in San Francisco. Davies did not attend.

● Hearst left an estate valued at $59.5 million to be divided by his wife, four sons, and a trust benefitting the Los Angeles Museum, the University of California, and other Hearst-supported organizations. The family's lawyers considered trying to squeeze out Marion Davies, for whom Hearst had set up a trust of thirty thousand shares of Hearst Corporation preferred stock. However, it became clear that a long court battle on the issue would be an embarrassing ordeal for all, so a compromise was struck: Marion would retain her shares, promising to keep her nose out of the Hearst businesses. The next day, her free delivery of Hearst papers resumed.

W. C. Fields

For fifty years film comedian W. C. Fields entertained millions of people with his juggling, sleight of hand, and meek, yet malicious characters. He managed a long career in spite of his unhappy personal life, ill health, and alcoholism.

● It's hard to know what to believe regarding Fields's early life. Fields had a penchant for exaggeration and tall tales. Maybe, as he claimed, he left home at age eleven and set up housekeeping in a plank-covered foxhole, with kids in the neighborhood providing him food. Or maybe he really left home at age nineteen with a thermos of coffee and a pile of sandwiches prepared by his mother, as his family claimed.

● In any event, it is agreed that Fields (who was born William Claude Dukenfield on January 29, 1880 or April 9, 1879, depending on which of his stories you believe) became obsessed with juggling at a young age. He enraged his father, who sold fruit and vegetables from a cart on the streets of Philadelphia, by habitually juggling quantities of produce into pulp and juice.

● Some of Fields's acting ability came from his mother, who was an excellent mimic and kept her family in stitches by standing in the doorway and conversing with passersby while muttering hilariously insulting asides to her family. And he seems to have picked up his famous nasal intonation from his father, an ill-educated immigrant from London.

● Fields claimed that booze was not to blame for his large, red-and-purple nose, but rather all the beatings he got from his father and neighborhood toughs.

● When Fields was thirteen he sold newspapers on the streets of Philadelphia. He developed a running patter, yelling out catchy stories of the day. However, Fields didn't bother with stories from the front page, instead looking for unusual articles and strange names that caught his eye. For instance, "Bronislaw Gimp acquires license for two-year-old sheep dog. Details on page 26." He also juggled folded newspapers. The act fascinated people and Fields sold a lot of papers.

● After a while, Fields opted for a suburban paper route. It was during this time that he cultivated his famous dislike of dogs. Fields claimed that he "was bitten on an average of every six houses [and] dogs would knock off their dinners and cross the street" to get him.

● Fields got his first paying juggling job in 1891. According to the story he told, he and a friend agreed to juggle at a strawberry festival put on by a Methodist church for thirty cents. After he was done juggling he tried unsuccessfully to get the deacon to pay up. Fields finally became so frustrated that he and his assistant stole thirty-one umbrellas which they pawned for $1.20. He resolved to henceforth perform only for Baptists.

● He spent several years as a petty thief and was a professional "drowner" on a pier in New Jersey. He was paid to pretend to drown every hour—the lifeguards would save him, drawing a crowd. Eventually he combined juggling and comedy and began making a mild success in vaudeville circuits.

● He married in 1900 and fathered a son, William Claude Fields, Jr. He never divorced his wife, Hattie, but never lived with her again after 1904.

● Having once been robbed, Fields didn't like to carry a lot of cash while on the road. So wherever he was, he'd open a bank account. He claimed to have seven hundred accounts in banks all over the world. His friend Gene Fowler said, "I think he lost at least fifty thousand dollars in the Berlin bombing. He had bank accounts or at least safe-deposit boxes in such cities as London, Paris, Sydney, Cape Town, and Suva." Usually these accounts were open under his real name but sometimes he used odd aliases such as Figley E. Whitesides, Sneed Hearn, Dr. Otis Guelpe, and (in Madrid, Spain), Señor Guillermo McKinley. After his death, only about three dozen accounts were located.

● Fields's juggling act became a big success. In 1915 Fields settled into a run with the Ziegfeld Follies on Broadway. In 1931 Fields was offered a movie contract with Keystone Studios. Because Fields was a Broadway star he asked for and got five thousand dollars a week. Used to being ripped off by promoters in his early years, he insisted on getting paid half of his weekly wages on Monday and the other half on Wednesday.

● Fields was very competitive. He couldn't stand to watch films by other comedians. Coaxed once into watching some early films by Charlie Chaplin, he started coughing and complaining of the heat. He left the theater after a few minutes. When someone asked Fields what his opinion was, he said, "The son of a bitch is a ballet dancer . . . and if I get a good chance I'll kill him with my bare hands."

● He was an excellent golfer but he loved to cheat. While a companion was trying to putt, Fields would invariably jingle change in his pocket, go into a coughing fit, or pretend to be slapping at flies. He wasn't above moving the ball if it wasn't in an advantageous position.

● Fields's drinking was legendary. He usually started the day with two double martinis, followed by a small breakfast. He drank martinis on the way to work and kept huge amounts of liquor in his dressing room. Lunch was usually a crab meat salad accompanied by more martinis. Both the studio and Fields kept up the story that he was drinking pineapple juice from his jumbo cocktail shaker. One day, when Fields was away, some pranksters put real pineapple juice in the shaker. When he took his next gulp he bellowed, "Somebody's been putting pineapple juice in my pineapple juice!"

• Fields had little patience for children, especially if he felt they were scene stealers. The most famous wee adversary was Baby Le Roy, a frequent costar. Fields knew there was nothing he could do against him; moviegoers were always going to focus on a baby, no matter what he came up with. But he did manage to get a little revenge one day. During a break in filming, Fields offered to give the toddler his orange juice, which he had spiked with gin. When the break was over, the baby was near catatonic. While pandemonium broke out on the set, Fields sat in a corner mumbling, "Walk him around, walk him around." And when the director finally got him roused but not energized, Fields shouted, "The kid's no trouper. Send him home."

• During World War II, Fields followed all of the developments passionately. He bought a world map and would stick pins on countries like Peru for no apparent reason. One afternoon he and fellow drinkers, actors John and Lionel Barrymore, Gene Fowler, and John Decker, got themselves so full of drink and patriotism that they decided to enlist that very day. They were well past their prime, and Lionel was in a wheelchair. They all told outrageous lies, shaving decades off their ages and wildly embellishing their military expertise. Finally, the young lady at the recruitment center put down her pen and asked if they had been sent by the enemy.

• From 1940 to 1945 Fields leased a Spanish-style house for $250 a month in the middle of Hollywood. He enjoyed the cheap rent and the environs but what irked him was the fact that he lived on DeMille Drive, and Cecil B. DeMille, for whom the street was named, was a neighbor whose home was at a slightly elevated level. All this led Fields to form an insane dislike for DeMille.

• One day, the body of two-year-old Christopher Quinn, son of DeMille's daughter and Anthony Quinn, was found floating face-down in a pond in Fields's front yard, possibly lured there by a toy sailboat that Fields floated in the pond. Fields, full of sadness, rage, and guilt, burned the boat and drained the pond.

• Fields successfully wrangled $25,000 from Universal for a plot idea written on the back of a grocery bill. The scribbles became his last movie, *Never Give a Sucker an Even Break*, for which he received screenplay credit under the name of Otis Criblecoblis. Other names he used for screenplay credits include Charles Bogle and Mahatma Kane Jeeves.

• In the 1930s his heavy drinking and general ill-health began taking its toll. He ended up in a sanitarium for several months. He went through a bad case of delirium tremens as he was forced to break his heavy, lifelong addiction to alcohol. After that he couldn't stand to be touched. Even the weight of bedsheets was painful, and they were forced to chloroform him to cut his fingernails.

• During this time, listening to the rain gave him some peace and helped him doze off. His companion Carlotta Monti simulated the rain by running a sprinkler on his house roof at night. During the day she would situate Fields under a large outdoor umbrella and turn the hose on it.

• Fields recovered enough to go into a successful radio career. He didn't lose his malevolent spirit, however. First of all, he engaged in a running "feud" with ventriloquist dummy Charlie McCarthy. On his own show, his sponsor was Lucky Strike cigarettes. The company's officers laughed along with the rest of the nation at Fields's stories about his fictitious son Chester—until one day when someone in the company figured out that his son's full name would be Chester Fields . . . the name of a rival brand of cigarette.

● Fields hated the "mawkish festivity" of Christmas. Christmas seemed to have it in for him as well—Fields died on Christmas Day 1946 from a massive stomach hemorrhage.

Richard Nixon

Richard Milhous Nixon, the thirty-seventh president of the United States, was the second president to face impeachment, and the first to actually resign from office.

• Richard Nixon was a mass of contradictions: He was raised a pacifist Quaker, yet as president he ordered more bombs dropped than any man in history. He made a career out of the fear of Communism, yet was the first to try rapprochement with China. He hated appearing on TV, yet won in 1968 because of it, being sold like soap in an advertising campaign that first used the flashy techniques that are commonplace now. He managed to get reelected in 1972 by a landslide, yet before his death was rated among the least popular politicians in recent history.

• Born in Yorba Linda, California, on January 9, 1913, to Frank and Hannah Nixon, young Richard was named after Richard the Lionhearted.

• His earliest memory was falling out of a horsedriven buggy that his mother was driving, slitting his scalp in a long angular cut that required stitches. From that point on until his death he combed his hair straight back to hide the scar even, he said later, regretfully, "when the vogue of parting hair on the left side came along."

• When he was seven, a younger friend had filled a jar with pollywogs, and Nixon wanted them. Nixon had a hatchet in his hand at the time, and he hit the boy in the head with it, leaving a permanent scar.

● Jessamyn West, Nixon's cousin who sometimes baby-sat him, described him as "not a little puppy dog, one you wanted to cuddle, though he may have longed for it. It didn't strike me that he wanted to be hugged. He had a fastidiousness about him."

● In first grade, his mother made a point of telling his teacher, "Never call him Dick—I named him Richard." Every day he wore a freshly starched white shirt with a black bow tie and knee pants, and his teacher was quoted as saying that she could not remember him ever getting dirty. He took great pains in brushing his teeth, was careful to gargle, and before he left for school asked his mother to smell his breath to make sure he would not offend anyone on the bus. He didn't like to ride the school bus, because the other children didn't smell good.

● He was a very solemn child who rarely ever smiled, and nobody can recall him ever really laughing. When the older boys made fun of him, Nixon cried bitterly. "I was the biggest crybaby in Yorba Linda," he admitted decades later. "My dad could hear me even with the tractor running."

● He was seriously uncoordinated, and too small for football, but his father wanted him to play so that nobody would think Nixon effeminate.

● For three summers Nixon was a barker for the "Wheel of Fortune" concession in the fair at nearby Slippery Gulch. He was quite good at it.

● Years later, Nixon liked to go on and on about his humble beginnings. Jessamyn West remembered it differently: "The idea that the key to Nixon was his early poverty is ridiculous. The Nixons had a grocery store, two cars, and sent their son to college. By some they were considered rich."

• His father lent him the money for his three years at Duke University Law School, and Richard had to pay back every penny. At school, Nixon led a monastic life in an abandoned toolshed in a heavily wooded area near the campus. It was an eight-by-twelve-foot shed, lined with corrugated cardboard for warmth. He did not date any girls for the entire three years. His nickname was "Gloomy Gus."

• In a foreshadowing of his future, he once broke into the dean's office to get an advance look at the grades.

• After he graduated and passed the bar exam, he bungled his first court case in a way that looked as if he were personally and unethically trying to gain a financial advantage. The case wound up costing the firm $4,800 in an out-of-court settlement. In the course of the proceedings, he was threatened with disbarment by a judge, who said, "Mr. Nixon, I have serious doubts whether you have the ethical qualifications to practice law in the state of California. I am seriously thinking of turning this matter over to the Bar Association." Nixon thought of abandoning the United States and setting up a law practice in Havana, Cuba. He actually traveled there to check out the possibilities before World War II interrupted his law career.

• After the war Nixon attempted to pass himself off as a veteran who had seen actual combat while stationed on Green Island in the Pacific. There is more data available on Nixon's poker playing—he made a great deal of money—than on any other single aspect of his war experience. Nixon also opened "Nixon's Snack Shack" near the airstrip, where pilots and their crews were able to get coffee, sandwiches, fruit juices, and occasionally liquor. From the war he received two citations for merit and three medals, but no battle stars.

• After the war, he considered going back to practicing law. Instead, he decided to become a politician. Through a series of outrageous, mean-spirited, but brilliantly opportunistic campaigns, he made a successful career of accusing opponents of being Communists. He rose meteorically in California politics, and quickly ended up in the U.S. House of Representatives on the House Un-American Activities Committee, a red-hunting group of dangerous buffoons, including proudly anti-Semitic John Rankin of Mississippi and John Wood of Alabama, an active member of the Ku Klux Klan. "It was," said George Reedy, covering the committee for United Press, "the worst collection of people that have ever been assembled in the entire history of American politics." With publicity from this job, during an era of anti-Communist hysteria, Nixon quickly got elected to the senate in time to join Joseph McCarthy's witch-hunts, and then became the premier candidate for vice president, placating the extreme right-wing who were unhappy with comparatively moderate Dwight Eisenhower.

• At thirty-nine, Nixon was the second youngest vice president. Only Dan Quayle was younger.

• Long before Watergate, Nixon counseled a friend, "You don't know how to lie. If you can't lie, you'll never go anywhere."

• In an interview, Truman called Nixon "a shifty-eyed goddamn liar." Nixon had applauded the decision to go to war in Korea, but later, seeing the war's unpopularity, blamed Truman for incurring American casualties.

• Nixon was never seen touching his wife, Pat, in public during his Washington years, except once, while standing in the back of a convertible, he put out his hand to steady her. There were rumors that they refrained from sex for years at a time.

• In 1958 Nixon traveled to Hong Kong and met Marianna Liu, a tour guide. They became inseparable and there were rumors of an affair—rumors that eventually ended up in J. Edgar Hoover's personal files. It became one of the bits of information that Hoover later used to keep his job when Nixon threatened to replace him.

● Nixon had a terrible temper and a salty vocabulary, which he almost always succeeded in keeping under control in public. Once though, during the 1960 campaign, he was sitting in the back seat of a car behind one of his aides, Air Force Major Don Hughes, during a long ride between cities. Frustrated and impatient, Nixon suddenly went into a tantrum, swearing and repeatedly kicking the back of Hughes's seat with both feet, refusing to stop. Hughes had the car stopped and got out until aides got Nixon quieted down again.

● After a meeting at Cornell University with a group of young college editors who had thrown some tough questions at him, he exploded at his staff and yelled at aide Ted Rogers, "You son of a bitch, you tried to destroy me in front of thirty million people."

● In 1963 Nixon joined the law firm of Mudge, Stern, Baldwin and Todd. In the beginning Nixon brought in the lucrative Pepsi-Cola account. Pepsi, long affiliated with Republican interests, re-hired Nixon as its lawyer after he lost the race for California governor. It was after this defeat that he announced angrily to the press that they "won't have Nixon to kick around anymore."

● Conspiracy theorists take note: On November 22, 1963, the day Kennedy was shot, Nixon was also visiting Dallas, attending a Pepsi-Cola convention. Months earlier Lee Harvey Oswald had put on his gun and told his wife, "Nixon is coming. I want to go and have a look. I am going to go out and find out if there will be an opportunity, and if there is, I will use the pistol." His wife finally talked Lee out of it.

● A "new Nixon" came back in 1968 and got elected to the presidency.

● Nixon was a bit strange, even before the pressure of Watergate investigations reportedly drove him to the brink of paranoia and insanity. He instructed the members of the White House staff not to talk to him or to his wife, even when greeted by them. He would not let the *Washington Post* be delivered to his home, so his daughters wouldn't see the political cartoons about him. As president, Nixon had the White House waiter hide a thirty-dollar bottle of wine in a napkin to be served only to him, while the other guests were given wine worth six dollars a bottle.

• Howard Hughes gave Nixon's brother Donald a "loan" for $205,000 that was never paid back. Later, the IRS reversed a previous decision to annul the tax-exempt status of the Howard Hughes Medical Institute, a dubious tax shelter Hughes had set up, legally declaring it a charitable organization. Because journalist Tom Braden questioned the Hughes loan, he was audited by the IRS every year Nixon was in office as president. To avoid further such embarrassments from his little brother, Nixon put Donald under electronic surveillance. There was evidence, in fact, that the Watergate break-in was an attempt to find out what the Democrats knew about Donald's embarrassing dealings.

• Nixon authorized secret investigations of the sexual and drinking habits of his political rivals and others on his "enemies list." He ordered twenty-four-hour surveillance on Edward Kennedy, telling his chief of staff, Bob Haldeman, "Catch him in the sack with one of his babes." However, when his own conduct was questioned, he answered indignantly, "A candidate's personal life and that of his family are not fair subjects for discussion unless they somehow bear directly on his qualifications for office."

• After his resignation because of the Watergate affair, Nixon managed to mostly rehabilitate his image into that of elder statesman. He died in 1995.

Charles Lindbergh

Charles Lindbergh became an American hero when he completed the first solo flight across the Atlantic Ocean in May 1927. However, what goes up, must come down . . .

- Charles Lindbergh was conceived on his parents' honeymoon and born on February 4, 1902. A few years later the family house burned down. His parents, having already acknowledged that they were temperamentally unsuited for each other, marked the occasion by splitting up.

- Lindbergh's father was a Republican congressman for a predominantly Roman Catholic district in Minnesota, so divorce would have meant political suicide. The family lived together during the winter months to keep up appearances for political campaigns and then Charles and his mother left for the rest of the year.

- While a new house was being built with insurance money, Charles and his mother lived on the third floor of a hotel in Little Falls, Minnesota. It was there that young Charles did his first aeronautic experiment: dropping the landlady's cat out of the third-floor window to see if it was true that a cat would always land on its feet.

- Lindbergh preferred learning on his own to a classroom setting. By virtue of being the "man of the house" three seasons out of four, he thought himself a level above his classmates. His mother encouraged that conceit, discouraging him from getting "too friendly" with the neighborhood kids. Dissatisfied with high school and alienated from his peers, he jumped at the chance to earn his senior year credit in a World War I farm-work program.

● Lindbergh's mother was a woman of culture and a school teacher whose expertise was in chemistry. She pushed her son into college. He immediately rebelled against both the educational system and his mother, who had decided to move in with him while he attended the University of Wisconsin. Lindbergh was less interested in learning than in spending time getting known around town as a daredevil motorcyclist.

● After three semesters Lindbergh dropped out to pursue his dream of flying airplanes. He left mom and alma mater behind and enrolled in a flying school far away in Nebraska. Only one problem: On his first flight up in the air, Lindbergh discovered that he had a fear of heights.

● He decided the way to overcome the fear was to become a "wing walker" for a carnival barnstormer, scrambling over the wings of a biplane while it flew over the crowds. It didn't work: every day he was absolutely terrified, and every night he awoke with nightmares of falling. He escalated his self-prescribed therapy by taking up parachute jumping in 1922, which enabled him to overcome his vertigo and nightmares.

● He put his experience with parachutes to good use a few years later when he began flying mail planes. He was forced to jettison out of four different planes in one year, setting a dubious world's record.

● After that eventful year Lindbergh got his own plane, a Curtiss "Jenny," with a top speed of seventy miles per hour, and began barnstorming all over the country. His mother joined him as an assistant and copilot. She had a profound impact on him, spoiling him for most women of his own age. He frequently expressed contempt for the frivolous young "flappers" of the era.

• A French businessman had offered a prize of twenty-five thousand dollars for the first flier or team that could make it nonstop from the United States to France. Lindbergh decided, like dozens of other young dreamers, to try for the prize.

• The plane he designed was put together by a new aviation company and was less than perfect. For one thing, his view was blocked by the plane's massive gas tank, so if he wanted to see straight ahead, he had to lean his head way over and look sideways. Also, the plane steered badly and tended to drop like a rock in a stall. He called it the *Spirit of St. Louis* because most of his financial backers were centered in that city.

• Getting ready to fly from New York, Lindbergh was appalled by the behavior of the press and the inaccuracies of their stories. He never trusted the press again. Photographers would shout, "Smile!" and he'd glower and snap back, "What for?"

• When Lindbergh crossed the Atlantic, he didn't carry a radio because it added too much weight. His navigation was an iffy thing. At one point near the end of his journey he spotted a fishing fleet, dove his plane down to within shouting distance, cut the engine, and screamed, "Which way to Ireland?"

• The first time Lindbergh met Anne Morrow he barely noticed her, but eventually he decided that this was a woman who met the high standards set by his mom. Their courtship began covertly and due to Lindbergh's adversarial relationship with the press, their marriage and the births of their children would invariably be reported days or weeks after the fact.

• Lindbergh had a reputation of being a bit of a prude. He abstained from any form of alcohol or tobacco. Before his famous flight, Lindbergh kept a list of rules that he examined every night to develop positive qualities or get rid of any flaws in his character. He would mark the attributes that he had fulfilled with a red cross and those he had failed with a black one. He would review this list every night until the number of red crosses more than outnumbered the black ones.

● The kidnapping and murder of his son, Charles Lindbergh, Jr., has been called the crime of the century. The officially accepted scenario of the crime is that Bruno Richard Hauptmann climbed a ladder to the child's room the evening of March 1, 1932. He took the child, leaving a ransom note on the windowsill, and on the way down the ladder accidentally dropped the child, killing him. He buried the child in the woods near the home, but acted as if the child was still alive by sending twelve other ransom notes. He received fifty thousand dollars in ransom money. Incriminating serial numbers led to Hauptmann's capture and a circuslike trial. He was found guilty and was electrocuted on April 3, 1936.

● Like the assassination of John F. Kennedy, people have come up with increasingly unbelievable theories about what "really" happened to the Lindbergh baby. One of the most unlikely was that the child died by accident (or was killed on purpose) at home and that the Lindberghs covered up the death by devising a kidnapping ruse. Someone outside the group—the Mafia, Hauptmann, or a mysterious someone else—took advantage of the Lindbergh's supposed plight and came up with ransom demands for a child they didn't have. The Lindberghs, fearing that they would be caught in their own lies, were forced to go along with the fiction and paid the ransom. Somehow (the story goes), Hauptmann got his hands on some of the ransom money, either as a conspirator or a dupe, and got killed for it.

● The Lindberghs moved to England in a self-imposed exile from the hounding of the American press. In June 1936 Lindbergh received an invitation from the American military attaché to Germany, Truman Smith, to tour the factories of Germany's air industry. Smith hoped that Lindbergh would act as an informant for the United States by reporting what he saw at German aviation centers.

● The Germans in turn hoped the same thing. They wished to use Lindbergh to spread word of the supposed invincibility of the German Luftwaffe, showing him "top-secret" plans and hangars filled with planes for the occasion. They told him outrageous lies about their factories' output and their planes' abilities.

● Their ploy worked. In a letter to Joe Kennedy, United States Ambassador to England, Lindbergh wrote that the German air fleet was stronger than all of the Allied forces combined. The story spread, and with each telling the German air force got bigger. By the time it got reported to the leaders of Europe, the German air fleet was supposedly ten times bigger than that of the rest of Europe combined, and defeat was the only possible outcome of getting into a war with Germany. This misinformation helped convince the prime ministers of France and England to sacrifice Czechoslovakia to Germany and to sign the Munich Pact.

● Lindbergh not only brought back inflated ideas of the German Luftwaffe but also a love for the National Socialist ideals. He found it troubling that American women were entering the workforce on what was considered equal terms with men. In his mind, a nation could not consider itself superior while its women were encouraged to leave the home. He considered the German women's ideal of *Kinder, Kirche, Kuche* (children, church, and kitchen) to be the proper one. Lindbergh also felt, like the Nazis, that the superiority of the northern European civilization was being threatened by other races.

● When France and England finally entered the war with Germany, Lindbergh returned to the United States to become the poster boy for the America First Committee, a nonintervention group, telling the American people that the United States should stay out of the troubles in Europe. As America moved closer to entering the war, Lindbergh's speeches got shriller and began to betray his racism and anti-Semitism.

• This prewar phase of Lindbergh's life has been labeled as the hero's fall from grace. He and Anne spent most of their time with members of the America First Committee, alienating their pro-Allies friends.

• Lindbergh was briefly considered for the position of secretary for air in FDR's cabinet, but was rejected because those around Roosevelt saw Lindbergh as untrustworthy, bordering on traitorous. Both sides of Lindbergh's and Anne's family—parents and siblings—disowned them during this time. It took the Lindberghs a long time to mend the fences.

• However, the debate was cut short by the bombing of Pearl Harbor. Once America entered the war, the American hero in Lindbergh came out again and he began to fly combat missions in the Pacific.

• Lindbergh had been so taken by the Nazis, he referred to the concentration camps as "ex–prison camps." He assumed that the people in these camps were being treated as fairly as any prisoner of war would be treated. When finally faced with the brutality of the death camps while touring Europe after the war, he finally admitted that he had been wrong.

• In the postwar era of his life, Lindbergh became a conservationist. On a trip to Vietnam as a brigadier general in the air force, Lindbergh engaged in a conversation with a local correspondent for one of the wire services. The exchange is recounted by Leonard Mosley in *Lindbergh: A Biography*:

"General Lindbergh," she said, "I hear you are not entirely happy with U.S. operations in Vietnam." "I don't know who gave you that impression," he said crisply. "I approve of any operations which prevent the spread of Communism in Asia." "Then does that mean you're in favor of defoliation?" she asked. "I hear you flew over the rain forests. Didn't it horrify you—the way they've been destroyed? All those trees. All those animals. All those birds and people." There was a silence. Then Lindbergh said: "I should hate anyone to think I approve of that. Once upon a time I thought George Washington was a good hero for American children, because when he cut down the cherry tree he admitted it later on. Now I'd have the story omitted from American history books. Even owning up doesn't excuse the cutting down of a tree."

● Lindbergh's year of reconciliation was 1973. In a spirit of apology, he wrote to many friends that he hadn't spoken to since his unpopular stand before World War II. In the summer of 1974 Lindbergh was rushed to a New York hospital with a fever of 104 and an advanced case of lymphatic cancer. On August 17, 1974, he was secretly flown to his home in Maui; a week later, Lindbergh lapsed into a coma. He died on August 26, 1974.

Joe DiMaggio

*Though his baseball career was a short one—only thirteen years—
"Joltin' " Joe DiMaggio, baseball's "Yankee Clipper," became one
of the most charismatic sports figures of the twentieth century.*

• Joseph Paul DiMaggio was born in Martinez, California, on
November 25, 1914. He was the eighth of nine children born to
Joseph (Giuseppe) and Rosalie DiMaggio, a Sicilian couple
who had emigrated to the United States at the turn of the century. Joe and his brothers Vince and Dom would all play baseball in the major leagues, playing for the first time together in
1940.

• As a small child, Joe had to wear steel leg-braces. The braces
fixed his knock-knees, but left him with weak ankles.

• When Joe was a few years old, the family moved to San Francisco. His first experience with baseball came on the playgrounds
of its North Beach. The kids played ball on what was called the
"horse lot" because a dairy company used it as a parking lot for
its horse-drawn milk wagons. The kids would scare off the horses
by throwing rocks at them, and then they would improvise a baseball diamond. "We used rocks for bases," said Joe, "and it was
quite a scramble among twenty of us kids to scrape up a nickel
to buy a roll of bicycle tape to patch up the ball each day." Joe
played bare-handed and used an old boat oar for a bat.

• At age sixteen, although he played a lot of baseball, he became seriously interested in tennis. The long hours of isolated drills necessary to hone those skills did not appeal to him, however, and he abandoned the sport almost as quickly as he had taken it up.

• In 1933 both Joe and his older brother Vince were playing for the California Seals, a minor league team. Joe was such an outstanding outfielder that Vince was soon considered expendable and shipped to the Hollywood team. Almost overnight Joe DiMaggio became the most talked about minor-league player in the country.

• In 1936 DiMaggio went to play for the New York Yankees in the American League, and in 1939 he won the league's Most Valuable Player Award.

• "If your legs are right," DiMaggio said, "your timing is right and everything else falls into line." Maybe so, but the injury-prone DiMaggio seems to have made it *in spite* of his legs. He seemed to have an "opening-game jinx"—he missed six of nine opening games because of injuries, mostly to some part of his legs, ankles, and knees.

• During World War II, DiMaggio traded his $43,750-a-year salary for $50 a month and an olive drab army–air force uniform. He played baseball in the service, too, until ulcers forced him to stop. When he was discharged three years later, he returned to the Yankees at his prewar salary.

• At the beginning of World War II, because his Italian parents were technically "enemy aliens," federal regulations said that they had to leave their North Beach home, since it was in a forbidden zone near the Pacific Coast. Eventually, though, President Roosevelt declared that Italians were no longer considered enemy aliens, and DiMaggio's parents were allowed to stay in their home.

• In postwar Japan the two most popular Americans were General MacArthur and Joe DiMaggio.

• Although DiMaggio authored two baseball books, his own reading interests focused on sports' pages and the comics. He would ask his friend Lefty Gomez to buy him comic books because everyone recognized him and he was embarrassed to be seen with the latest *Superman* and *Batman* offerings.

• DiMaggio didn't like to be photographed, but he knew the value of publicity. He timed his public appearances skillfully, never quite receding, yet never becoming overexposed.

• DiMaggio had been extremely bashful and shy when he was younger, so once he began getting famous, he devoted much energy to making up for his lost time with the ladies.

• He met his first wife, Dorothy Arnold, in 1937. Once they were engaged, DiMaggio announced that he didn't know exactly when the wedding would take place, just that it would not take place during baseball season.

• Joe, twenty-four, and Dorothy, twenty-one, were married in November 1939 in downtown San Francisco. So many people attended the wedding that the city's health director, himself an invited guest, took the precaution of having an ambulance at the site in case of any medical emergencies.

• Dorothy divorced him in 1944, asking for custody of their son, $500 a month alimony, and $150 a month for child support. When she tried to have the amounts raised later, the judge turned her down, telling her that she had made a mistake in divorcing DiMaggio in the first place.

• DiMaggio missed his son, and Dorothy, too. DiMaggio continued to see her, and people thought they might remarry. It took Marilyn Monroe to get her out of DiMaggio's system.

• DiMaggio met Monroe at the San Francisco restaurant Villa Nova, and the two hit it off. After sleeping with Monroe for the first time, he sent her flowers. The couple was married on January 14, 1954, at San Francisco City Hall. The Roman Catholic Church refused to recognize DiMaggio's divorce from Dorothy and automatically excommunicated him.

● On the couple's wedding night, DiMaggio asked the desk clerk if their room had a television. Sex was one of Monroe's favorite forms of recreation, and—she later confided to friends—DiMaggio spent too much of their time together fixated before a television set, and not enough tending to her sexual needs. Still, DiMaggio was said to be an adroit, compassionate, and arousing lover. Monroe called DiMaggio "Joe the Slugger" and said, "Joe brings a great bat into the bedroom." She told friends that DiMaggio had the finest male body she had seen.

● Years later, DiMaggio told another Hollywood actress that he was aware that he had a great body, focusing his boasts on a particular organ. For DiMaggio's next birthday, the actress sent him a mirror and a ruler.

● While Monroe and DiMaggio were courting, a calendar containing nude photos of Monroe became an object of cult frenzy. Soon the images were being marketed as an ashtray design, on highball glasses, and on cocktail trays. DiMaggio couldn't accept that showing off her body was part of her job, and he heatedly suggested that Monroe dress more conservatively. She began wearing relatively modest clothing when they were together.

● Monroe said that she and DiMaggio were sexually compatible. But there were other problems. He was neat, and she was sloppy. He was private, repressed, and possessive; she was outgoing. Each was willful. Each had a temper. Each was a star.

● The marriage lasted only nine months. Monroe had two or three affairs, all brief, all casual, late in the marriage. On October 27, 1954, Monroe appeared at a courthouse in Santa Monica, California. It was as civil as was allowed under divorce law at the time: She briefly and impersonally described DiMaggio's silences, coldness, and indifference. DiMaggio did not contest her statement, nor did he mention her infidelity. Monroe was granted a divorce on the grounds of "mental cruelty." They remained friends after the divorce.

● After Monroe's apparent suicide on August 4, 1962, DiMaggio arranged everything for her funeral. DiMaggio was convinced that Frank Sinatra, with whom he'd been close friends in the 1950s, had carelessly helped Monroe along the way to destruction, and he barred Sinatra from her funeral. He also barred almost everyone else from Hollywood, including Sinatra's cronies, Dean Martin and Peter Lawford.

● DiMaggio was completely torn up by Monroe's death, and friends think he never got over her. He continued to send flowers to Monroe's grave three times a week for ten years, and, thirty years later, still refuses to discuss the relationship in public.

Liberace

How many pianists could mount a successful Las Vegas stage show? Not many. Pianist Liberace, famous for his humor, candelabra, and flamboyant stage costumes, was one of a kind.

- Born in 1919 in West Allis, Wisconsin, Liberace was, like Elvis, the only survivor of twins.

- Liberace's mother was such a fan of film star Rudolph Valentino that she named Liberace's brother Rudolph Valentino Liberace. Liberace's full name was Wladziu Valentino Liberace, but his friends called him Lee.

- The pianist recalled his mother's love as "completely suffocating and damn near incestuous." She was always touching him, kissing him, unaware that her son was rendered nearly physically nauseous by her unwanted intimacies. He escaped by playing the piano, because he knew that his mother would not interrupt his practice sessions.

- When Liberace was in his teens his father, Salvatore, deserted the family. The son didn't see his father for decades, until Salvatore was very old and sick.

- At school, Liberace was recruited to accompany silent movies that were shown in the auditorium.

• Liberace always knew he wasn't like other boys. When, at age ten, he began to have crushes on male teachers, he didn't know what to do or think.

• He was playing piano in a bar when he met a football hero from the Green Bay Packers. Liberace said that he lost his virginity when the man offered him a ride home one night and seduced him.

• Liberace took extreme measures to keep his homosexuality secret. Before he began his television show, few questioned his sexual preference, but the intimacy of the medium revealed his inflection and mannerisms and launched much speculation and many tasteless jokes. But it didn't matter because his target audience—ironically, mostly women of his mother's age—loved him just the way he was.

• To silence speculation about his sexual preferences, Liberace began spending his evenings with Sonja Henie, a Norwegian-American figure skater and actress.

• In one of Liberace's books he included his answers to some of the questions the media would occasionally ask him. When asked, "Have you had a face-lift?" he replied, "Not yet. But if you think I've already had one, it means I can still wait until my friend and authority on the subject, Phyllis Diller, tells me it's necessary." Liberace had already had at least two face-lifts by then. In answer to the question "Is that your real hair?" Liberace replied, "The hair is real, but the color only my hairdresser knows." The hair *was* real, but it had grown on someone else's head. In reality, he had started balding in his thirties and had already lost most of his hair. And when asked why he hadn't married, he answered, "I'm still looking for the right girl."

• The pianist's idea of a vacation was to hit all the garage sales and flea markets he could find. Liberace eventually had three warehouses filled with everything from furniture to china. He kept buying houses so he could furnish them with his antiques and other finds. After his death, Christie's auction house of London held a three-day auction in Los Angeles to dispose of more than twenty thousand of his items, from trinkets to dozens of candelabras to mirrored pianos to Rolls-Royces.

● During his shows, Liberace made ten or more costume changes, dressing in floor-length coats and capes. One of his favorite coats was virgin fox with a sixteen-foot train, which cost $300,000.

● His costumes were also famous for their glitz: "I support the entire Austrian rhinestone business," he said.

● Between his heavy costumes and piano playing, Liberace sometimes lost as much as five pounds during his act.

● He attacked hecklers with a series of remarks and gestures. One of his favorites was to raise the middle finger on one hand and, still grinning, look directly at the heckler, asking, "How do you like the ring on this finger?"

● When Mae West was asked what she wanted for her birthday she replied, "Just bring me Liberace." Liberace appeared at her door on her birthday with a huge red bow across his chest and yelled, "Surprise! I'm your birthday present!"

● Liberace was generally gracious to fans, usually giving autographs freely except in two situations: If eating, or in the men's room, he would ask the autograph seeker to come back when he had finished.

● The pianist loved dogs and eventually had twenty-six. When one died, he would cry inconsolably.

● When Liberace played Radio City Music Hall in 1985, he set a fifty-three-year attendance record for the theater. Already in pretty bad shape from the ravages of AIDS, he put on twenty-one performances, each more than two hours long. He began each of them with one of his more spectacular entrances, using a harness under his costume to fly over the audience and across the stage.

• The last years of Liberace's life were embroiled in legal wranglings with a former live-in lover, Scott Thorson. Liberace first met Thorson in 1977, when Liberace was fifty-seven and Thorson was eighteen. The two men lived together for five years, during which time the musician looked into the possibility of adopting his young lover. He paid a plastic surgeon to have the young man made over to look like himself.

• But when Thorson returned home to attend his foster mother's funeral, Liberace moved a new young man into their bedroom. Thorson sued the musician, claiming that Liberace had promised him in front of witnesses that he would take care of Thorson for the rest of his life.

• After some wrangling, Thorson signed an agreement settling for $75,000 (of which his lawyer got a third), three cars, three dogs, and his own clothes.

• The agreement he signed also specified that Thorson would give up any other claims against Liberace. But on October 14, 1982, he again filed suit against Liberace in Los Angeles County Superior Court, trying to win palimony.

• Thorson and his lawyers began revealing embarrassing facts to the press, apparently thinking that Liberace would settle in order to keep his sexual life private. On November 2, 1982, the *National Enquirer*'s front page had a picture of Scott and Liberace, with the banner headline LIBERACE BOMBSHELL—BOYFRIEND TELLS ALL. The article covered the story of their love affair, the plastic surgery, the promises of lifetime support, the proposed adoption, Liberace's new relationship, and Thorson's subsequent eviction from Liberace's life.

• Liberace retaliated by giving an exclusive interview to the *Globe*, another major tabloid. He insisted that gays were out to "assassinate" him. He portrayed Thorson as a disgruntled former employee who had been fired in 1982 because of his use of drugs and misuse of firearms.

• In early autumn 1986 Liberace offered Thorson an out-of-court settlement. Thorson still was not told what motivated the offer; Liberace's attorney simply said that he just wanted to put an end to the dispute. Both men signed a final agreement on December 3, 1986.

• By this time, rumors about Liberace's ill-health had begun circulating through the entertainment industry and the gay community. He taped an interview with Oprah Winfrey for her Christmas show that year. Even heavy makeup couldn't hide the fact that he looked almost as bad as Rock Hudson had during Hudson's final public appearance.

• The *Vegas Sun* scooped everyone with its January 24, 1987, headline: LIBERACE VICTIM OF DEADLY AIDS. Liberace's attorney immediately issued a vigorous denial, saying that the pianist didn't have AIDS, that he suffered from emphysema, heart disease, and anemia. His personal physician announced that his illness resulted from a "watermelon diet" and anemia.

• Liberace died on February 4, 1987. Shortly after Liberace's body was embalmed, the Riverside County Health Department formally rejected his physician's death certificate and ordered an autopsy, which California law requires when there is suspicion that someone has died of a contagious disease. The county coroner revealed the true cause of Liberace's death—AIDS—in a nationally televised press conference.

Judy Garland

"The most talented woman I ever knew," said Bing Crosby. "She was a great, great comedienne and she could do more things than any girl I ever knew. Act, sing, dance, make you laugh. . . . There wasn't a thing that gal couldn't do—except look after herself."

- The girl who became "Judy Garland" was born Frances Ethel Gumm on June 10, 1922, to Ethel and Frank Gumm, who performed in vaudeville shows throughout Minnesota.

- According to Garland, Ethel, already the mother of two girls, took great delight in telling stories about trying to abort her with home-remedy abortion methods like "rolling down stairs and jumping off tables." When those failed, her parents hoped at least that the baby would be a boy. It wasn't, and hoped-for "Francis, Jr." became "Frances."

- Frances's father was a homosexual who had thought marriage might "cure" him. It didn't, and the relationship between Ethel and Frank was alternately strained and stormy. Discussing her childhood later, Garland referred to her mother as a "real-life wicked witch of the West." The relationship with her sisters was similarly rocky. Her father was her main support, and at age fourteen she was devastated when he suddenly died. Perhaps that helps explain why some of the men she married were much older than she was. Some were homosexuals. At least one, Vincente

Minnelli, was both. (Her daughter Liza Minnelli continued this latter tradition when she married openly gay Peter Allen.)

● Frances made her stage debut at the age of two for a Christmas show at a local theater where her father performed. She sang "Jingle Bells" and "When I Take My Sugar to Tea" and, basking in the applause, she wouldn't leave the stage, and her father had to carry her off. (Years later, her daughter Lorna Luft also made her stage debut singing "Jingle Bells" at one of her mother's concerts.)

● Frances became a regular part of the family act, which her ambitious mother hoped would go beyond the limited theatrical world of Minnesota and maybe even into the movies. In 1926 the family moved to Lancaster, a distant desert suburb of Los Angeles, looking for warmer weather and bigger worlds to conquer (and, according to some accounts, to escape a scandal involving Frank and a local boy).

● The Gumm Sisters began performing wherever they could find a venue in the hope that they might be "discovered." It was becoming clear that the star of the group was seven-year-old Frances, called "Little Miss Leather Lungs" and "the little girl with the great big voice" because she could be easily heard without a microphone. (Louella Parsons was only one of several reviewers who thought Frances might actually be an adult midget.) The sisters got a place on a local radio show, and appeared in several forgettable musical movie shorts starting in 1929. The family all but split up at that point, with Frank staying in Lancaster to manage a movie theater, and Ethel and the girls based in Los Angeles and traveling.

● To polish their skills, the Gumm sisters were enrolled in a talent school, Mrs. Lawlor's School for Professional Children, where a twelve-year-old boy named Joe Yule, Jr., developed a crush on ten-year-old Frances. A few years later, the two met again at MGM Studios; by this time her name was Judy Garland and his Mickey Rooney.

• The sisters got the Garland name from comedian George Jessel in 1934. When Jessel introduced them at Chicago's Oriental Theatre before the featured movie, he complained, "Mrs. Gumm, I can't go out and keep introducing your girls as the Gumm Sisters. That's ludicrous. It gets a laugh, and you're not a comedy act. You've got to change your name." To what? she asked. He thought it over, and then in the next show introduced them as the Garland Sisters. Where'd Jessel get the name? There were several stories (including that he named them after a New York drama critic); however, here's the most likely: *Twentieth Century* was the featured movie that week. In it, the character played by Carole Lombard decides to change her name from Lily Plotka to something more glamorous: Lily Garland.

• Ethel decided the sisters needed glamorous first names as well. Frances became "Judy" from a Hoagy Carmichael song by the same name. (It was a system that worked again years later when Ethel suggested a name for Judy's first daughter from an Al Jolson song, "Liza.")

• On September 27, 1935, at age fourteen, Garland split from her sisters and signed a seven-year contract with MGM that started her at one hundred dollars a week. She was profoundly insecure about her looks, being shorter and plumper than the movie-star ideal. It didn't help that she had a slight curvature of the spine and that her boss, Louis B. Meyer, greeted her each day with "how's my little hunchback this morning?" Nor the fact that she had to carry portable caps for her teeth and rubber disks to make her nose turn up.

• Garland's father, semireconciled with the family, died early on Ethel's birthday in 1935. Later that night, to the grieving family's horror, guests from as far away as Grand Rapids started showing up at the house bearing brightly wrapped gifts and a festive attitude because Frank had arranged a surprise party for Ethel.

• Garland's first big break was a memorable scene in *Broadway Melody of 1938*, in which she plays a teenage fan singing "Dear

Mr. Gable" to a photo of the film star. Gable hated the song from the first ("Goddamn brat, you've ruined every one of my birthdays," he told Garland at a Warner Brothers party eleven years later. "They bring you out of the wallpaper to sing that song, and it's a pain in the ass.") It didn't help that the title was an in-joke at his expense: People in the studio knew that he was receiving a barrage of letters from a woman who claimed that he was the father of her child, each beginning with "Dear Mr. Gable . . ."

• Garland's problem with drugs began at age fifteen, with studio-supplied Benzedrine to keep her weight down, phenobarbital to counteract the Benzedrine at night to let her sleep, then more Benzedrine to wake her up again the next morning from her drugged sleep. Over the following years she began popping dozens of pills a day, and eventually began suffering from depression, paranoia, and malnutrition. Studio officials, who monitored every other aspect of her life, conveniently ignored her drug addiction as she raced through movie after movie. Later, the strategy backfired as her pill taking made her so erratic that she became impossible to work with.

• Garland was the second choice for *The Wizard of Oz*, purchased by MGM in response to the surprise success of Disney's *Snow White and the Seven Dwarfs*. They wanted Shirley Temple, but 20th Century Fox wouldn't lend her. There was much discussion that having a well-developed sixteen-year-old playing a little girl might not be believable. This objection was overcome with the help of breast flatteners, a well-laced corset, and a strict diet.

• *Oz* went way over budget, eventually costing $2.77 million, and making it the third-most expensive movie ever filmed up to that time after *Ben-Hur* and *The Good Earth*. Garland wasn't responsible for that overrun, since she performed like a trouper and was paid only $9,649 for her nineteen weeks of work (some reports had it that even Toto was paid more). The movie also ran long, so studio bigwigs cut one song near the end, "The Jitterbug," and nearly axed "Over the Rainbow" as well.

- Garland dated Jackie Cooper when she was a teen, and had sex with him once, but preferred older men. At age seventeen she fell in love with bandleader Artie Shaw, twenty-eight and twice divorced at that point. She often snuck out to spend the night with him. However, he suddenly eloped with Lana Turner, and so she turned her attention to his friend David Rose, who eventually became her first husband in 1941. Because Rose and Garland worked opposite hours, he'd bring an organ down to the side of the pool and work in his bathing suit while she and her friends swam. She got pregnant, had an abortion, and filed for divorce after eight months.

- Garland, unsure of her sexual attractiveness, began going to wild Hollywood parties, even trying some lesbian relationships. In 1943 Garland had an affair with Tyrone Power, who generally preferred men. Starstruck, she kept unwashed the champagne goblets he drank from, and even the corks from the bottles. That wasn't all she kept: She ended up having another abortion. The relationship broke up when she discovered that he was reading her passionate love letters aloud to his Marine buddies.

- She was the first actress to have a psychiatrist constantly on the set with her while she was working on a film.

- Garland got together with Vincente Minnelli when he directed her in *Meet Me in St. Louis*. It was also the first movie in which Garland started getting difficult on the set—not showing up on time, leaving the set early with "migraines," and overusing booze and pills. She married him because she wanted a stable, older man, even though she complained about Minnelli's asexuality with her (to a point that she had an affair with Orson Welles before her marriage and several others, including Yul Brynner and Mario Lanza, after). Still, Garland managed to become pregnant during her honeymoon, and Liza May Minnelli was born on March 12, 1946. The couple separated in 1948.

- Because Garland had a strong fear of pain, she had all of her children by cesarean section.

• She was also utterly terrified of flying. When forced to, she fortified herself with drinks before hugging her legs to her stomach in a sitting fetal position.

• She was also morbidly afraid of horses. In *The Harvey Girls*, set in the Old West, a scene with a horse had to be rear-projected behind her close-up so she wouldn't have to be beside the real thing.

• She also had severe stage fright all her life. She tried hypnotism. Each night the doctor would come to her room and intone a posthypnotic suggestion to put her into a state of relaxation: "Irish mail." She tried it a few nights before deciding to go back to her old way of coping: Irish *whiskey*.

• She was a very quick study, able to glance at a page of script and perform the lines without error, and also able to pick up a dance routine just by watching someone perform it a few times.

• In the spring of 1949 she underwent the first of a series of six shock treatments in the hope that it somehow would help her drug addiction. It didn't. She started hiding pills around the house and studio. When necessary, she'd panhandle barbiturates and Benzedrine from friends and crew members.

• Once, while shopping, Garland's friend Lee Gershwin asked casually if she had any plans for the evening. Garland replied jovially, "Yeah, I think I'll slash my wrists." Gershwin thought she was joking. She wasn't. It was one of more than twenty suicide attempts.

• Garland was scheduled to be in *The Barkleys of Broadway* with Fred Astaire but was fired for erratic attendance and over-dramatic behavior and replaced by Ginger Rogers. A few weeks into the filming, Garland suddenly appeared on the set in full makeup and costume, shouting abuse at Rogers.

• Garland was next kicked out of the lead of *Annie Get Your Gun* and replaced by Betty Hutton. Her contract with MGM was suspended in May 1949. Since she was broke, the studio lent her nine thousand dollars and paid forty thousand dollars to get her addiction treated at a prestigious clinic in Boston. It helped . . . for a few weeks.

• During the shooting of *Summer Stock* she sometimes hallucinated from the mixture of pills and spent days at a time unable to perform. But she was always healthy enough for the cast parties. "The same woman, who the day before was incapable of uttering a sound, would show up and sing her heart out for hours," said costar Gene Kelly. "As long as the cameras weren't turning, she'd be fine."

• She was fired from *Royal Wedding* and replaced with Jane Powell. Her contract was suspended again, and then terminated in 1950.

• Garland did some radio shows but her debts were rapidly mounting because she continued to live lavishly despite little or no income. Her reputation for being difficult had pretty well spread through the entertainment industry, so she had trouble even booking live shows.

• At age twenty-eight she found she no longer had a career. In England, however, she was still beloved. She sang and danced in a long and extremely successful run at the Palladium. (Over the years, Garland returned there whenever her standing in the United States took a nosedive.) Garland had had a crush on British actor Robert Donat since she was a girl, and so she was thrilled on opening night to get an envelope from him. But instead of congratulations on her performance, he had written a note recommending his psychiatrist.

• While touring in Dublin, her dressing room had windows that opened onto the parking lot. Each night, before and after each show, she threw open the windows and sang a song or two for the people who couldn't afford to pay. The manager of the Manchester theater where she performed thought she was a pathetic creature, usually drunk or high and looking bewildered. He said her manager, Sidney Luft, would push her onto the stage, saying, "Get out there, you drunken bitch." What was amazing was that, onstage, she could (usually) pull herself together, talk coherently and entertainingly, and stay in control of that amazing voice.

● After Garland's triumphant tour in England, she returned to the States and had the first of about a dozen "comebacks." (She herself complained good-naturedly, "Every time I come back from the bathroom, someone announces that I've made a comeback.") She played the Palace in New York to sold-out houses. The show ran for nineteen weeks, and, according to *Variety*, it could have sold out for nineteen more. She went on to a triumphant four weeks at the Los Angeles Civic Auditorium.

● She was singing at the Greek Theater in Los Angeles when a moth flew into her mouth during "Over the Rainbow." "Now in the middle of 'Get Happy' you can go ptui!" she'd say, telling the story, "but not during 'Over the Rainbow.' " Without losing a beat, she tucked it under her tongue, and continued singing.

● Before her divorce from Minnelli, Garland discovered that she was pregnant by new love Luft. She had an abortion, her third. In June 1952, pregnant again, she married Luft and hired him as her manager.

● Daughter Lorna Luft was born on November 21, 1952. A few days later, suffering from postnatal depression and high on Seconal and Dexedrine, Garland tried to slit her own throat. The doctor, who had dealt with her halfhearted suicide tries several times previously, warned her, "Judy, you keep this up and one of these times you're going to hurt yourself." Five years later she interrupted the afternoon television viewing of eleven-year-old

Liza and a school friend to tell them that Mommy intended to commit suicide. When Liza followed her and started pounding on the locked bathroom door, screaming, "Mama, don't kill yourself!" a butler rushed in and broke down the door.

● Twice, she nearly died when she fell asleep or passed out while smoking, starting major fires.

● In 1953 Judy was offered a role with James Mason in *A Star Is Born*. Because it was a time when movie studios were trying to compete with television, the movie was almost filmed in 3-D; when that idea was rejected, the studio scrapped a lot of film footage, at a cost of three hundred thousand dollars, and began reshooting in extrawide CinemaScope. Mason's wife, hearing rumors that her husband and Garland were having an affair during filming, responded philosophically, "If they are, she'll get thin and the film will be finished quicker."

● Garland was nominated in 1955 for an Oscar for Best Actress in *A Star Is Born*, but she was in the hospital with newborn son Joseph Wiley Luft on the night of the Academy Awards presentation. They set up cameras and mikes in her hospital room to record her reaction in case she won. (She didn't.)

● The screenplay for *The Three Faces of Eve* was written with Garland in mind. But she refused to do it, perhaps because the story of out-of-control multiple personalities was too close to life. Joanne Woodward took the role instead, and she won an Oscar.

● Garland loved hamburgers with peanut butter.

● Garland was terrified of live television, but, pressured by money problems, she signed up with CBS for a series of specials. The night before the first broadcast, she overdosed on sleeping pills and was still badly slurring her words during the afternoon dress rehearsal. When the cameras started, she was still shaky, but by the second song was in good shape.

• In 1956 *The Wizard of Oz* was shown for the first time on TV which, despite the fact that only a handful of homes had color TV, was a big success, becoming an annual event.

• Garland's triumphant TV specials led to a series in 1963 which she hoped would go long enough to finally solve her financial difficulties. Unfortunately, CBS put it up against *Bonanza*, the most popular show on television. Judy's ratings were better than expected, but not high enough to keep the show from being canceled after twenty-six shows.

• Garland continued her successful concert tours. When she went to Australia, customs officials confiscated all of her beloved drugs. She acquired replacements on the black market, but the dosage levels were foreign to her, playing a role in some of her out-of-control moments on that tour.

• "It got to a point that I was a virtual automaton—with no memory," she told an interviewer years later. "I played some very big dates in 1958 and 1959, but I don't remember any of it." She also became obese. At the end of 1959 Luft persuaded two doctor friends to impersonate musicians and covertly examine her, since she wouldn't see a doctor. During the course of the evening, one reached over and felt her shoulder, confirming his suspicion that Garland was waterlogged, which meant that there was something wrong with her kidneys or liver—or both. They took her to a hospital and found that she had acute hepatitis and that her liver had swollen to four times its normal size. Over the next seven weeks they drained more than twenty quarts—five gallons—of excess liquid from her body. No more hard liquor, her doctors said, but they let her drink Blue Nun Liebfraumilch. While in the hospital, she managed to persuade Random House to advance her thirty-five thousand dollars for her autobiography, which she began but never finished.

• She left the hospital feeling better than she had since she was a teenager. She was relatively sober and using only moderate doses of Ritalin, a mild mood elevator. (This moderation wouldn't last long—she'd soon be taking twenty and then forty of them a day instead of the recommended dosage of three.) She went into a studio and quickly recorded twelve songs with no difficulty, and went to London and began another series of concerts, taking time out to campaign for John F. Kennedy on U.S. military bases in Germany.

● With her turbulent private life and melodramatic public role, she developed a following of gay men and became a favorite model for female impersonators. Like Christians in Rome drawing fish in the sand to identify themselves in a hostile world, gays— heavily persecuted at the time, both socially and by law-enforcement officials—began using "a friend of Dorothy's" as a code phrase, referring to her most enduring and endearing role.

● Garland had been a friend of vaudevillian Fanny Brice (in fact, Brice had been the one who had suggested over lunch, based on her own career, that Garland go to London whenever propects were dim in the United States). The movie script of Brice's life, *Funny Girl*, was written specifically with Garland in mind, but Garland turned it down and Barbra Streisand got the role. She did, however, take a small part as a German hausfrau in *Judgment at Nuremberg*, the beginning of another of her comebacks. A two-disk record album, *Judy at Carnegie Hall*, shot to number one and stayed there for thirteen weeks, then lingered on the Top 40 chart for seventy-three weeks.

● She recorded a leading role for *Gay Puree*, a full-length animated cartoon and appeared in several more dramatic roles in films, including *I Could Go On Singing*, a semiautobiographical study filmed in England of a difficult and bedeviled music star.

● Once again she drove cast and crew crazy. She became angry that she didn't have a private toilet in her trailer/dressing room as specified in her contract. The ladies' room was just a few steps away; however, to make a point, she'd storm into the nearest studio business office, order the hapless occupant out, and use the wastebasket as a toilet.

• Meanwhile, her marriage to Luft went through a series of separations and reconciliations on its way to an eventual divorce. She also lost his services as a manager. The agency she hired to replace him defrauded her of hundreds of thousands of dollars.

• Liza began making a success of her own career. Garland's reaction was at least as competitive and despairing as it was supportive. Two days after throwing a seventeenth birthday party for Liza, who had just gotten a part in an off-Broadway musical, Garland nearly killed herself with another overdose of barbiturates. She skipped the opening night of Liza's musical. Later, to get Liza to quit the show and move back to the West Coast, Garland hired Liza's boyfriend to be on her TV show's staff. When mother and eighteen-year-old daughter played the Palladium together, Garland constantly upstaged her, playing competitive tricks such as continually jerking Liza's microphone toward her mouth as if she didn't know how to use it properly.

• In 1963 Garland was blackmailed by someone who had a picture of her lying topless and unconscious on a gurney, having her stomach pumped after one of her suicide attempts. She paid fifty thousand dollars for the negative and the prints, which she burned.

• Garland had little loyalty to old friends, family, and coworkers. For decades, after Mickey Rooney's career went into a deep hole, she avoided him. "Don't let that asshole in here" was her reaction when he dropped by unannounced at her house for a social visit. Later, though, when she realized a reunion would make a good stunt for her weekly TV show, she invited him to be her first guest.

• By 1966 Garland was more than $100,000 in debt, not counting the more than $400,000 she owed in back taxes. She began moving in with friends whenever possible, even camping for three months on the living-room floor of one of Liza's friends. When she arrived in New York to appear on the *Merv Griffin Show*, a producer trying to book accommodations was surprised that she was blacklisted from all the major hotels for having repeatedly skipped out on hotel bills. She ended up staying with the producer's parents.

● She needed money and so accepted a role in *Valley of the Dolls*, playing a part modeled to a large extent on Ethel Merman, with whom *Dolls* author Jacqueline Susanne had had a flagrantly public affair. Ironically, another character, the pill-popping neurotic played by Patty Duke, was largely based on Garland herself. However, once she found out what the movie was about, she became ambivalent about appearing in it and, after several days of showing up late, cowering in her dressing room and refusing to come out, and then not showing up at all, she was fired.

● She decided it was time to try to write her autobiography again. She contacted a ghostwriter, who got an inkling that she wasn't planning to tell the whole, unvarnished truth when she recounted some harrowing stories of her life and then said, "Isn't it remarkable that with all the horror, with all that I've been through, I never drifted into pills or booze?" The project quickly fell through.

● Before she died she married men who were substantially younger than her. The first was Mark Herron in 1964 (and again in 1965 when it was revealed that she was still legally married to Luft in 1964). She liked to accompany him on his trips to gay clubs (she enjoyed being the only woman there, surrounded by fawning, handsome young men). When she divorced him in 1966, she claimed their marriage had never been consummated. She had an affair with a woman in 1966, barely avoiding a scandal. In 1969, a few months before her death, Garland married Mickey Deans.

● By the end of her career her shows were characterized by long, rambling monologues to disguise the fact that her voice was disappearing, and that she couldn't remember the words to her songs. The once adoring crowds that had long tolerated her peculiarities began heckling her, to her deep distress.

• Garland died from an overdose. Deans, her last husband, discovered her still sitting on the toilet in her bathroom. He had run out of the house the night before after a screaming battle. By the time he arrived home the next morning, rigor mortis had already set in. She was forty-seven years old and $4 million in debt.

• At Garland's funeral comedian Alan King turned to Liza Minnelli and got a smile when he whispered, "This is the first time your mother has ever been on time for a performance."

George S. Patton

George Smith Patton, Jr., was a no-nonsense four-star general in the U.S. Army who led victorious battles in Mexico, World War I, and World War II. With good reason people called him "Old Blood and Guts."

● George S. Patton, Jr., was raised in an upper-class family in southern California at the end of the nineteenth century. Patton's maternal grandfather, Benjamin D. Wilson, had been the first mayor of Los Angeles. A paternal grandfather had been a Confederate colonel in the Civil War. Combining his family history and his own obsession of reading about great military leaders, Patton felt that joining military life was inevitable.

● He was dyslexic and kept out of school so other kids wouldn't make fun of him. His father taught him at home. The first school he attended was the Virginia Military Institute, the alma mater of Patton's father and grandfather, in 1903. The following year he gained admittance to West Point, but he had to repeat his first year.

● Patton thought that a strong sex drive went with being a soldier. Once, when his wife, Beatrice, wrote that she was picturing him doing his favorite pastime—reading—he was clearly miffed and replied, "Darling One . . . What in the Hell do you mean by 'Doing what I like best to do—reading.' I would rather a damn sight look at something else than a book, and you know what it is, too. It looks like a skunk."

● He started an affair in 1937 with his niece (by marriage), Jean Gordon, that was to last for several years. She called him "Uncle Georgie."

● Patton participated in the Olympic games in Stockholm in 1912. His event was the modern pentathlon, and he finished a respectable fifth place, despite the fact that he fainted twice: once in front of the royal box during the cross-country run and the other at the end of the three hundred-meter swim (he had to be fished out of the water with a boat hook).

● Patton developed a strong belief in reincarnation and déjà vu. Oftentimes he would visit a battle site in Europe and recount ancient battles, and announce that he had been a participant in such battles in a previous life, serving as, for example, a Roman soldier or an officer under Napoleon.

● Once, during World War I, he urinated in the foxhole of another division commander to show his contempt for "passive defense." He was extremely aggressive and frequently told his troops that he saw nothing noble in death—it was better to kill others than to die for your country.

● The French had invented a light tank and the U.S. army obtained some prototypes to try out. Patton got the job of working with them, in part because he spoke French fluently and could read the manuals.

● Patton's fluency in French wasn't always a virtue. He created a headache right before the campaign in French North Africa during World War II. As the American ships headed for the coast of Morocco, Patton started reading propaganda leaflets that were meant to be dropped behind enemy lines. He went into a rage, shouting, "Some goddamn fool in the States forgot to put the accents in this thing! In 'fidele' the accent gràve is missing from the middle e and the accent acute is missing off the e in 'l'amitie'!"

Seven hours later, as American troops began storming the shore, a group of soldiers was still on the ship adding accent marks by hand.

● Patton was the first man to lead a motorized vehicle into battle in a 1916 skirmish against Mexican bandit Pancho Villa. Soon after, he started the First Light Tank Battalion. To his disappointment, peace came to Europe before his boys could see any action, in large part because American tank designs still had a few bugs in them. For example, one manufacturer submitted a prototype that was run by a steam engine. Of 23,405 tanks ordered from American manufacturers during World War I, only 26 were delivered before war's end.

● In 1932 about twenty thousand World War I veterans marched on Washington, demanding partial payment of their war bonuses (approximately fourteen hundred dollars each), but were refused by Congress. Out of work and depressed, many lingered, setting up camps and living in abandoned buildings. Afraid of anarchy, Hoover ordered the army to clear the place out. Patton, executive officer of the third Cavalry, was eager to jump into the fray and kick "those Bolsheviks" out of town. He was effective—too effective, some say. He finally got to use his tanks in battle, flattening the camps and chasing the campers. The rout lasted only two days, but the images of young soldiers beating and teargassing down-and-out veterans and burning their belongings was to haunt the army for a decade.

● While stationed in Hawaii before World War II, Patton's first division commander judged him unfavorably as "invaluable in war . . . but a disturbing element in peace." Patton considered this high praise indeed.

● While in Hawaii, Patton composed a paper laying out the precarious position of the American presence in the Pacific. He predicted that a Japanese attack on Pearl Harbor was not only possible, but probable, and would be disastrous to the United

States. The date of his report was April 26, 1935 . . . six years before his predictions came true.

• When World War II started, Patton was assigned to the tank corps again. The army was slow in providing spare parts or funds to repair broken-down tanks. One of Patton's mechanics, annoyed, mentioned that it shouldn't be so difficult—most of the parts needed were ordinary things that could be ordered from the Sears Catalog and adapted. Patton immediately contacted Sears Roebuck and put in a series of orders, writing checks from his own bank account (one order was known to cost him eight hundred dollars, but the total amount he spent was a secret he took to his grave).

• Patton was disgusted when he first visited his headquarters in England. He was assigned to an apartment that had until recently belonged to a high-priced call girl. Between the pink and frilly feminine furnishings and the mirror on the ceiling above the oversized bed, he figured it was assigned to him by some spiteful rival.

• Patton had a certain way with words, especially evident when he addressed his troops:

War is a killing business. You've got to spill their blood, or they'll spill yours. Rip your bayonets into the bloody bowels of the enemy, or shoot 'em in the guts.

It is a popular idea that a man is a hero just because he was killed in action. Rather, I think a man is frequently a fool when he gets killed.

There is only one tactical principle which is not subject to change. It is: To use the means at hand to inflict the maximum amount of wounds, death, and destruction on the enemy in the minimum time . . . Battles are won by frightening the enemy. Fear is induced by inflicting death and wounds on him . . . The larger the force and the more violence you use in the attack, whether it be men, tanks, or ammunition, the smaller will be your proportional losses.

• During the invasion of Italy, he ordered the mules of a poor Sicilian shot because they were blocking his passage over a bridge.

• In August 1943 Patton committed the unthinkable. In two separate evacuation hospitals in Sicily he slapped two enlisted men across the face with his gloves. Both men had complained of lost nerves and Patton became enraged. He couldn't stomach the idea of the "truly wounded" having to look at men he considered cowards. Patton (who still thought he had been right) was forced to apologize to the staff of each hospital, the enlisted men who had been slapped, and all the divisions stationed in Sicily. The incidents put the brakes on his rise in the military, because Eisenhower thought him too unstable to go any higher in the chain of command.

• However, the mental instability that made Patton fearful in hospitals also made him fearful to the enemy. Since he was one of the few Allied generals who genuinely terrified the Germans, Eisenhower didn't want to let him go, but couldn't fully trust him in a position of responsibility. His solution: For much of the war Patton was used as a decoy, moving from place to place with high visibility to confuse the Germans, who figured that he would be part of any major push into Europe. He was assigned to a "phantom army" in England that consisted of realistic-looking inflatable rubber trucks and landing craft that were moved all over the country in the dead of night to make it look like the main D day invasion would take place in southern Norway. The Germans were so taken in that when the real invasion started in France, they held back critical defenses because they wanted them in place for when Patton's "real" invasion started.

• A few weeks before D day, Patton was told by Eisenhower (then supreme Allied commander of the Normandy invasion) and others to keep a low profile. Unfortunately, he was invited to give a small speech in Knutsford. In an unrehearsed oration, Patton said, "Since it is the evident destiny of the British and

Americans to rule the world, the better we know each other the better job we will do." Regrettably, he failed to mention the Russians, our allies at the time. This caused such an uproar that Patton's ability to command was once again called into question.

• Finally, he was put in charge of a tank corps and, plotting out strategies on Michelin tourist maps, made a series of bold moves that changed the course of the war. In less than ten months his armor and infantry roared through France, Belgium, Luxembourg, Austria, Czechoslovakia, and then finally into Germany.

• On the way, Patton was continuously in danger from shelling, strafing, and bombing. In the middle of one scorched, scarred, and burning landscape, with the sound of explosions around him, he threw out his arms and looked to the skies as if bathing in a warm spring rain. "Could anything be more magnificent?" he shouted to the soldiers around him. "Compared to war, all other forms of human endeavor shrink to insignificance. God, how I love it!"

• Patton demanded a high level of spit and polish even on the front lines. He hated Bill Mauldin's popular cartoons of unshaven, slovenly, dogfaced soldiers and tried to get them banned from *Stars & Stripes*. When he complained to Dwight Eisenhower, the general, a Mauldin fan, laughed him off.

• In April 1945, nauseated by the appalling sights he witnessed at the Ohrdruf Nord concentration camp in Germany, Patton forced the mayor and his wife of the neighboring town to tour the camp. Later that day, the couple hanged themselves.

• In an interview he drew a comparison between the Nazi Party and the Republican and Democrat Parties of America. The ensuing worldwide uproar came as a complete surprise to him. The purpose and politics of the war seemed to bypass Patton completely. His only concern had been the fighting, not the reasons for it.

• In postwar Germany Patton became somewhat confused as to the point of denazification. He thought it pointless to get rid of

German workers who were so capable and efficient at their jobs (especially at "just taking orders"), and started seeing the former enemies as allies in the next war—against the Communists of the USSR. Though the American government covertly adopted the same strategy, he was relieved of his position.

● During a parade review, shortly after termination of hostilities in Berlin, he was scowling at a Russian general across the reviewing stand, who sent a translator over to Patton to invite him for a drink after the show. "Tell that Russian son of a bitch that I regard them as enemies and I'd rather cut my throat than have a drink with one of my enemies." The translator nervously conveyed the message, and the Russian general smiled broadly and responded. The translator returned and told Patton, "The general says he feels exactly like that about you too, sir. So why, he asks, couldn't you and he have a drink after all?" They did.

● On December 8, 1945, one day before he was scheduled to return home, Patton was traveling near Mannheim, Germany, with a friend. In a freak accident, an army truck collided with Patton's limousine. No one sustained any injuries but Patton. He was thrown forward from the backseat, got partially scalped by the interior roof light, and crashed into the front-seat divider, breaking his nose and neck. Paralyzed from the neck down, he was immediately hospitalized, but died on December 21 of pulmonary edema and congestive heart failure.

● Two weeks after Patton's death, Jean Gordon gassed herself to death in her apartment. A family story, possibly spurious, had it that one of Gordon's aunts found a message pinned to her dress reading, "I will be with Uncle Georgie in heaven and have him all to myself before Beatrice arrives."

Alfred Hitchcock

Alfred Hitchcock is considered one of the best movie directors who ever lived. Later, largely because of his TV show, he also became an unlikely TV star in his own right despite (or because of) his deadpan beagle face and portly body.

- Alfred Hitchcock was born on August 13, 1899, in Leytonstone, England, just outside of London, not far from the scene of the Jack the Ripper murders. His parents called him Fred, which he detested. Fred was replaced by an even more repellent nickname in school, "Cocky." He called himself "Hitch."

- His father was a successful produce and poultry dealer, which meant that there were plenty of eggs around the house. Alfred developed a lifelong dislike for eggs. In *To Catch a Thief* Jessie Royce Landis extinguishes her cigarette in the middle of an egg yolk. In *Shadow of a Doubt* a man enjoying a fried egg suddenly stabs the yolk, releasing a flood of goo onto his plate. "To me," said Hitchcock, "it was much more effective than oozing blood."

- When Hitchcock was six, in punishment for some minor transgression, he was sent to the police station with a note. The officer in charge read it and then locked him in a cell for five minutes, saying, "This is what we do to naughty boys." From that point on, Hitchcock had an irrational fear of police, even refraining from taking out a driving license because he did not want to get in trouble with traffic officers.

• Hitchcock had a compulsive need to clean up after himself from childhood on, to the point of always drying a washbasin and polishing the taps after washing his hands.

• Hitchcock learned the art of suspense from Jesuit priests. He went to a Catholic boarding school, St. Ignatius College at Stamford Hill, until age fourteen. The Jesuits were noted for their fierceness in corporal punishment, carried out with a cane of hard rubber. The refinement of this punishment, however, was psychological. Once the errant child was sentenced to corporal punishment, he could choose when it should be administered: first morning break, lunch time, midafternoon, or the end of the day. Naturally, most children put off the fateful moment as long as possible. The suspense of anticipation made the punishment much worse.

• He became obsessed by maps and train schedules. By age sixteen he knew the geography of New York by heart from maps. His favorite reading was railway timetables and Cooke's travel folders, and he prided himself on being able to recite from memory all the stops on the Orient Express.

• During World War I an air raid left him with a vivid memory of going into his mother's room at home to see if she was all right: "The whole house was in an uproar, but there was my plump little mother struggling to get into her bloomers, always putting both her legs through the same opening and saying her prayers, while outside the window shrapnel was bursting around a search-lit Zeppelin. Extraordinary image!" The detail of the bloomers he recalled years later and slipped it into the opening sequence of *Dial M for Murder.*

• Hitchcock demonstrated a talent for drawing and got a job in the advertising department of an engineering firm. Years later, when he needed a logo for his TV show, he drew the now-famous line caricature of himself in profile.

● When Hitchcock was twenty, he was offered a job by a movie studio, Famous Players–Lasky Company, designing the title cards for silent films.

● Hitchcock had never been out with a girl other than his sister before he met his wife-to-be, Alma Reville, in her early twenties. He was shy with girls, and did not know many of the basic facts of life, having been kept, like most young men of his time, in discreet ignorance by his family and his teachers. Reville was a tiny, vibrant woman who was one day younger than him, but who outranked him at Famous Players. Eventually he was promoted to a film production position, and then he introduced himself to Reville. She said, "Since it is unthinkable for a British male to admit that a woman has a job more important than his, Hitch had waited to speak to me until he had a higher position."

● He and Reville were returning from business in Germany on an overnight boat on a dark and stormy night. She was lying down in her cabin, not feeling well. Hitchcock appeared at her door and, after making a couple of practical remarks about the job in hand, quite out of the blue asked her to marry him.

● On a film location at the ocean, he was told that the actress could not go into the water, because it was "that time of the month." Hitchcock said, "What time of the month?" Someone pulled him aside and gave him a careful and detailed description of periods and the physical processes of women. He was twenty-six and engaged to be married, and was flabbergasted that he had never heard of such a thing.

● He learned fast. Tallulah Bankhead was adamant about not wearing any underwear, and saw no reason to change her ways just because she had to climb up a tall ladder every day to get into the water tank where *Lifeboat* was being filmed. This daily ritual began to attract larger and larger throngs of technicians and bystanders. Eventually this news got back to the executive producer, Darryl Zanuck, who asked Hitchcock if he could do something about it. Hitchcock's reply was, "Willingly. Of course it will have to go through the proper channels, and I don't know which to go through—makeup, wardrobe, or hairdressing?"

● Hitchcock and Reville were married on December 2, 1926. The newlywed couple moved into a top-floor flat at 153 Cromwell Road, in West London, ninety steps up. She had begun as his assistant director. Reville did the script adaptations for six of his films and wrote or collaborated on ten of his screenplays.

● *Blackmail* was his first sound film, and the first in which Hitchcock made a cameo appearance. He appeared in thirty-six of his fifty-three films.

● Hitchcock loved playing practical jokes. Some were harmless, but others demonstrated a sadistic streak. During a stage performance, he once put a full-grown workhorse into the tiny dressing room of his friend, Gerald du Maurier.

● One of his favorite types of joke was the elevator gag. Right before getting onto a crowded elevator he would start telling a story, something like, "Of course, I didn't know what was going on. It was dark, and there was a knife on the ground and so I picked it up. It was just then that I noticed splotches of blood on the blade, and presently I felt wetness around my feet. I was standing in a pool of blood. Then I saw the body. Well, what could I do? My fingerprints were all over the knife and there were no witnesses. So I reached into my pocket and . . ." Hitchcock would suddenly exit the elevator midstory, leaving all the other passengers hanging.

● Other gags he played: He'd have gigantic pieces of furniture installed in friends' tiny flats while they were away. He once had a model of himself made and then floated it on the Thames River to see people's reactions.

● He actually felt he had gone too far in his joking when he paid a studio prop man to let himself be handcuffed overnight. Immediately before the handcuffing, Hitchcock gave him a drink liberally spiked with a strong laxative. The next day, the man had soiled himself and a considerable area of the floor.

● Hitchcock once set up a dinner party where everything that was to be eaten or drunk was blue. There was blue soup, blue trout, blue chicken, and blue ice cream. "It seemed like such a pretty color, I couldn't understand why hardly anything we eat is blue."

● He liked Peter Lorre because he was strange, and fascinating to work with. Hitchcock even worked around Lorre's frequent absences when he snuck off to shoot up more morphine.

● When Hitchcock began hosting a TV show, he despised having to break up his stories with television commercials, and he let the public know it with witty jabs at the sponsor like "Just as no rose is complete without thorns, no television show is complete without the following commercial," and "When I was a young man, I had an uncle who frequently took me out to dinner. He always accompanied these dinners with minutely detailed stories about himself. But I listened, because he was paying for the dinner. I don't know why I am reminded of this, but we are about to have one of our commercials."

● Because Hitchcock would outline his entire film in advance, scene by scene, he seldom wasted footage. (In contrast, most filmmakers typically shoot ten feet of film for every foot they use.) As a result, he often brought his pictures in under budget. Another benefit was that Hitchcock's stingy footage afforded no opportunity for studios to rearrange his shots and scenes.

● He drank large quantities of tea on the set. When he finished a cup, he would hurl the cup behind him to let it shatter where it would. It was a drain on the porcelain, but a calculated way to keep his crew on its toes.

● Having started as a virgin husband at twenty-seven, he began a life of celibacy at the age of forty-two. He was quoted as saying, "Sex has never interested me much. I don't understand how people can waste so much time over sex. Sex is for kids, for movies—it's a great bore."

● The management of Warner Brothers, hit hard by TV, demanded that Hitchcock film *Dial M for Murder* in 3-D. To do so required a huge, cumbersome camera that interfered with his crane shots and other Hitchcock cinematography trademarks. After all that trouble, the 3-D fad passed and the film was released as a regular "flat" film.

● Hitchcock tended to develop crushes on his leading ladies, especially "cool blondes." They apparently did not reciprocate. He introduced Grace Kelly to Prince Rainier and became jealous when they hit it off. He was invited to their wedding, but did not attend.

● Hitchcock was watching the NBC *Today* show when he saw a commercial for Sego, a diet drink. He was immediately smitten with the blonde actress, Tippi Hedren, and tracked her down for his next movie, *The Birds*.

● Hedren was delighted to get the part, but Hitchcock's continuous attention became disconcerting. He assigned three crew members to follow her around and report on her activities. He constantly pulled her aside for longer and longer "story conferences." He continually sent small gifts and love notes, and under the pretense of preparing for a complicated makeup session, he had a life mask made of her that he kept in his office. Eventually, when it became clear that she didn't share his interest, he sent her five-year-old daughter an elaborate doll of her mother, dressed as the character she played in *The Birds* . . . and packed in a coffinlike pine box.

● Hitchcock and Reville made an unusual Hollywood couple. They lived in the same house in Bel Air throughout their marriage. She did the cooking, and employed only a cleaning lady to help with household chores. The extravagances in their home were a huge eat-in kitchen with a walk-in freezer and complete wine cellar.

● During the filming of his fifty-third and final feature, *Family Plot*, Hitchcock suffered a heart attack and had a pacemaker installed. He had it done with a local anesthetic so he could watch the operating procedure. He bounced back from his surgery, happy to show his scar and relate the gory details.

● Afterward, he was amused to find that his pacemaker set off alarms at security gates in airports.

● When he used a public toilet and another man entered the room, he would quickly raise his legs within the stall "so that no one could tell there was anyone there."

● In Switzerland he saw a little boy walking with a priest who had his hand on the boy's shoulder and was talking very seriously to him. Hitchcock said to his companion, "That is the most frightening sight I have ever seen." Hitchcock then rolled down the window of the car and yelled, "Run, little boy, run for your life!"

● He received dozens of prestigious awards in his lifetime, but he never received an Oscar for best director. He was nominated five times: *Rebecca* (1940), *Lifeboat* (1944), *Spellbound* (1945), *Rear Window* (1954), and *Psycho* (1960).

● On April 29, 1980, Hitchcock died in his home in Bel Air. His estate was estimated in excess of $20 million. These included major holdings in city and county bonds issued by Los Angeles and San Francisco, ownership of oil wells in four states, gas wells in Canada, and 150,000 shares of MCA stock. Among his effects were 2,250 head of cattle at the Hitchcock Hereford Farms, sixty-six cases of wine, and twenty-nine major pieces of art.

Adolf Hitler

To this day, we struggle to understand how this son of a petty civil servant managed to convince an entire nation to go along with his dreams of world conquest and racial superiority.

- Adolf Hitler, born April 20, 1889, is undoubtedly one of the most puzzling personalities of our time. He became a vegetarian and purportedly loved animals (he even left bread crumbs for the mice in his apartment), played games with children, and lovingly offered gold watches to friends who promised to quit smoking, yet sentenced millions of men, women, and children to death without a second thought.

- Hitler's father, Alois Hitler, was the illegitimate son of Maria Anna Schicklgruber. Maria worked for the Frankenreithers, a Jewish family, as a servant. There has been speculation that Alois's father was the nineteen-year-old son of the family. While postwar research casts some doubt on this story which portrays Adolf as one-quarter Jewish, Hitler himself feared that it might be true and tried to cover up any evidence of the matter. Whether true or not, the Frankenreither family financially supported Maria until her son was fourteen.

- Hitler's father had three wives (but divorced only one of them), seven or eight children, and at least one more child out of wedlock. One wife was thirteen years older than him, another twenty-three years younger, and one—Hitler's mother—was his foster daughter. Hitler's godfather was a Jew named Prinz.

● Hitler was not born in Germany, but rather in (at that time) Austria-Hungary.

● Hitler's sister Paula claimed that Adolf got a sound thrashing every day from his father. Although Alois was strict, it was not clear that he was any more so than the average German father of that period.

● Hitler idolized his mother and personally nursed her during her last few weeks as she lay dying of cancer. Her physician, Dr. Edmund Bloch, was a Jew. After her death in 1908 the grieving Hitler promised the doctor he would be forever grateful for the care he took of his mother.

● At age eight Hitler attended a Benedictine monastery school. He longed to become an abbot, but barely escaped expulsion when he was caught smoking. The monastery's coat of arms, displayed in various parts of the school, prominently featured a swastika.

● Hitler hated school and his teachers hated his insolence. When he finally finished high school he celebrated by getting so drunk that he fell into unconsciousness. When he awoke he could not find his graduation certificate to show his mother. He returned to the school to get a duplicate. The headmaster was waiting for him with his original certificate. It had been torn into four pieces and used as toilet paper. The humiliated future führer then made a vow to touch alcohol never again.

● Hitler was a voracious reader of Karl May's Western novels, which were very popular in Germany at the time. May was a German who had never visited the United States, so he made up facts about the geography and the habits of American cowboys and Indians. Hitler later claimed that everything he knew about America came from May's books, and that he got the idea for

concentration camps from reading about American Indian res-
ervations.

● Hitler's half brother Alois, Jr., served time in jail for thievery on
at least two occasions and was a bigamist. He was banished to a
concentration camp in 1942 because he talked too much about
Hitler as a youth.

● Hitler's first youthful love was Stephanie Jansten. He composed
a number of love poems in her honor including one he called
"Hymn to the Beloved," and apparently falsely believed from her
last name that she was Jewish. In spite of his passion and his
confession to his best friend that he would jump off a bridge into
the Danube to commit suicide, taking Stephanie with him, he
never once got up the nerve to talk to her. It wasn't until many
years later that she discovered she had once been the object of
the führer's ardor.

● Unable to get into art school, Hitler moved to Liverpool, England, to avoid the draft. However, on a visit to Vienna, the authorities caught up with him, and he entered the army just as
World War I was breaking out. He was a message runner in those
pre-radio days, and was awarded the Iron Cross for bravery under
fire, thanks to the recommendation of his commanding officer,
Hugo Gutmann, who was Jewish. By this time Hitler, however,
was already deeply anti-Semitic.

● While in the army, he loved sketching and painting bombed-
out buildings.

● One month before Germany surrendered he was blinded by a
chlorine gas attack and didn't fully regain his sight until the war
was over.

● During the 1920s Hitler took lessons in public speaking and in
mass psychology from Erik Jan Hanussen, an astrologer and fortune teller. Hitler was a strong believer in astrology, telepathy,
graphology, phrenology, and physiognomy, and usually sought
supernatural advice when making decisions.

• He also believed he was under divine protection. This feeling had been reinforced during the war when he was in a trench eating lunch and a voice told him to get up and move to a different spot. A few minutes later a stray shell fell and everyone who was in the place he had left was killed.

• Hitler was secretly financed by German industrialists and various German princes, who believed the Nazis were the best group to stop the rising support of Communism that threatened their fortunes. They contributed a reported twenty-five million gold marks in the years before the Nazis took over Germany. In return, Hitler discreetly changed the party platform which had been up to that point against capitalists and royalists.

• Angela, Hitler's elder half sister, was the only family member he had any contact with in his later years. She was once the manager of the Mensa Academia Judaica in Vienna. During an anti-Semitic student riot, she defended the Jewish students from attack by beating Aryan students with a club from the steps of the kitchen.

• Hitler was a very ordinary looking man with a mincing walk. His strongest physical asset was his eyes, which were blue verging on violet, with a depth and glint that made them almost hypnotic. In his earlier days he wore a pointed beard, often unkempt, and had broken, rotten teeth. He began wearing the famous little moustache during World War I. More of a British style than a German one, he may have adopted it in imitation of English officers, whom he grew to admire during his years at the front.

• Hitler's nickname was "Wolf." Only a handful of people were ever allowed to use the name. His favorite dogs were Alsatians, which in German are called "Wolfhuende." His French headquarters was named Wolf's Gulch. In the Ukraine he called his headquarters Werewolf, and in East Prussia, Wolf's Lair.

• Angela's daughter, Geli Raubal, was a pretty woman who, in her twenties, lived with Hitler during his rise to power. Nineteen years younger than Hitler, she was by all accounts the only woman he ever loved. Hitler made her pose for nude drawings, which were later stolen and bought back from a blackmailer, and reportedly whipped her with a bullwhip. She is quoted as telling a friend, "My uncle is a monster. You would never believe the things he makes me do."

• He was insanely jealous of her. When his chauffeur confessed to him that he and Reubal were lovers and wanted to marry, Hitler flew into a rage and fired him. One night, after a loud public fight, she apparently killed herself with a shot from Hitler's revolver.

• When Hitler learned of her death, he decided to become a vegetarian and made a vow never to eat meat again. He went into a deep depression and threatened suicide. An associate, Gregor Strasser, took heroic measures to keep him alive, a fact he regretted three years later when Hitler ordered his execution.

• He threatened to kill himself many times, always allowing someone to save him. When in jail for the first time, he decided to starve himself to death. A visiting party member convinced him that he should at least think the decision over clearly, and that to be able to think clearly it was necessary to have some food. He gobbled rice hungrily.

• Eva Braun, his final mistress, was a product of a convent school. She was only seventeen years old when Hitler began to take her out. Once, after seeing photographs of Hitler in the company of other women, Braun also shot herself, severing an artery in her neck. She survived.

• In 1935 Braun became despondent when Hitler's preoccupation with international affairs left little time for her. She again attempted suicide, this time by swallowing twenty sleeping pills. Her sister Ilse found her in a coma and saved her. Angela was his housekeeper at this time. She despised Braun, refused to shake hands with her, and referred to her as "the stupid cow."

Because Hitler continued to bring Braun to his chalet, Angela gave up her housekeeper post and got married.

● Conjecture about Hitler's sex life abounds. Hitler had only one close friend during his late adolescence, a sensitive artist and musician, August Kubizek. They were inseparable and some believed they carried on a sexual relationship. Hitler did an architectural drawing of a house in which the two might live together, sharing their interests in art and music.

● One former army associate claimed that, in the army, Hitler was never promoted past lance corporal because of alleged pederastic practices. He also claimed that while in Munich, Hitler was guilty of offenses under Article 175 of German military code which deals with pederasty.

● Many men in his inner circle, including Rudolf Hess and Ernst Röhm, were homosexuals. One of the rooming houses in which Hitler lived in his younger days was a notorious pick-up site for homosexual trysts.

● Some rumors claimed Hitler was impotent, others that he got pleasure from women defecating and urinating on his face. We do know that Hitler had a keen interest in pornography.

● Hitler also had an incredible sweet tooth and consumed large quantities of pastries and as much as two pounds of chocolate in a day.

● Hitler did not like to be alone. He would frequently summon aides to sit with him in the middle of the night while he rambled on about anything that came to his mind. There was an unwritten rule among the aides that no one would ask a question lest Hitler go off on another tangent.

● When Hitler visited Mussolini to try to arrange a pact against Russia, he became very disillusioned about the professionalism of the Italian navy when he saw the sailors' laundry flying from the ships' masts.

• After a nine-hour meeting in 1940 with Spanish dictator Franco, Hitler remarked to Mussolini he would rather visit a dentist and have three or four teeth taken out than repeat the ordeal.

• By 1937, when the rest of the world didn't even consider environmental degradation a significant problem, Hitler was mandating antipollution devices on factories in the Ruhr. All new factories, like those that manufactured Strength-Through-Joy cars (later renamed the Volkswagen), were required to install antipollution devices.

• During the Balkan campaign, Hitler's special train carried a separate car for the führer's cow.

• Dr. Erwin Giesing, who treated Hitler after an aborted assassination attempt by German generals, was one of the few men Hitler trusted after the affair. However, Giesing wrote in his diary that he had once tried to kill the führer by giving him a double dose of cocaine. The attempt went undetected, and Hitler remained alive.

• A chronic queasy stomach caused Hitler to fear he had cancer. The Rumanian dictator Antonescu shared Hitler's plight with stomach ailments. He sent his Jewish cook, Fraulein Kunde, to the führer. When Himmler asked Hitler about the propriety of having a Jew as a cook, he ordered his aides to "Aryanize" her, making her officially not Jewish.

• At the end of the war, when Hitler decided to commit suicide rather than fall into the hands of the Russians, his first act was to poison his favorite dog, Wolf.

Frank Lloyd Wright

Frank Lloyd Wright was perhaps the most famous and influential architect ever. His buildings fit tidily and unobtrusively into the environment. His private life, however, did not exactly follow suit.

• Frank Lloyd Wright was born in Richland Center, Wisconsin, on June 8, 1867. However, he consistently lied about his age, claiming to be two years younger than was indicated by the date on his birth certificate.

• Wright was a self-admitted "mama's boy" who was kept home from school and taught by his mother. He didn't get along nearly as well with his clergyman father. Still, he credited his father's playing of Bach and Beethoven on the organ as an aid in developing his aesthetic sense. Later in life he fought with his mother at almost every turn about his career and marriage. Wright did not attend the funeral of either parent.

• Wright entered the University of Wisconsin at age eighteen. The school didn't teach architecture, so he studied engineering.

• Catherine Tobin was the first girl he kissed (and he was twenty-one before that happened), and she became his first wife. They had six children.

• Wright began working as a draftsman in Chicago in 1887, but quickly landed a job designing houses for the Adler and Sullivan architecture firm. Wright, under the burden of some heavy debts, was also designing houses on his own, bypassing the firm. His boss, Louis Sullivan, disapproved of this moonlighting.

● In 1909 Wright ran off to Europe with Mamah Cheney, the wife of a wealthy client. Tobin, however, refused to divorce him.

● Wright returned to Wisconsin, opened his own office, and lived with Cheney in a house he called Taliesin. A bizarre tragedy struck on August 14, 1914, when servant Julian Carleton went berserk. He murdered seven people, including Cheney and her two children, and burned down the house. Carleton then swallowed hydrochloric acid, which burned his throat sufficiently to prevent him from eating or speaking and he died of starvation seven weeks later. No explanation was ever provided for the crime.

● A few months after Cheney's death, Wright took Miriam Noel, a sculptress, as his mistress. Nellie Breen, a housekeeper who Wright had fired, intercepted some of their letters and had them published in Chicago newspapers. As a result, under the Mann Act and because of trips the two had taken together, Wright was charged in federal court with transporting a woman across state lines "for immoral purposes." Charges were eventually dropped.

● The on-again, off-again affair with Noel lasted several years and they married just days after Tobin granted Wright a divorce in 1922. Wright's short marriage to Noel was unhappy. She became schizophrenic, and Wright left her three months later.

● Wright was always short of cash and eventually went bankrupt. To make ends meet, Wright acted as a dealer in Japanese prints. "Wrieto-San," as he became known to the Japanese after building the Imperial Hotel in Tokyo, was not above "improving" some of the prints, using colored pencils and crayons.

● In 1924, although still married to Noel, Wright began seeing Olgivanna Milanov Hinzenberg. Wright tried unsuccessfully to divorce Noel. In December 1925 Hinzenberg gave birth to a daughter, Iovanna.

- In September 1926 Noel attempted to sue Hinzenberg for $100,000 for alienation of Wright's affection. In response, Wright and Hinzenberg went into hiding in Minneapolis, taking along Iovanna and Svetlana, Olgivanna's daughter from her marriage to Russian architect Vlademar Hinzenberg. Vlademar, spurred on by Noel's lawyers, obtained an injunction to prevent Olgivanna from taking Svetlana out of the country. He then tried to secure custody of Svetlana on the grounds that by having a child out of wedlock with Wright, Olgivanna was unfit to be a mother.

- Vlademar also posted a $500 reward for Wright's arrest on charges of having "abducted" Svetlana. A sheriff, accompanied by a media entourage and lawyers, arrived at Wright's Minneapolis cabin. Wright was arrested and spent two nights in jail, and then was released.

- Prosecutors discovered that Wright and Olgivanna had gone to Puerto Rico on vacation just after Iovanna's birth, which amounted to a technical violation of Olgivanna's status as an alien resident. Once again, Mann Act charges were filed against Wright, but were dropped a few weeks later. Although there were rumors of other fleeting affairs in Wright's life, he spent the rest of his life with Olgivanna.

- Throughout the melodramas of his personal life, Wright designed innovative buildings. He became the leading practitioner of a style known as the prairie school, using low-pitched roofs and extended lines to blend a building into the landscape instead of challenging it.

- In 1916 Wright traveled to Tokyo to design the Imperial Hotel. To keep it safe from Tokyo's constant earthquakes, he floated the building on a bed of mud. While there, his son, John Lloyd Wright, was inspired by an antiearthquake building technique he saw and adapted it on a smaller scale, inventing the popular American toy Lincoln Logs.

● While Wright became recognized abroad as a significant talent early in his career, it took decades for his ideas to gain acceptance in this country. Finally in the 1930s, commissions started pouring in.

● Wright designed a number of unusual buildings, such as a gas station in Cloquet, Minnesota, a Rolls-Royce dealership in New York City, and a dress shop in San Francisco that became the model for the Guggenheim Museum. He had a whimsical approach to designing. For a clothing manufacturer in Grand Rapids, he designed a house without closets so that all clothing would have to be displayed out in the open.

● In 1935 Wright was approached to construct a campus for Florida Southern College. Students earned a portion of their tuition by helping to mix and pour concrete for slabs and walkways, as well as manufacturing the concrete blocks that were used to construct the buildings. The students also contributed urine. It was collected daily, mixed with salt and muriatic acid, and applied to the copper Wright used as decoration throughout the college, quickly oxidizing it to a soft blue-green color.

● Ultraconservative writer Ayn Rand modeled a character in *The Fountainhead* after Wright, based on the idea that he embodied the individualism, greed, and selfishness that she believed to be virtues. Wright—much more politically liberal than Rand—was not flattered. In fact, he made a great public display about being insulted by the characterization, and once took an opportunity to publicly chastise her.

● In another public encounter at the "21" club, Rand addressed Wright as "Master" and lectured him on her political views, which Wright found—or pretended to find—tiresome. She had him design her a house, and they met several times in both New York and Los Angeles, but the house was never built.

● Rand asked him to prepare the architectural drawings for use in the movie version of *The Fountainhead*. He demanded

$250,000, plus the right to reject the script or the sets—she turned him down.

● In 1943 Wright met Baroness Hildegard Rebay von Ehrenwiesen (known as Hilla Rebay) who was the driving force behind the creation of the Guggenheim Museum, in New York City. Rebay was not only a young German artist, but an amateur physician as well. She had many unusual notions about the dangers of "dead teeth" and the virtues of bloodletting. Under her influence, Wright (by then in his midseventies) had his teeth removed and replaced by dentures. Both Wright and Hinzenberg had big black leeches applied to their throats in order to "drain poisonous old" blood from their bodies and prompt the manufacture of "pure, new" blood.

● Wright died on April 9, 1959, at Taliesin West, the complex he built in Arizona. Both he and Hinzenberg are buried there. One of Wright's best-known descendants is his granddaughter, actress Anne Baxter. Two other grandchildren are also architects.

Marie Curie

*Marie Curie discovered radium and won two Nobel Prizes. When
asked to write an autobiography, she said, "It will not be much
of a book: 'I was born in Warsaw of a family of teachers. I married Pierre Curie and had two children. I have done my work in
France.'"*

● Marie Curie was born Marya Sklodowska on November 7, 1867,
in Warsaw, Poland. She was the youngest of five children.

● Poland was occupied by Russia at the time, which made Russian the official language, replaced Polish officials with Russian
ones, and declared the country to be the Russian province of
Vistula Land. Marie's father, a professor, lost job after job to Russian nationals sent to "Russify" Poland, pushing his large family
into poverty. In the middle of Saxony Square in Warsaw, the Russian tsar had placed a monument to "Poles faithful to their sov-
ereign." Marie considered these "faithful Poles" traitors, and she
made a point of spitting on the monument whenever she passed
it.

● In a small apartment filled with family members and her
father's students, Marie learned to concentrate by blocking the
world out. Once while reading a book at the dining room table,
lost to the world, her siblings built an arch of chairs over her
oblivious head. When she finished she stood up and the structure
tumbled around her. When her older brothers and sisters stopped

laughing, she said blankly, "That's stupid," and walked out of the room.

• When Marie was a child, her oldest sister died of typhus. Her mother died of tuberculosis when Marie was eleven. Although raised in the church by her devout mother, she began to have doubts about the god who let such things happen, and left the church for good in her teens.

• She graduated from secondary school first in her class at age fifteen, and promptly had a nervous breakdown, brought on by the strain of high expectations, extreme pressure, and a deep dread of reciting lessons in front of the class. To soothe her nerves, her father sent her to live with relatives in the country with a firm order that she refrain from books and studying. It was, by all accounts, the happiest year of her life.

• When she returned, Marie and her sister Bronia risked exile in Siberia to attend an illegal nationalistic school called the "Floating University," which met in different attics, basements, and living rooms each week to avoid the police. It was there that she learned the philosophy of "positivism," based on logic, observation, and science.

• Marie and Bronia both longed to go to Paris to study, since women were excluded from Russian universities. Each saved as much as they could by tutoring, but that wasn't a lot, and it became clear that it would take many years before they could each acquire enough to complete a degree. Marie proposed that her sister, being three years older, should go to Paris with their pooled savings. Marie, meanwhile, would take a governess job providing room and board so all of her salary could be forwarded to Bronia. Then, when Bronia completed her five-year medical course, she could then pay for Marie's education. Bronia agreed.

• Marie found a well-paying position she liked with a family called Zorawski as governess to their two youngest children. After a year, the family's eldest son, Casimir, came home for the holidays. He and Marie fell in love and he told his parents they planned to marry. His mother fainted at the thought because "one does not marry a governess" and his parents forbade the union. Marie, needing the job, continued working for two more years as if nothing had happened. She started a clandestine school and began teaching the children of illiterate factory workers how to read and write. She continued her study of science and chemistry, reading textbooks into the night.

• Bronia got married to a man who had completed his medical degree. Since Bronia had only her last year's exams left, she wrote that Marie could move in and attend the Sorbonne if Marie had enough money for the year's tuition. Marie, still dejected over Casimir, exhausted from overwork, and worried about her ailing father, told Bronia she couldn't leave Poland yet.

• Marie returned to Warsaw and the Floating University. She had access to a lab for the first time, where she soon discovered her love of experimental research. She was finally happy again. Casimir, still in love with Marie, arranged to meet her in the mountains at Zakopane for two days. Casimir asked his parents again if he could marry Marie, and they refused again. Marie told Casimir that she was ready to get on with her life, and immediately wrote to Bronia asking if her offer was still open. She packed her clothes, food for the three-day trip, her books, a bag of caramels, and a wooden stool so she wouldn't have to pay extra for a seat, and took off across the continent. She signed up for courses at the Sorbonne a few days before her twenty-fourth birthday.

• Distracted in her sister's apartment and wanting to live closer to school, Marie moved to a new place. Very poor and not knowing how to cook, she survived on bread and butter, tea, fruit, radishes, and an occasional piece of chocolate. She rarely had enough coal to heat her apartment, and stayed up studying until two every night trying to keep up with the class that was taught in French, a language she barely knew. She fainted regularly from lack of food and sleep, and woke up panicked because she feared that she would flunk out. Instead, she ranked first in her class in achieving her master's degree in physics in 1893, and second in her class in obtaining a masters in math in 1894.

• While working on her math degree, Marie needed more lab space. A professor suggested that the head of the Paris School of Physics and Chemistry, Pierre Curie, might lend her a workroom. Pierre had already formulated what is still known as Curie's Law, concerning how magnetic properties are changed by temperature.

• From the first moment, there was literally a chemistry between the two. On their first date, he presented her not with candy or roses, but with a scientific article he had written.

• At the end of the year Pierre proposed, but Marie declined, still scared by her first love affair and not wanting to desert her country and her family. During the summer, while home in Poland, Marie received eloquent and logical letters from Pierre, explaining how both their work would be enhanced by teaming up. He even offered to move to Poland if she would marry him. His scientific method worked: She finally agreed to marry him, and returned to Paris.

• They were wed at city hall in Sceaux, Pierre's hometown. They took the bus to the ceremony, and didn't have the money to buy rings. Marie wore a new navy-blue suit, chosen for its practicality once the ceremony was over. One of their wedding gifts was a generous check from an affluent relative which allowed them to buy two bicycles. On their honeymoon they toured France. Cycling became a favorite pastime, even when Marie was eight months' pregnant with her first child, Irène. (This was cutting it a little too close—she had to take the train back to Paris where she barely beat "*le stork*.")

• They spent nearly every waking hour alone together, most of it working or reading silently side by side. They thought it an ideal relationship.

• Marie decided to become the first woman in Europe to earn a doctorate in science. She needed a doctoral thesis subject and chose to study a phenomenon that Henri Becquerel had recently discovered in uranium, which she named radioactivity. She tested every known element and found that thorium also emitted radiation. Pitchblende, a substance from which uranium was extracted, turned out to have more radiation than its thorium and uranium content would account for, leading Marie to decide that there must be an as-yet-undiscovered radioactive element in the pitchblende.

• Pierre dropped his own work to study radiation with Marie. She soon isolated one of two new sources of radiation, a new element that she named polonium, after her country of origin. Several months later she and Pierre announced that they'd discovered the second of two new elements, radium.

• The Curies used their small savings to purchase and transport pitchblende residue from the St. Joachimsthal mines in Bohemia. Marie melted and processed the tons of pitchblende a basinful at a time.

• In 1901 Pierre Curie and Becquerel described the burns they'd gotten from radiation, yet the skin that grew back was healthy. Doctors found that radiation destroyed skin-cancer cells, and the skin grew back free of the disease, setting the stage for radiation therapy.

• Marie finally got around to finishing and defending her doctoral thesis on June 25, 1903, after putting it off for years in favor of the research itself.

• In 1903 Henri Becquerel and the two Curies shared the Nobel Prize in physics for the discovery of radioactivity.

• Marie chose not to seek a patent for her radium separation process. She sent the information free to anyone who asked. She had no desire to be rich, and did not want to deny people the medical benefits of her discoveries.

- In late 1904 Pierre was finally given a chair in physics, a lab, and three employees at the School of Physics and Industrial Chemistry in Paris. He hired Marie as his lab chief. For the first time, Marie started getting paid for her work.

- Then tragedy occurred. In April 1906, while attempting to cross a street, Pierre slipped and fell into the path of a heavy wagon containing military goods. The driver was unable to stop it in time; a rear wheel crushed Pierre's skull.

- After Pierre's death, there was no one capable of running the lab except Marie. It was therefore decided that she should be given his chair in physics and the lab. Marie studied his notes, and began teaching exactly where Pierre had left off the year before.

- The former president of the Royal Society of Scientists, William Thomson, Lord Kelvin, published a letter saying that radium was not an element. Marie had so far only extracted salts of radium, so she decided to prove radium's existence by separating it from its chlorides and bromides. It took her four years to produce a gram of pure radium metal. (This was not the first time Lord Kelvin had been wrong. He also stated flatly that "Radio has no future," and "Heavier-than-air flying machines are impossible.")

- Marie next established the "curie," a unit of measurement for radium, defined as the "quantity of emanation in equilibrium in one gram of radium."

- Marie was nominated for induction into the French Academy of Science. During the stormy debate, an academy member thundered that "women cannot be members of the Institute of France!" Thanks to prejudice against her as both a woman and a foreigner, she missed being elected by two votes.

- In 1911 Marie fell in love again. Unfortunately, it was with a married man. Her colleagues knew something was up when she began wearing dresses instead of black suits and started fixing up her hair. The source of this change, Paul Langevin, had already separated from his wife, but Marie was accused of husband stealing in Madame Langevin's writ for a legal separation. Her legal documents quoted heavily from passionate letters from Marie, excerpts of which were published in the newspapers which were already full of antiforeign sentiments in the tense time before World War I. Marie, a highly visible target, received death threats and public harassment. The dean of the Faculté des Sciences threatened to withdraw Marie's chair at the Sorbonne. His daughter, who was hiding Marie and her daughters to protect them from outraged citizens, said she would never speak to him again if he did. He didn't.

• While in hiding, Marie's spirits were raised on December 1911 when she was awarded the Nobel Prize in chemistry for the isolation of pure radium. She was the first person to win the Nobel Prize twice.

• Due to the effects of radiation, both Curies had been in poor health most of their adult life. Marie became quite ill with a high fever and kidney problems. She stayed with a friend in England, using the name Madame Sklodowska, until she could return to her work in December 1912.

• At the beginning of World War I, Marie saw the need for x-ray facilities in the combat zones. She went to women she knew in Paris, asking them to lend their cars to the war effort. She turned them into portable field labs, which became known as "Little Curies." Marie drove one of them throughout the war, running the x-ray machine while the doctors operated. She also established two hundred radiological rooms around the country and trained nurses to run them. Her gram of radium was put to medical use. Every week she "milked" it for the gas it gave off and sent vials of the gas to medical facilities to cure scars and skin lesions.

• Marie died on July 4, 1934, of a high fever brought on by her lifelong radiation exposure. Her last clear words were "I want to be left alone," before her speech became unintelligible babbling, addressing people long dead. Dr. Claude Regaud, head of the medical branch of the Institute of Radium, said, "Madame Curie can be counted among the eventual victims of the radioactive bodies which she and her husband discovered."

Oscar Wilde

Oscar Wilde was the darling of society and a leader of the aesthetic movement in Europe. He wrote a number of poems, a controversial classic novel, The Picture of Dorian Gray, *and plays, including* The Importance of Being Earnest *and* Lady Windermere's Fan. *His quick wit and talent for shameless self-promotion launched him to stunning fame . . . before a court case plunged him into stunning notoriety.*

• Oscar Fingal O'Flahertie Wills Wilde—poet, playwright, self-proclaimed aestheticist, and quotemaster extraordinaire—was born in Dublin on October 16, 1854. After a public school education, he went to Oxford, where he deliberately went to work to abandon his Irish brogue. He adopted a stately, leisurely English accent in which he delivered perfect sentences that seemed to have been written, according to poet W. B. Yeats, "overnight with labour and yet all spontaneous."

• Both of Wilde's parents had been famous and controversial. His father, William, was a brilliant eye and ear surgeon in Dublin who wrote several groundbreaking medical textbooks. As he became well known, former patient Mary Travers began hinting publicly that he had raped her after knocking her out with chloroform two years earlier. She used the threat of an embarrassing fuss to extort money from the doctor "to move to Australia." She didn't go, however, and continued making accusations.

- Oscar Wilde's mother, Jane, was known to most at the time as "Speranza," the pseudonym she used when writing tirades for the Irish Nationalist cause. Stung by the accusations against her husband, she wrote a letter to Travers's father saying that Mary was making "unfounded accusations." Mary sued Jane for libel, but was awarded only one farthing in damages.

- At age twenty-one, Wilde became a Mason, just as his father had been. Within a few months he moved up two "degrees" to the level of Master Mason. (He was unnerved while in jail years later when another prisoner gave a secret Masonic distress sign that obligated Wilde to come running to help.)

- While Wilde was at Oxford, he had heterosexual sex for the first time. He probably had already been introduced to homosexual sex years earlier, as had most schoolboys in all-male English boarding schools. His partner at Oxford was "Old Jess," the campus prostitute. He contracted syphilis. The mercury treatment, ineffective but widely used at the time, blackened his teeth. Wilde began a habit of talking with his mouth hidden behind his hand. The "treatment" also left his syphilis unchecked, and the disease eventually killed him.

- Wilde moved to London in 1878 and started a very good friendship, possibly an affair, with actress Lily Langtry. This was shortly before she also began an affair with the Prince of Wales, "Edward the Caresser."

- Wilde also had a fling with Catholicism at the time, enjoying the spectacle and theatrics of its ceremonies. He seriously considered leaving his Protestant roots. What stopped him short, besides the fact that he'd have to resign from the Masons, was money. His half brother, recently deceased, had been sufficiently alarmed by Oscar's papist leanings to add a codicil to his will withholding Oscar's portion of the inheritance if he should convert to Catholicism within five years.

● Wilde published a modestly controversial volume of poetry in 1881. Some thought it indecent, but a reviewer in *Punch* sniffed, "The author is Wilde/But his poetry's tame." Wilde shifted his attention to writing plays shortly after.

● Wilde spent a year touring America as a lecturer on his theories of aestheticism and the place of beauty and the arts in everyday life. On the sophisticated East Coast, college students came to his lectures to jeer at his longish hair and foppish dress, which featured a dark purple sack coat with lacy wrists, knee breeches, black stockings, and buckled shoes. The newspapers satirized him. "If you survive yellow journalism, you need not be afraid of yellow fever," Wilde told the *New York Times*. "In the old days men had the rack; now they have the Press."

● He was thrilled when he made a pilgrimage to visit Walt Whitman and the grand old poet, who, making no attempt to conceal his homosexuality, gave him a lingering kiss on the lips.

● One of Wilde's most famous bon mots may or may not have really happened. Although it sounds like something he would have said, no contemporary account records his reputed exchange with a customs agent in New York Harbor: "Have you anything to declare?" "I have nothing to declare except my genius."

● During his yearlong American tour, Wilde traveled thirty thousand miles and appeared in thirty-four states and territories, giving six lectures a day throughout the East, South, Midwest, West, and Canada. To everyone's surprise, he found a rapt audience in many small frontier cities and towns, charming an entire town of miners in Leadsville, Colorado. "They were polished and refined compared with the people I met in larger cities back East," Wilde wrote. "The revolver is their book of etiquette. This teaches lessons that are not forgotten."

● P. T. Barnum attended his second lecture in New York, leading to an unfounded rumor that Wilde would tour with Barnum's circus.

• Joking that he had "succeeded in civilizing America," Wilde returned to England. Wilde's mother suggested that he should find a nice girl with money to marry and settle down. The girl part was not what Wilde had in mind, but money sounded good to the perpetually strapped young man. He figured he could play the role of husband as well as that of dashing young man, and that marriage might stop some of the unsavory rumors about him, so he began shopping around.

• Lily Langtry was out of the question. She was already married, was as financially strapped as he was, and had several well-heeled lovers ahead of him. One of Wilde's prospects, Florrie Balcombe, turned down his proposal of marriage and married *Dracula* author Bram Stoker instead. He then turned his considerable charm on Constance Lloyd, telling her, "With your money and my brain we could go far." In November 1883 he proposed and she accepted. They were married the following May, and the long-suffering Lloyd bore him two sons before the two stopped having sexual relations in 1886. They remained technically married until her death in 1898.

• Wilde's sex life, meanwhile, had gone elsewhere. He started a longtime, intensely romantic love affair with a young man, Lord Alfred Douglas. The two were not just lovers, but became friendly rivals in sexual competitions with young male prostitutes. Douglas's father, the marquis of Queensberry, demanded to see Wilde and sent him a calling card addressed to "Oscar Wilde Posing as a Somdomite [*sic*]."

• Wilde filed suit against the Marquis for libeling him. The Marquis defended himself against the charge by offering convincing evidence that his allegations were absolutely true. Wilde withdrew his suit, but as a result of the publicity, he was immediately prosecuted by the state for "sodomy and other acts of gross indecency" under a new law that made consensual homosexual acts between males illegal. (When it was pointed out that females weren't mentioned, Queen Victoria reportedly said, "No woman would do that.") The judge announced, "There is no worse crime than this," and sentenced Wilde to the maximum sentence of two years at hard labor.

● Most of the time he was imprisoned he was not allowed to write, and had few books to read. He suffered badly from physical ailments of gout, anemia, constant diarrhea, and an infected inner ear. He believed that he was losing his mind. During the brief times that he was allowed paper, he wrote *The Ballad of Reading Gaol* and *De Profundis*.

● Lord Douglas was never prosecuted, thanks to strings that his influential father pulled. He had been the one to encourage Wilde to sue his father when wiser friends advised otherwise; he and a brother had also promised to finance the legal costs, which they did not. He spent the rest of his life publishing books dedicated to "exposing and smashing Wilde's cult and the Wilde myth" and claiming that he had never participated in homosexual acts.

● After Wilde was released, he left England, never to return. He also never wrote anything for publication again. He lived in relative poverty, depending on the few friends who hadn't deserted him to keep him sheltered and alive, entertaining them still with flashes of his wit. He died in Paris in 1900.

Malcolm Forbes

Malcolm Forbes inherited Forbes magazine from his father, but made it over in his own image, using the self-proclaimed "Capitalist's Tool" as a platform to make a fortune, hobnob with the rich and powerful, become famous . . . and meet cute young hunks.

• Malcolm Stevenson Forbes managed to charm the pants off politicians, Hollywood celebrities, business leaders, and the press. That's why everybody came to his parties . . . and how he managed to keep his homosexuality secret from the public, although it was fairly well known among those close to him. His "romance" with Elizabeth Taylor afforded him publicity and provided a cover for his constant gay cruising to the point that not even the tabloid press mentioned it in his lifetime.

• Forbes was given a thirty-five dollar duplicating machine for his thirteenth birthday. He published his own newspaper, co-edited by schoolmate George Shultz, Ronald Reagan's future secretary of state.

• He printed his last school newspaper after he inadvertently published an off-color joke, innocently unaware, he said, of the sexual innuendo. The joke was: "Did you hear about the absent-minded professor who kissed the trolley good-bye and then jumped on his wife and went to town?" School officials considered kicking him out for this outrage; instead, they merely shut the offending newspaper down.

● As a child, Forbes did not want to succeed his father (founder of *Forbes*), he wanted to become president of the United States. (His son, Steve, later used his inherited fortune to pursue the Oval Office himself.) Forbes ran several times for political office. After being elected a state senator from Somerset County, New Jersey, he retired from politics after losing a bid to become governor of New Jersey.

● Forbes enlisted in World War II by cheating on his eye exam (he wore contact lenses), but he was eventually discharged. Before his discharge, he earned a Bronze Star and a Purple Heart.

● Forbes's biggest contribution to what had been his father's business magazine was the Forbes 400, the annual list of America's richest citizens, designed to compete with the Fortune 500 list of companies. When Forbes first started it, at least eighty people threatened to sue to keep their fortunes private. Others begged and even tried bribes to stay off, not wanting family members, business associates, criminals, and tax collectors to know. Forbes insisted that his staff report the facts, regardless of appeals and threats.

● At first it was hard to amass the information, since so much wealth is so well hidden. Finally, *Forbes* reporters found out that while rich people were reluctant to talk about their own wealth, they loved to talk about others', and they usually were accurately informed about who owned what. By playing tycoons against each other, the magazine was able to come up with reasonably accurate estimates of everyone's wealth.

● Once they were on the list, however, new concerns arose. One secretive developer who was incensed that he was on the first list surprised *Forbes* editors with a demand that he be put on the second: "If you take me off, it'll make me look bad. I got no choice but to stay on this fucking list."

● Ironically, Forbes himself, one of the four hundred richest Americans, insisted at first that he not be listed on his own list, citing the same arguments—the IRS and potential kidnappers—

that other subjects had tried. His editors insisted that for credibility, he had to be included, so for a compromise, he was always listed at the four hundredth position, but without a valuation of net worth.

• Although he married and fathered five children, he preferred the carnal company of young men, many of whom were employed at his own magazine. Behind a hidden door in his plush office at *Forbes* magazine, Forbes built a secret apartment. The apartment featured artwork depicting mostly naked men, reputed to be one of the world's largest and best collections of erotic art. He would casually invite a young male employee in to use the sauna.

• After having sex, he would invariably tuck a hundred dollar bill into the pocket of the young man.

• In fact, young men were frequently given suggestions by senior employees on how to rebuff Forbes and still keep their jobs. The most popular ploy was to conversationally make some reference to a (sometimes nonexistent) spouse or fiancée.

• Forbes was a collector, amassing the world's largest collection of Fabergé eggs, as well as other Fabergé objects. Some three hundred were on display at a museum in his office building that also housed a toy-boat collection, presidential papers, and honorary degrees that Forbes had collected over the years. Around the world he stashed his other collections: toy soldiers (he had more than one hundred thousand) in Tangier, Morocco; Victorian art in the family's house in London, England; hot-air balloons at a château in Normandy, France. He also collected Harley-Davidsons and even sponsored his own motorcycle gang.

• Forbes loved to give parties for advertisers, politicians, and famous people. In 1987 he threw a party at his home in Far Hills, New Jersey. One hundred twenty-one bagpipers and drummers and a kilted Forbes marched through an artificial mist out of the woods and into a Scottish village erected for the occasion. The reputed cost of the party, including expensive gifts to the eleven hundred guests, was $2 million . . . all written off his taxes as a business expense, of course.

● The punch line to the party, however, came at the end of the year. All of the *Forbes* employees were summoned to a Christmas event to watch the videotape of the party most had not been invited to. Before showing the tape of one of the most conspicuously lavish extravaganzas of the decade, Forbes opened with a little speech about rough times ahead, profitability being way down, and how all the employees would have to tighten their belts in the coming year.

● In 1989 Forbes chartered three planes—a Concorde, a 747, and a DC-8—to ferry eight hundred "close personal friends" and one hundred ten reporters to his home in Morocco for three days. Also at a reported cost of $2 million, this party featured six hundred drummers, acrobats, and belly dancers, and had three hundred turbaned Berber horsemen. Most worked for free by orders of Moroccan dictator King Hassan. The king also arranged for dozens of beggars and other unsightly Tangerine citizens to disappear into jails for the party weekend.

● For the guests, the nadir of the event was the Hotel Solazun, where the air-conditioning didn't work. For the normally rich and pampered, this was traumatic. Said gossip columnist Liz Smith, "Some of it was like taking an un-air-conditioned bus trip with seven hundred people to Ardmore, Oklahoma, over the dog days." Forbes's reaction was "What did they expect? That I should build them a hotel?"

● Two months before his death, Forbes was confronted at a Christmas party by writer Al Weisel. Weisel suggested that it was important for famous gay people like Forbes to come out of the closet to be a role model for gay teens, who have a horrendous sense of hopelessness and a high suicide rate. Forbes reacted angrily, stating that his private life was nobody else's business, and walked away.

● Forbes died in his sleep on February 23, 1990. He left a fortune of between $700 million and $1.23 billion.

● After Forbes's death, his magazine staff was notified that, under terms of his will, they would all receive one week's pay and all debts to the company of under ten thousand dollars would be forgiven.

Queen Victoria

During her reign of sixty-four years, the longest of any English monarch ever, Queen Victoria ruled over a nation undergoing changes of a monumental nature.

● Alexandrina Victoria didn't realize that she might become queen of England until she was nearly eleven. Little "Drina" was made aware by way of a piece of paper that had been discreetly slipped into a book on English kings and queens. It outlined the succession of the English monarchy. "I am nearer the throne than I thought," she said, and broke into tears. She was third in line, but she knew it was not for long—her uncle, King George IV, was gravely ill, and her other uncle, who would shortly become King William IV, was in poor health, too.

● Victoria's father and the king's brother, the duke of Kent, had died shortly after her birth in 1819, leaving his family with a royal pedigree and a mountain of unpaid debts. Victoria and her mother were given sanctuary at Kensington Palace and there she spent a dreary childhood, being schooled in the classics and Latin, little suspecting that she was being groomed in case she was needed for the throne.

● "Drina" became queen in June 1837, a month after her eighteenth birthday. Her first act was to banish the name Alexandrina from all official uses. The name was in honor of Alexander I of

Russia, who had consented to be the child's godfather. She never liked it much.

● Her coronation was chaotic and personally painful. It lasted five hours. There had been no rehearsal, so the officiators and the soon-to-be queen were continuously whispering, "What do we do now?" to advisors. The bishop skipped a page in his guidebook and announced the coronation over; as the queen and witnesses proceeded outside in confusion, he had to call them back to finish the ceremony. The crown weighed nearly three pounds and its sharp metallic edges cut into Victoria's head; she nearly dropped the orb; an eighty-two-year-old lord stumbled down the flight of steps at the altar; and the new queen nearly screamed with pain when the archbishop jammed a ceremonial ring onto the wrong finger, postponing the evening festivities while she soaked her hand in ice water in order to remove the ring.

● The press at the time reported a plot to poison the young princess by her "wicked" uncle Ernest, Duke of Cumberland, the claimant to the throne in line just after Victoria. In reality, the so-called Cumberland Plot was actually an invention of the paranoid and ambitious Sir John Conroy, who had insinuated himself into a position of advising and controlling Victoria's mother during the years before Victoria ascended to the throne. Conroy spread rumors and suspicion through the court and the press, wanting to advance his position.

● Conroy earlier had had an affair with King George IV's sister, Princess Sophia, and had taken over control of her finances. At his instigation, Sophie prevailed on her brother to bestow a knighthood on Conroy, and later she secretly gave birth to his illegitimate child.

● Victoria hated Conroy personally, especially the control he had over her mother. When she became queen, she edged him out of power. Later in life, Victoria dismissed the Cumberland Plot as the result of "Sir John's own invention . . . Utterly false."

• After officially moving to Buckingham Palace, an address she seldom frequented (she thought the Windsor Palace airier and healthier), the young queen soon had to deal with a political crisis that became a tempest in a chamber pot, the "bedchamber crisis." When the majority party in Parliament changed from Whig to Tory in 1839, the new prime minister, Sir Robert Peel, attempted to carry out a longstanding custom: appointing new ladies of the bedchamber for the queen as a political plum. Victoria would have none of it. She viewed the ladies as her personal attendants. When she refused to make the requested changes, Sir Peel refused to form a new government. This let the existing Whig government—under her first prime minister, personal mentor, and first love, Lord Melbourne—remain in tenuous power. The Tories did not regain control of Parliament until two years later.

• Victoria also resisted Parliament's urging that she rush off and get married. She had been unofficially betrothed to her first cousin, Prince Albert of Germany, for several years, but was in no hurry to tie the knot. Many viewed this reluctance as evidence of her attachment to Lord Melbourne and the wags filled the air and the pages of the *Times* with rumors of Victoria's preoccupation with him. "The simple truth in this case is that the queen could not endure the thought of parting with Melbourne, who is everything to her," wrote Charles Greville, a member of the court. "Her feelings, which are *sexual*, though she does not know it, and are probably sufficient to bear down all prudential considerations." In truth, her affection for him was genuine, his influence profound. This had some unfortunate effects.

• Although Melbourne was a Whig and trained the young queen in Whig philosophy, he was actually quite conservative. He viewed most social change as evil, and saw most public discontent as the product of a malicious minority of rabble, usually Irish, probably Socialist, and often both. He harshly prosecuted trade unionists and other rabble-rousers, pushing through a ban on "illegal secret oaths," punishable by seven years of exile in Australia, which he enforced selectively. Victoria, once generally tenderhearted toward the unfortunate, grew to echo much of this sentiment.

● In the area of social reform, the queen, despite being an avid reader of Charles Dickens, was unable to fathom the poverty and despair that accompanied industrialization. She was staunchly opposed to socialism in any form and believed that anyone could improve his station in life with a little pluck and determination. She disapproved of legislation to alleviate the condition of the poor and abolish child labor. (Melbourne told her that it kept children "out of mischief" to be working twelve to fifteen hours a day in factories at age six.) On several occasions, the Salvation Army requested and was refused funds from the Privy Purse, her discretionary fund.

● When it became clear that marriage was the only way to fully rid herself of the influence of her mother and the hated Conroy, Victoria finally married Albert. The two had an unusually happy life together for English monarchs, going beyond the call of duty by producing nine offspring, belying the modern view of Victoria as a grumpy, unsmiling prude. The twenty-one-year-old Victoria described her honeymoon in her diary: "I *never, never* spent such an evening!! My dearest dearest dear Albert sat on a footstool by my side, and his excessive love and affection gave me feelings of heavenly love and happiness I never could have hoped to have felt before! He clasped me in his arms, and we kissed each other again and again! His beauty, his sweetness and gentleness—really, how can I ever be thankful enough to have such a *Husband*! . . . To be called by names of tenderness I have never yet heard used to me before was bliss beyond belief!"

● Although Albert was from Coburg, Germany, he served the realm admirably, acting as a chief architect for the Great Exhibition of 1851, en route to which many Britons got their first train ride. Despite early opposition from many members of Parliament and other nobility for being German, and despite becoming the object of howling ridicule for approving the design of a huge, all-glass Crystal Palace, the exhibition's huge success gained Albert the respect of the nation.

● Albert was instrumental in preventing war with the Union during the opening months of the American Civil War. Personnel from a Union ship had boarded a British ship and arrested two Confederate envoys, James Mason and John Slidell. The decidedly pro-South Parliament called it an act of war and pressed for an armed response. Albert managed to soften the response, avoiding an armed showdown over the issue, and prevented the British from entering the war on the Confederate side, which would have almost certainly resulted in France's joining the Union side in exchange for a restored Quebec.

● Albert's death in 1861 at age forty-two left the nation bereft of one of its more able statesmen and sent Victoria into a period of mourning from which some contemporary observers say she never fully recovered. Victoria was devoted entirely to him. Her duty to continue the royal lineage done, she never saw reason to remarry.

● Over the next twenty years Victoria was said to have consulted with a spiritualist by the name of John Brown, who had been a stable hand at the royal estate of Balmoral in Scotland. While the story that Victoria actually participated in séances with Brown (or other mediums) is questionable, Brown's influence, and her attachment to him, is undeniable. Usually dressed in kilts, Brown became Victoria's closest personal servant; rumors began to fly that she had secretly married him. Brown's apparent intimacy with the queen was observable at almost all public functions as he attended her. In her personal correspondences she often referred to Brown in endearing terms such as "my dear one" or "my kind friend." Whatever the true nature of the relationship, Brown was unquestionably the queen's closest friend until his death in 1883.

● In 1887 her Golden Jubilee was celebrated in royal style with parades, concerts and general hoopla. Although she was criticized widely in the press for her continued seclusion, she was still admired by her people. During an age of constant change, she represented stability and abundance to a people who enjoyed an average life span of only about forty years, and who, if they wished to have two surviving children in the family, would have to give birth to on average seven.

● Victorian England was a time in which everyday speech was peppered with profanity. Brothels flourished, and taverns were plentiful. Table manners were decidedly lacking. The British government decided to fund an educational campaign to correct the bad habits of those from the lower classes who were now joining an emerging middle class. How much did the beloved monarch figure in these massive changes? Actually very little, but her name continues to be firmly attached to the campaign of bringing gentility to the new middle class. By 1887 the influence of the middle class reached deeply into parliamentary circles for the first time.

● Victoria had a lifelong fondness for novels, considered a lowbrow form of writing when she was young. Her admiration for the work of Charles Dickens inspired her subjects to read him as well, bringing to public consciousness some of the more enduring literature of the period.

● Victoria was a great believer in new technology and proclaimed riding in railroad cars to be great fun (although a little fast at 18 mph).

● She abhorred smoking and banished it from all rooms at the royal residences save for a billiards room at the far end of the castle. A gentleman wanting a cigar following a meal in the royal household "had better be prepared for a long walk," as one dinner guest remarked.

● "If only they knew me as I am," Victoria lamented on the eve of her Diamond (sixtieth) Jubilee in 1897. The previous year she had surpassed George III as the longest reigning monarch, and the nation's affection for her bordered on worship. The decade of the 1890s had seen her more and more detached from the affairs of state and more involved with the affairs of her children and grandchildren.

● Victoria held a lifelong disappointment in her eldest son, Prince Albert Edward. In fact, there was some speculation that she willed herself to live so long just to keep him from becoming king for as long as possible. Edward, more popularly known as "Edward the Caresser," continually confirmed his mother's worst opinion by becoming involved in a series of scandals. Of her son "Bertie," as she called him, the queen wrote on May 24, 1900 (her eighty-first birthday), "God has been very merciful and supported me, but my trials have been manifold."

● In January 1901 the queen died and an era passed with her. The British Empire had already reached and passed its zenith. She outlived twelve prime ministers and was queen mother to five generations of Britons, and imprinted an age which is inexorably linked to her name.

● Victoria wrote two thousand five hundred words in her journal every night, filling 122 volumes in her lifetime. After Victoria's death, her daughter, Princess Beatrice, named as her literary executor, fulfilled the title all too literally. She decided that most of Queen Victoria's journal was not suitable for general reading and burned all but a few volumes of childhood reminiscences, destroying a priceless historical treasure chronicling nearly all of Britain's nineteenth century.

Rudolph Valentino

Rudolph Valentino was the first male Hollywood heartthrob. Women swooned when he came on the screen, and when he died at the peak of his career, millions of women mourned. It was the best career move he ever made—had he lived into the sound era, his career probably would have nosedived.

● Rodolfo Alfonzo Raffaelo Pierre Filibert Guglielmi di Valentina d'Antonguolla was born in Castellaneta, Italy, on May 6, 1895, the third of four children. His mother was believed to be French; his Italian father was a veterinarian.

● He had a scar on his right cheek from playing with a shaving razor at the age of five. He told people it was inflicted during a duel, which he, of course, won.

● His family was affluent enough to send the children to school. Rodolfo skipped out and wandered through the olive groves and orchards, with his head in the clouds, imagining himself as a great adventurer, a sailor, a brave warrior. In response, his father beat him regularly. His father died when Rodolfo was nine years old, leading him to hope that the death would cause enough financial strife to end his schooling. No such luck.

● Rodolfo was something of the village scourge, refusing to attend church or work, raiding orchards, spitting, cursing, and fighting. His mother once locked him out of the house and he threw rocks at the door and windows.

● His mother sometimes called in an uncle to apply extra persuasion—in the form of heavy-handed beating with a thick leather belt. It was useless. He refused to work or study, and certainly refused to stop chasing girls.

● He and a relative finally convinced his mother that it would be better for the whole family if he went to America to live with some relatives who had moved to New York City. On December 9, 1913, he set sail as a steerage passenger on the *Cleveland* with a single American dollar sewed into the lining of his jacket. He was eighteen.

● He did not speak English when he arrived in America. For six months he did menial jobs. He hated them all, and was usually fired for insolence.

● By the summer of 1914, Valentino spoke English well enough to seek work outside the Italian quarter. He moved into a stable garret adjoining the Long Island home of millionaire Cornelius Bliss, for whom he was employed as one of six gardeners on the estate. He was given free room, board, and six dollars a week. He was soon fired.

● He began hanging around dance halls and cabarets and was surprised that women, seeing his oily good looks, assumed that he was a gigolo and started offering him money to dance with them, sit with them, and even make love to them. This was his kind of work.

● Valentino, ever the professional, spent hours in front of a mirror perfecting a smoldering-eye look and used generous applications of brilliantine on his thick hair to keep it slickly combed to his scalp.

● He was an instant success with the unescorted female customers, both young and middle-aged. There were sometimes fights between the women as to who would get him. Almost overnight he became the most popular dancer at Maxim's, a famous nightclub, making seventy dollars a week.

● His name was too hard for the ladies to remember, so he started using "di Valentina."

● He was arrested for "white slavery"—being a pimp and possibly a blackmailer—and spent at least three days in jail in 1916, but the records disappeared from the New York City police files in 1921, apparently the result of bribes from his movie studio at the time.

● One of his lovers divorced her husband—and then killed him. Valentino decided that he might be implicated and deported, so he quickly left New York, headed for San Francisco and then Los Angeles. Almost exactly four years after his arrival in America, he arrived in Hollywood.

● His first movie role was in *The Married Virgin*, for which he received fifty dollars a week to play . . . a gigolo and blackmailer. The picture was never released. His next two roles featured him again as a gigolo and blackmailer. Within a few years, he played an Italian count, an Irishman, and an Apache dancer. The minor roles barely kept him alive and his creditors were publicly humiliating him. He started fixing cars at a local garage.

● One night at a party he met and romanced actress Jean Acker. They met over the next few nights and she suggested that he change his name to Rudolph Valentino, letting him hold her hand and kiss her a few times, but nothing more. He impulsively proposed marriage one night, and she accepted. The next day they had a small wedding ceremony. That night, he unlocked the hotel door and bowed, preparing to carry her over the threshold. Instead, she smiled, ducked into the room, and slammed the door in his face. She explained that she married him out of pity and asked him to go away.

• A few months later Acker would go to the courts for a legal separation, accusing Valentino of abandoning her, abusing her, and making no attempt to support her. She demanded three hundred dollars a month maintenance and fifteen hundred dollars in attorney's fees. Valentino countersued for divorce and two years later was granted it on the grounds that she had deserted him.

• Meanwhile, Valentino finally got his big break, playing the lead in *The Four Horsemen of the Apocalypse* in 1921. The director, once opposed to the casting of the unknown Valentino, began noticing in the daily rushes that the camera loved his face and that Valentino dominated every scene he was in. The director rewrote the script to make Valentino's part larger. The movie was a masterpiece, and Valentino became a star.

• He made up a fictitious family history for the biographers. He said that his father had been a captain in one of the crack Italian cavalry regiments. He said that he himself had gone to the Royal Military Academy. In reality, the closest he'd ever gotten to the academy was traveling through France when he was a teenager.

• Valentino had a cauliflower ear on his left side, which he hid with makeup for long shots, and made sure only his right side was photographed on closer shots.

• He got the best advice in his career from actress Natacha Rambova, who told him to always befriend the lighting technicians. "Forget the director, forget the cameraman, the 'juicers' can make you look stunning—or dead," she told him. From then on, Valentino made a point of greeting the lighting technicians at the beginning of every shoot.

• In *A Society Sensation* he was required to jump off a pier to save the girl. He did so, and nearly drowned, not knowing how to swim.

• *The Sheik* was a runaway success. Suddenly sheik fashions became chic fashions for both men and women, and Vaseline experienced a significant sales boost as a hair application. The movie also inspired a number of popular songs, including one which Valentino despised, "The Sheik of Araby."

• Valentino married Rambova before his divorce from Acker was final. He thought that if they got married in Mexico it would be all right. Two days after they returned home, the marriage was reported in the newspapers and Valentino was thrown in jail, charged with bigamy. It was discovered that Rambova was very ill when they returned from Mexico, and that the marriage had never been consummated. Therefore, his attorney said, the marriage had not taken place at all. Valentino was cleared of the bigamy charge. On March 14, 1923, they tried again and were legally married.

• Valentino became interested in spiritualism and the occult. He believed that his dead mother was sending messages to him. He had a personal spirit "guide" named Black Feather.

• He was a bad driver, once spinning off an Alpine road, and coming to rest with one wheel hanging off the cliff. He drove into a telephone pole in Bologna.

• After becoming famous in the United States, Valentino went back to what he hoped would be a triumphant homecoming in Italy. He was very disappointed to learn that the customs officials did not know who he was, and there were no smiles, handshakes, and welcoming greetings for the returning hero. Instead, there was a delay, and a charge for taking in too many cigarettes. His movies had not yet made it to his homeland.

• He received nine hundred fan letters a day, some with undergarments inside, asking him to touch them, preferably with his lips, and return them to the sender. Other letters included nude photographs and detailed descriptions of what the women wanted to do with him.

• He grew a beard, which caused a storm of protest among his admirers. His fan club sent him a letter warning him that if he kept his beard, wives all over the country would urge their husbands to follow suit, and this would utterly deface America and make its citizens difficult to distinguish from Russians. They threatened to boycott his next picture if he kept the beard. He shaved it off.

• For a long time Valentino had suffered from what he called "indigestion," and constantly took bicarbonate of soda to ease the pain. He didn't like doctors and refused to see one. On August 15, 1926, shortly before noon, he collapsed in his room, clutching his stomach, writhing and moaning in agony. He was taken to the hospital where he was operated on for acute appendicitis and a gastric ulcer.

• While recovering from his surgery, Valentino developed an infection. It was septic endocarditis, a poisoning of the wall of the heart, for which there was no treatment or cure. He died at 12:10 P.M. on Monday, August 23, 1926. He was thirty-one.

• When news of his death spread, women began weeping, moaning, and fainting. At least one committed suicide.

• Valentino had asked to have his body publicly displayed. Tens of thousands of weeping women stood in line for hours to catch a glimpse of it. Riots broke out around the funeral home, local businesses were vandalized, a nearby auto dealership was destroyed, and a frenzied mob broke through the front window of the mortuary and nearly overturned Valentino's coffin.

• Actress Pola Negri, claiming without any evidence that she and Valentino had been secretly "engaged," stole the show, wearing exquisite mourning clothes and fainting on cue anytime reporters and photographers were nearby.

• In May 1930 a memorial to Valentino was unveiled in Hollywood's De Longpre Park. It was a symbolic bronze nude, standing on a globe, with its head gazing toward the sky. After being toppled twice from its pedestal, it was removed by the park staff for safekeeping.

● Every year without fail until 1972, on the anniversary of Valentino's death, a great mass of beautiful flowers would arrive at his tomb. The flowers have not arrived since then—presumably the anonymous sender died that year.

● A mysterious "Woman in Black" would also appear every year on the anniversary of Valentino's death. There was much press speculation about her identity. It turned out that publicist and film producer Russell Birdwell had hired an extra for five dollars to "mourn" at Valentino's grave for a movie scene he was filming. The scene ended on the cutting room floor, but the extra had enjoyed the attention she had gotten and began appearing at the grave on her own each year. Ironically, years later, Birdwell became a journalist with the *Los Angeles Herald-Express* and was assigned to do a story on the woman and, if possible, discover her identity. In the story he finally confessed his role in starting the tradition, but his article was pretty much ignored by the press and public who preferred the "mystery." Meanwhile, the silent, mysterious Woman in Black began multiplying—one year six of them showed up.

● In a way, Valentino's death was a good career move. The one record he made in his life was suppressed because his high, reedy voice did not match his image. If he had survived the advent of the talkies, his career probably would not have.

J. Edgar Hoover

J. Edgar Hoover was America's premier law-enforcement agent for five decades. He was also its chief blackmailer and unelected despot. Ironically, there is evidence that he ignored America's worst criminals because he himself was being blackmailed.

- "On Sunday January 1, 1895, at 7:30 A.M. J. Edgar Hoover was born to my father and mother, the day was cold and snowy but clear. The Doctor was Mallan. I was born at 413 Seward Square, S.E. Wash. D.C." wrote thirteen-year-old J. Edgar in his diary. He had already discarded his first name, John, and started his habit of keeping tabs on people. He began systematically filing away accounts of the personalities and habits of his teachers and friends, and the clothing sizes of his loved ones.

- Little Edgar was a "high-strung" and "glum" child, "sickly and excessively fearful, clinging to his mother whenever he could," according to people who knew him. He was mortally ashamed of his father, Dickerson Hoover, Sr., who suffered from clinical depression and was in and out of asylums for years until his death.

- After college Hoover used his government job to avoid being drafted into World War I. Fifty years later he would incessantly persecute Vietnam War draft resisters.

- Hoover considered proposing marriage to a woman he identified only as "Alice" in the waning days of World War I. She, however, ran off with a returning veteran with whom she'd corresponded during the war. Hoover claimed that after that the only "love in his life" was his dog, Spee De Bozo, in the 1920s.

● Hoover's mother had unsuccessfully tried to keep her other son from marrying and moving away, but her grip on Edgar was much firmer. He lived with her until her death in 1938, when Edgar was forty-three.

● After his mother's death Hoover sought out the company of Lela Rogers, Ginger Rogers's mother. Four years older than Hoover, Lela's ultraconservative political views were a perfect complement to his. Marriage was never seriously considered, but Hoover and Lela remained friends until her death in 1955.

● Hoover also claimed to have had a "relationship" with Dorothy Lamour. They met for the first time in 1931 when she was performing at The Stork Club in New York City. After his mother's death, they also became close friends and remained so for decades.

● Hoover made a career out of anti-Communism, which began in 1919 when he was an ambitious desk jockey in the Bureau of Investigation (the "Federal" had not yet been tacked to its name). He began amassing files on suspected "Bolsheviks," cross-referencing half a million names at a time when the country had only 110 million people. The day after his twenty-fifth birthday, Hoover celebrated with the biggest "Red Raid" in America's history, in which ten thousand people were arrested in one day by simultaneous raids all over the country by bureau agents and local police. Most of the suspects were found to be innocent and eventually released, and the bureau took a great deal of heat for its police-state tactics. Still, the raids did the trick—party membership, eighty thousand strong before the raids, dwindled to six thousand after 1920, and continued to plummet down to twenty-eight hundred by 1971, a large percentage of whom were FBI informants.

• After that raid Hoover refused to release membership figures so that people wouldn't know how weak the Communist Party really was. He told Abba Schwartz, assistant secretary of the State Department, in 1963: "If it were not for me, there would not even be a Communist Party, because I've financed the Communist Party in order to know what they are doing."

• William Sullivan's job in the FBI was monitoring the Party. He suggested in 1970 that Hoover release membership figures to show that the FBI was winning the war against subversion. "How do you think I'm going to get my appropriations out of Congress if you keep downplaying the Communist Party?" Hoover asked him angrily in 1970. Years later, after Hoover was safely dead, Sullivan announced that the "Communist threat" had long been "a lie perpetrated on the American people."

• Hoover considered Supreme Court Justice Felix Frankfurter "the most dangerous man in America" for his support of civil rights. Hoover kept a file on Frankfurter for fifty years, and bugged his offices and those of at least eleven other Supreme Court justices.

• Hoover never voted in an American election. In fact, he never even registered to vote. He claimed to be apolitical, but in fact was a staunch supporter of the right wing of the Republican Party, feeding its candidates dirt on opponents. In the 1920s he began the practice of keeping politicians under surveillance, and regularly used what he found to blackmail and punish anybody who might threaten his power. He also rewarded political friends and allies, often failing to fully investigate charges against them.

• Hoover kept his best secrets in files named Sex Deviate, Cointelpro, Official and Confidential, Personal and Confidential, June Mail (a name chosen for its innocuous sound), and—most cleverly—Do Not File, designed so he could claim with technical truthfulness that there was "nothing in FBI files" about the agency's illegal break-ins, dirty tricks, threats, and details about politicians' sex lives.

● Like Oscar Wilde, Hoover was a member of the Masons. He reached its highest level (thirty-third degree) by age sixty. He gave preferential hiring to Masons when they applied for jobs in the FBI.

● And like Oscar Wilde, he, too, was apparently homosexual. Hoover wrote hundreds of increasingly explicit and infatuated letters to his young protégé, Melvin Purvis. Things didn't work out, however (the handsome young man turned out to be a latent heterosexual). The last straw was when Purvis started getting publicity for capturing some high-profile criminals, threatening to overshadow Hoover. Purvis was forced out of the FBI. For a long time afterward, Hoover used the FBI to harass Purvis, getting him fired from jobs, spying on him, and spreading false stories about him to the press. Purvis committed suicide in 1960.

● Hoover's next big infatuation centered on Clyde Tolson, a rookie agent. Tolson, a handsome and ambitious man five years younger than Hoover, was slavishly willing to do Hoover's bidding in and out of the office. In an unheard-of three years, Tolson advanced all the way to assistant director.

● The two men became inseparable, traveling together on taxpayer-financed junkets. They dressed alike, and every day they ate the same lunch for free from the same restaurant. Its owner, Julius Lulley, was often repaid with Hoover's odd sense of practical jokes. Once, when Lulley's wife complained to Hoover that Lulley wouldn't buy her a fur coat, Hoover had one of his agents get a picture of Lulley with another woman and used the threat of showing it to his wife to convince Lulley to shell out the money.

● The romance between the two men was the source of a great deal of speculation within the organization. In the 1960s, agents joked regularly about "J. Edna" and "Mother Tolson." One agent, Guy Hottel, had been a close friend to both. When he retired, he developed a drinking problem. When drunk, he liked to tell stories of sex parties with the boys at Hoover's house. Hottel's wife would call the FBI whenever he went on a bender; they would send a Teletype message to the police to pick him up and bring him in for protective custody at FBI headquarters until he sobered up.

● The FBI came down hard on anyone caught spreading rumors about Hoover and Tolson. Even civilians were not immune. One woman was shocked when she was visited by FBI agents after telling her bridge partners that Hoover was gay; they bullied her into calling her friends and withdrawing the assertion.

● Several authors who were writing less-than-complimentary books on the FBI found themselves victims of mysterious burglaries in which the intruders ignored valuables and carried away manuscripts and research materials. If that didn't stop them, FBI agents would lean on their publishers, or even bookstore owners, hoping to suppress the books. It usually worked.

● For decades, despite evidence that was obvious to everybody else, Hoover claimed there was no such thing as "organized crime." He refused to allow the FBI's resources to be used to fight the Mob, instead going after "communists" and petty criminals. Why? According to author Anthony Sommers in *Official and Confidential: The Secret Life of J. Edgar Hoover*, it was because the Mob had very explicit photos of Hoover and Tolson having sex, and information about an arrest of Hoover in New Orleans on a morals charge in the 1920s.

● In 1959 a citizen's action group, the Fund for the Republic, raised $4 million to help fight organized crime. Its president contacted Hoover for advice on how to spend it, sending a list of prominent mafioso. Hoover said flatly that none of the Mob bosses on the list were known to the FBI. He suggested that the money would be better spent for a study of why blacks committed a disproportionately high percentage of violent crimes.

• Sommers writes that dozens of people were witnesses to Hoover and Tolson's relationship. Some say they saw the two men holding hands discreetly in one of the FBI limousines that taxied them around. In 1978 Ethel Merman, a Hoover confidant for more than three decades, came out against Anita Bryant's antigay campaign. "Some of my best friends are homosexual," she said. "Everybody knew about J. Edgar Hoover, but he was the best chief the FBI had."

• Hoover was sufficiently troubled by his gay impulses that he began seeing a psychiatrist about it in 1946.

• One of the more lurid stories about Hoover comes from Susan Rosenstiel, the wife of mobster Lewis Rosenstiel, who often met with Hoover for social and lobbying purposes. Rosenstiel claimed that Hoover helped her husband bribe a number of congressmen to pass a law that helped his liquor business in 1958.

• That same year Rosenstiel discovered her husband and rabidly anti-Communist lawyer Roy Cohn in bed together one morning. The secret out, her husband and Cohn, who decades later died of AIDS, eventually invited her to a party at the Plaza Hotel in New York. It was a very intimate affair, the most memorable part of which was seeing Hoover dressed in "a fluffy black dress, very short, with flounces, lace stocking and high heels, and a black curly wig. He had makeup on and false eyelashes." Cohn introduced Hoover to Rosenstiel as "Mary," and whispered that she should pretend not to recognize him. She left after the men started having sex with two young boys whom Cohn had hired for the night.

• A year later Rosenstiel was invited to another party at the hotel. This time, she said, Hoover had a red dress on and a black feather boa around his neck. "He was dressed like an old flapper" from the 1920s. Hoover had a Bible, she said, and had one teenage boy read from it while another fondled Hoover, "wearing rubber gloves."

● A set of photos of Hoover dressed as a woman at a party had reportedly circulated through the gay community of Washington, D.C., ten years earlier. People who had seen them characterized Hoover as looking like "a remarkably ugly woman."

● Police investigated a child porn and gay-teen prostitution ring in Los Angeles in 1969, at a time when Hoover and Tolson were visiting the area on another of their "inspection tours." The cops were surprised to hear from several different teen boys that they had been picked up by Hoover and Tolson in an FBI limousine. According to one fifteen-year-old, Hoover lectured him about his long hair before having sex with him. Fifteen men were indicted in that investigation, but not Hoover, Tolson, or any of the ring's other celebrity clients.

● Ironically, one of Hoover's favorite smears, offered without any apparent evidence against a number of personal enemies—including Martin Luther King, Adlai Stevenson, and three top aides of Richard Nixon—was that they were homosexuals.

● He learned his lesson from being blackmailed by the Mob, says Sommers. For four decades he had agents collect every allegation of sexual, political, or financial misconduct they could find on every politician in Washington. Every president from Roosevelt on wanted to retire Hoover—but backed down when they saw what he had on them. John and Robert Kennedy, whom Hoover despised, were particularly vulnerable to the volume of information Hoover had on their womanizing. In fact, some accounts have it that it was Hoover who used his clout to demand that JFK choose Hoover's friend and ally Lyndon Johnson as his running mate. (Some conspiracy theorists have postulated the next logical step—that the reason he insisted was because he intended to make sure that Kennedy wouldn't finish his term.)

● Hoover traveled outside the United States only twice in his life: one trip just over the border into Canada, and one just over the border into Mexico. That was enough—he just did not trust foreigners.

- His fear of germs was second only to that of Howard Hughes. He installed a special ultraviolet lighting system that he believed would kill viruses, and kept a servant on staff to swat flies in his office.

- Hoover purposely avoided any contact with persons having moist palms, and recruits so afflicted were screened out. The same was true for recruits who had pimples, or were bald, or who had political beliefs more liberal than Hoover's. Three recruits were fired because they had small heads; another because his ears stuck out.

- He also refused to hire black agents. Robert Kennedy pressured him on this in the 1960s, and as a result Hoover "promoted" his black servants on staff, calling them "agents" while they performed the same menial duties as before. When he died, the FBI had only seventy black agents out of a total of six thousand.

- Hoover absolutely despised Martin Luther King, and was enraged when King won the Nobel Peace Prize in 1965, an honor that he himself coveted. Shortly before King was to pick up his prize in Sweden, Hoover had an unmarked parcel sent to King's wife. It contained a tape of King allegedly having sex with another woman, along with an anonymous note to King threatening to expose him to the world and suggesting that suicide was the only honorable way out.

- King was demoralized for several months. The FBI stepped up the pressure, harassing King with anonymous phone calls, threats, and midnight false-fire alarms. Hoover gleefully reviewed the wiretap transcripts for signs that the constant badgering was having an effect; one transcript quoted King telling a friend, "They are out to break me, out to get me, harass me, break my spirit." King fell into a period of insomnia and deep depression. Finally, he rallied and decided that the cause was just, and that "we are not going to let Hoover and the FBI turn us around."

● When King was killed three years later by a sniper, Atlanta FBI agents cheered; one shouted, "We finally got the son of a bitch!" Hoover "personally" took over the investigation. The first day he spent getting his photo taken for public relations purposes. The next day, as he had the day after Kennedy's assassination, he went to the race track for the day. In the weeks that followed, he failed to show up for meetings with the attorney general on the subject.

● The fingerprints of James Earl Ray, a small-time criminal and prison escapee, had immediately been found on the scene, as well as a radio with his prison number on it. But it took two weeks for the FBI to issue an alert for him. For the next two months, Ray traveled around the country. He was finally caught in London, on the day of Bobby Kennedy's funeral.

● Ray was carrying a large amount of cash when he was arrested, the source of which still has not been explained. He never went to trial. He confessed to acting alone as part of a plea bargain, but later recanted and claimed that the FBI was involved and he had gone along under the threat that they'd harm his family.

● For years afterward Hoover continued to smear King as a "Communist and a scoundrel," leaking information and copies of the FBI's King sex tapes. His new goal became trying to stop Congress from making King's birthday a national holiday. His efforts were successful for several years; King's birthday wasn't honored until 1982.

● Hoover had the FBI laboratory invent a heated toilet-seat for his use.

● Hoover was ashamed that he was only five feet seven inches tall. He concealed this by wearing custom-made elevator shoes. In his office, his extrahigh chair was set on a slight platform; visitors were ushered to a low couch.

• Hoover felt that female criminals were far more vicious and dangerous than males. He also told the New York Round Table that female criminals always have red hair—if not naturally, "she either adopts a red wig or has her hair dyed red."

• Persistent rumors around Washington, D.C., especially prevalent in the black community, had it that Hoover was mulatto, "passing" for white. It has been suggested that Hoover's special persecution of gays and blacks was his way of trying to counteract the rumors.

• Hoover absolutely loathed Eleanor Roosevelt, claiming that the reason he never married was "because God made a woman like Eleanor Roosevelt." He called her "a nigger-lover" for her pro–civil rights stands. What survives of her FBI file runs 449 pages, including Hoover's suspicions that she was having sex with men and women all over Washington. (There is some evidence that she may have had an affair with one of her bodyguards and journalist Lorena Hickok, but Hoover took it several steps further, documenting suspicions that she was involved with her black driver, her doctor, an Army colonel, two leaders of the National Maritime Union, and various left-wing leaders.)

• Hoover authorized the promiscuous use of wiretaps around the country. However, whenever he had to give testimony in front of Congress he would have all but one—the tap on the Communist Party headquarters—turned off for the day so he could truthfully testify that the FBI was doing no illegal wiretapping.

• Both Hoover and Tolson had a passion for horse racing, and Hoover's interest bordered on addictive. He would schedule "inspection tours" of local offices to follow racing schedules. He loved betting heavily on the horses legally and illegally through bookies. Members of the Mob, grateful for his inattention toward their activities, regularly gave him hot horse-tips and then fixed horse races so that his two hundred dollar bets would win as often as not.

● During the student unrest of the 1960s, Hoover established the COINTELPRO program which set up activists for arrests on trumped-up charges, started fights at peaceful protests, sent anonymous letters to employers and family members of legal protesters, coaxed otherwise law-abiding activists to commit illegal acts, printed phony documents to stir up violence between black militant allies, and incited his Mob contacts to have comedian and black activist Dick Gregory beaten up.

● Nixon's secret goon squad, the "Plumbers," led by E. Gordon Liddy, twice reportedly turned the tables on Hoover and broke into his house on a "black bag job" of their own, trying to find the incriminating files that prevented Nixon from replacing him.

● One report has it that in the Plumbers' last break-in at Hoover's house, shortly before his death, a poison of the thiophosphate genre was placed on Hoover's personal toilet articles. The effects of this highly toxic compound? Massive heart failure.

● On May 2, 1972, Hoover was found dead next to his bed. He had been in good health, and had had no previous heart problems. The cause of death was officially "hypertensive cardiovascular disease" and no autopsy was done. When undertakers arrived shortly after, they found fifteen to twenty men in suits ransacking books and papers, and emptying out drawers.

● Before his death, Hoover somehow amassed millions of dollars on a civil servant's pay ($43,000 a year was his peak salary). Although he projected an air of incorruptibility, he made a lot of money from unethical and illegal dealings. Hoover received hundreds of thousands of dollars in illegal gifts and accommodations, some from Mob-connected individuals, and he and Tolson used FBI library and recreation funds for their own uses.

● Hoover left all his earthly belongings to Tolson, bypassing relatives and other friends. Tolson died a recluse in 1975. He was buried, by mutual request, ten yards away from his former boss.

The Beatles

John Lennon, Paul McCartney, George Harrison, and Richard "Ringo Starr" Starkey produced records as the Beatles for only seven years—from 1963 to 1969. Yet their early music still sounds fresh, and their extensive influence on popular music continues three decades later.

• In the beginning of Beatlemania the Beatles' audience was primarily young (and often screaming) teen girls. The group was considered a joke by most adults, and they themselves didn't take their careers too seriously. Lennon said, "It's fun . . . but it can't last long." Starr's goal was to make enough money to open his own hair salon.

• In 1960 the group first called itself the Quarry Men, then the Silver Beatles. Founders Lennon and Stu Sutcliffe were art students in college when they started, Harrison was still in high school, the drummer was Pete Best, and McCartney performed under the stage name Paul Ramone because, he said, "it sounded really glamorous, sort of Valentino-ish." (Nearly two decades later, the Ramones took their group name from this, with each member adopting "Ramone" as a surname.)

• The band's early years were rough. One of their first engagements was accompanying a stripper named Janice in a club in Liverpool's brothel district. One night, as the Beatles played at a ballroom in Neston, a group of "teddy boy" gang members kicked a sixteen-year-old to death on the dance floor in front of them.

● The group traveled to Hamburg, Germany, where they figured they could make a living in the night scene. Hamburg was a rough town at the time, known in the early 1960s as the gunrunning center of Europe. Sutcliffe was once dragged offstage and kicked in the head by a gang of toughs before Lennon dragged him back to safety. Sutcliffe died two years later, on April 10, 1962, from a cerebral hemorrhage which might have been brought on by the attack.

● During their Hamburg era, when they were required to play eight- to twelve-hour days, the band began using amphetamines, first Preludin ("prellies"), then Purple Hearts and Black Bombers.

● By the end of 1962 the group took to showing their contempt for the drunken Hamburg audiences by making lyrical changes, singing "A Taste of Honey" as "A Waste of Money" and "Shimmy Shimmy" as "Shitty Shitty."

● Lennon bought a pig for a pet; shortly after, he threw it out a top-floor window to its death, shouting, "Look, a flying pig."

● Lennon had shoplifted in Holland the harmonica he played on "Love Me Do."

● At manager Brian Epstein's instruction, the Beatles began wearing matching collarless suits designed by Pierre Cardin in place of black leather pants and jackets which, Epstein said, made them look like Nazis.

● That the Beatles were "antimaterialistic," said McCartney, was "a huge myth. John and I literally used to sit down and say, 'Now let's write a swimming pool.' " They wrote the first Rolling Stones hit single, "I Wanna Be Your Man."

● McCartney idolized Little Richard and adopted many of his vocal mannerisms. Apparently Little Richard was also fond of McCartney: According to a member of the Beatles' touring crew, at their first meeting, "Richard chased McCartney round and round the dressing room, Paul just managing to keep one step ahead. . . . Richard got on much better with Brian Epstein."

• Cynthia Lennon gave birth to Julian while John was watching bullfights in Barcelona on holiday with Epstein. For years it was rumored that John and Epstein had had an affair on their vacation. Manager Spencer Mason is quoted as saying, "we all knew what happened," without elaborating. Apparently, it was a sensitive subject: At McCartney's twenty-first birthday party, disc jockey Bob Wooler teased a drunken Lennon about the Barcelona trip. Lennon alleged that Wooler called him "a bloody fag." He responded by battering Wooler in the face and breaking three of Wooler's ribs.

• As Beatlemania began exploding across England, the September 10, 1963, *Daily Mirror* carried a first appraisal of the Beatles: "The stone-age hair style boys are as nice a group of well-mannered music makers as you'll find perforating the eardrum anywhere." The *Daily Telegraph* slammed the group, saying Beatles-induced mass hysteria was filling empty heads just as Hitler had done. Sir Edward Boyle, education minister, said, "The Beatles have no future." British disc jockey Brian Matthews stated, "If the Beatles made a disc of themselves snoring for two minutes, it'd go to number one." The Chicago label Vee Jay released the Beatles' first U.S. single, "From Me to You"/"Thank You Girl," misspelling the group's name as "The Beattles."

• The Beatles' second British album, *With the Beatles*, was released on November 22, 1963, the day John F. Kennedy was assassinated. The following day, comedienne Dora Bryan released "All I Want for Christmas Is a Beatle," the first Beatles parody/tribute record. (The Beatles parodied back a Christmas recording for their fan clubs with "All I Want for Christmas Is a Bottle.")

• McCartney not only dated actress Jane Asher, he moved into a bedroom in her family's upper-class home. He began writing hit songs for her brother, Peter Asher, for his duo, Peter and Gordon. He lived there until Jane caught him in his bed with another woman.

● Ed Sullivan first became aware of the group via a news report on Beatlemania filed from England by Walter Cronkite. After their first Sullivan show appearance, Sullivan's orchestra director, Ray Bloch, predicted, "They won't last longer than a year." The TV critic for the *New York Times* sniffed, "They hardly did for daughter what Elvis did for her older sister or Frank Sinatra did for mother."

● Cassius Clay (later known as Muhammad Ali) was to fight Sonny Liston for the championship in a few days. The group tried to meet Liston, who refused to have anything to do with "a bunch of faggots." They instead met Clay. He bossed them around for the photographers, commanding them to the canvas with "Get down, you little worms!" Lennon, however, got the last laugh (see the chapter on Muhammad Ali, page 34).

● On August 28, 1964, in a room at the Delmonico Hotel, New York, Bob Dylan introduced the Beatles to marijuana.

● Given the opportunity to meet Noel Coward in Rome, only McCartney went; Lennon declared he had no interest in meeting "that old poofter." Coward was "charmed" by McCartney, but aware he'd been snubbed by the other three Beatles. He wrote, "The message I would have liked to send them was that they were bad-mannered little shits."

● Because they couldn't be heard over the blare of the crowds at their concerts, Lennon would sometimes scream obscenities instead of lyrics into the microphone. According to a member of the entourage, hookers were plentiful on tour, and "there were orgies in every town. It's only a miracle the press didn't get hold of it."

● Or did they? In New York, Epstein entertained a group of "rent boys" (male prostitutes) at a party in his suite at the Plaza. A photographer for one of the tabloids lowered himself down the side of the hotel in a bosun's chair. The resulting photos of the party were quietly bought out of the marketplace.

• While on tour of the Philippines, Philippine First Lady Imelda Marcos invited the group to meet her at the palace, but Epstein, citing fatigue on the group's behalf, ignored the invitation. A mob, angry at this affront, greeted Epstein and the band at the airport, punching, kicking, and spitting on the group. They fled the country without being paid.

• The Beatles were awarded membership in the Member of the British Empire (MBE) Order, an honor that would allow them to put "Sir" in front of their names, if they so chose. A number of previous MBE recipients, including several army officers, resigned theirs in protest. Sir John Lennon responded by saying that, while the soldiers had gotten theirs for "killing people," the Beatles got theirs for entertaining; thus, Lennon said, "I'd say we deserved ours more."

• The Guinness Book of World Records cites McCartney's "Yesterday" as the most-recorded song in history, with over eleven hundred known versions to date. McCartney worked out the music before deciding on words, using a temporary nonsense verse that began, "Scrambled eggs, oh how I love your legs."

• Even after the success of "Yesterday," when the Beatles were stretching their creative abilities, not everybody was impressed. Broadway songwriter Richard Rogers said of their music, "I find it monotonous . . . nothing creative or original about it . . . their music won't last." In *Hi-Fi Stereo Review* magazine, a reviewer wrote of *Revolver*, "They are finally as hip, as revolutionary, as new and urgent, as Elvis Presley in his ten-year-old gold lamé suit." Reviewing *Magical Mystery Tour* in the same magazine, Rex Reed called the album, "Repulsive . . . revolting . . . creepy . . . stagnant."

• In June 1966 Lennon was quoted in *Redbook* as saying, "We're more popular than Jesus now," resulting in Beatle bans and record burnings, primarily in the southern United States and South Africa. Ironically, he was misunderstood; the quote came from a longer section in which he was actually deploring the decline of spirituality in the modern world.

● After the Beatles quit touring—their final concert was August 29, 1966, at San Francisco's Candlestick Park—Epstein began existing on "a diet of pills, booze, and dangerous, often painful one-night encounters with the rough trade he picked up outside the military barracks in Knightsbridge," according to a Beatles' staffer. In late 1966 Epstein attempted suicide with sleeping pills.

● Lennon got deeply involved with LSD, estimating that he had taken one thousand trips by November 1966. Consequently, Lennon gave up much of his creative control over the group and it became "Paul's band" more than Lennon's as the Beatles entered the studio to record *Sergeant Pepper's Lonely Heart's Club Band*.

● The first Beatle album had been recorded in one sixteen-hour session on February 11, 1963, at a cost of $1,120. Less than three years later, *Sergeant Pepper* required an unprecedented seven hundred hours of studio time to record, at an unheard-of cost of $68,750.

● Starr complained that "with *Sergeant Pepper* I felt more like a session man. . . . Everyone says that record is a classic, but it's not my favorite album."

● In 1967 McCartney was buried in criticism for his opinions on drugs, as quoted in *Life*: "[LSD] opened my eyes. It made me a better, more honest, more tolerant member of society." He smoked pot, he says, on "almost a daily basis," and observed that "pot is milder than Scotch." During the making of *Sergeant Pepper's* he snorted cocaine, but soon quit using that drug.

● When Epstein expressed an interest in writing his autobiography, Lennon suggested he call it *The Queer Jew*. In fact, the working lyrics of "Baby You're a Rich Man" included a chorus in Epstein's honor, "Baby, you're a rich fag Jew."

• Convinced that he was soon to lose his job managing the group, Epstein committed suicide with an overdose of Carbrital sleeping pills on August 26, 1967. The *Financial Times* estimated Epstein's wealth at the time of his death at $19 million. None of the Beatles attended Epstein's funeral, "aware that their presence would have turned the service into a circus."

• Lennon met Yoko Ono on November 9, 1966. When Cynthia Lennon went on holiday to Greece, she returned to find that Ono had moved into the Lennon home with John. Just prior to Cynthia's trip, John had listed for her over three hundred women he'd slept with during their marriage, "singers, film stars, Playboy bunnies, the wives of friends," as he put it.

• Bored trust-fund baby and sometime groupie Linda Eastman flew to London in May 1967 to meet the Beatles, with her romantic eye set on Lennon. She settled for McCartney instead and married him a year later. Despite having even less musical talent than Ono, she joined his post-Beatles band Wings.

• The Beatles spent early 1968 in India with the Maharishi Mahesh Yogi. Many of the "White Album" songs were written in India during this period. After Lennon became disillusioned with the jet set holy man, he wrote a song called "Maharishi" with lyrics like, "Maharishi/You little twat/Who the fuck do you think you are. . . ." The lyrics were later toned down and, in order to avoid legal problems, the song's title was changed to "Sexy Sadie."

• Lennon began taking heroin to even out his constant LSD trips. In November 18, 1968, Lennon and Ono were busted for possession of 219 grams of cannabis resin. The following month the couple released *Unfinished Music No. 1—Two Virgins*, the cover of which featured Lennon and Ono in the nude. EMI's Sir Joseph Lockwood refused to distribute the album, saying, if the cover was (as Ono claimed) art, "why not show Paul in the nude—he's much prettier."

● McCartney got the blame for breaking up the Beatles in 1970, but Lennon had been thinking of doing the same thing: "Since 1966, I was always looking for a reason . . . I didn't have the guts to do it." Starr had quit for several days, before being coaxed back, during the tense White Album sessions (that's McCartney drumming on "Back in the USSR)." In 1969 Harrison also quit for a few days after McCartney criticized his playing.

● Lennon was killed in 1980 by a crazed fan, leaving widow Ono as the richest woman in the world. (Another crazed fan, Charles Manson, had a houseful of people killed a decade earlier in the hope that it would bring on the race war he thought the Beatles had predicted in the song "Helter Skelter.") At least two Americans committed suicide in the wake of Lennon's murder.

Winston Churchill

"We shall fight in the fields and in the streets, we shall fight in the hills; we shall never surrender." Winston Churchill was the leader of England during World War II. Jauntily flashing the V sign to photographers, his bulldog face personified the brave defiance of the plucky Brits.

• Winston Churchill's mother, Jennie, was an American whose own mother claimed both Iroquois blood and a direct descent from a lieutenant in Washington's army. Jennie was two months pregnant with Winston when she got married in April 1874. Afterward she had a number of lovers, including the Prince of Wales and William Gladstone. (George Moore, the Irish novelist and Jennie's confidante, claimed to know the names of two hundred of her lovers.) Rumor had it that her husband was not the father of Winston's younger brother, Jack.

• In part because Jennie's sexual popularity helped smooth the way, Lord Randolph, Winston's father, quickly moved up in London political circles. By his late thirties, Randolph had become chancellor of the exchequer and was expected to become prime minister. However, he started acting erratically and suddenly resigned from his position over a minor disagreement with party leaders. It turns out that Randolph had moved into the second stage of syphilis and was slowly declining into madness and paralysis.

• During much of his parents' unfolding drama, Winston Churchill was away at boarding school. At St. George's Ascot, his student days were characterized by a teacher as "one long feud with authority" by "the naughtiest little boy in the world." Once, after being flogged for stealing sugar, he took the headmaster's straw hat and kicked it to pieces.

• At Harrow School Churchill was placed with the group of boys who were considered dunces. The schoolmaster liked to place him periodically in the front of the class and announce, "Look at the stupidest boy at Harrow who is the son of the cleverest man in England."

• When Churchill was fourteen years old, his father inspected Winston's collection of nearly fifteen hundred toy soldiers, which Winston had arranged in an attack formation. Lord Randolph asked if Winston would like to join the army. Winston was pleased, thinking his father had been impressed by the attack formation. Later, though, he discovered that his father had suggested the army because he didn't think Winston was smart enough to become a lawyer . . . or anything else of consequence.

• Churchill was deeply excited by war. When British troops were sent to Afghanistan to teach the "lesser breeds" the folly of wanting independence, Churchill used his family connections to join them. He conspicuously rode a white pony up and down the front lines. He wrote his mother, "Bullets—to a philosopher, my dear Mamma—are not worth considering. Besides, I am so conceited I do not believe the Gods would create so potent a being as myself for so prosaic an ending."

• Churchill's military career was in large part motivated by political ambitions. "Being in many ways a coward, there is no ambition I cherish so keenly as to gain a reputation for personal courage . . . I feel that the fact of having seen service with British troops while still a young man must give me more weight politically," he wrote to Jennie. "I do not care so much for the prin-

ciples I advocate as for the impression which my words produce
& the reputation they give me."

• Lord Randolph sunk into complete helpessness and died at
age forty-six. Jennie married Captain George Cornwallis-West,
who was young enough to be her son—in fact, exactly sixteen
days older than Winston.

• After his mother remarried, Churchill decided he should think
about matrimony himself—but not too quickly. Clementine Hozier (his future wife), on being introduced to Churchill, said, "He
never uttered one word and was very gauche—he never asked
me to dance, he never asked me to have supper with him." The
next meeting, years later, on hearing Hozier hadn't read his newly
published biography of his father, he asked, "If I send you the
book tomorrow, will you read it?" She agreed, but he never sent
the book. The third meeting went better, and eventually they
were married. Churchill was thirty-three.

• All indications are that Churchill, horrified at the effects of
syphilis on his father, had eschewed sex before marriage. Instead,
he put his energies into the pursuit of power and glory, switching
parties whenever it suited his personal ambitions. After marriage,
however, sex was another story. He reportedly had a son in
France, who he never acknowledged.

• It was also rumored that he had an affair with Doris Lady Cas-
tlerosse; if true, Churchill's son Randolph followed in his dad's
footsteps years later by having an affair with her also. (Her outraged husband called Randolph and said, "I hear you're sleeping
with my wife." Randolph replied, "Yes, I am, and it's more than
you have the courtesy to do.")

• In a report to his government Churchill gained a reputation for
astuteness by predicting World War I years before it happened.
He wasn't always so politically smart. He completely misread the
Russian revolution, seeing Czar Nicholas as a tragic hero being
brought down by "a group of international Semitic conspirators"

(even though soon-to-be exiled Trotsky was the only Jew among the Soviet leaders). In 1932 Churchill ignored the rise of the Nazis in Germany while proposing that England should deal harshly with a menace of a different sort—pacifist Indian activist Mahatma Gandhi. He found it "nauseating," he said, that this "seditious Middle Temple lawyer" might actually "stride half-naked up the steps of the Viceregal Palace . . . to parlay on equal terms with the representative of the King Emperor."

● Melancholia, what we now call clinical depression, was a family trait, apparently inherited through at least five generations of ancestors. (The family motto was *Fiel pero Desdichado*, "Faithful but Unfortunate.")

● Churchill referred to depression as his "black dog" and discovered to his fascinated horror that aggression relieved it. He became a bully as a child, and found great excitement in his political duties when they involved bloodshed. As home secretary he sent the army to brutally supress striking miners and "anarchists"; at the beginning of World War I, he confessed to Hozier, "Everything is tending towards catastrophe and collapse. I am interested, geared up, and happy. Is it not horrible to be built like this?"

● He attempted to resign his post in exchange for the rank of major general, saying that his political career was nothing in comparison with military glory: "My God, this is living history! Everything we are doing and saying is thrilling—it will be read by a thousand generations, think of that! Why, I would not be out of this glorious, delicious war for anything the world could give me." In response to the paunchy forty-year-old's request, Britain's defense minister just laughed. (Two decades later, Prime Minister Churchill, sixty-one years old, overweight, and dependent on a cane to walk, firmly intended to land with British troops on D day. He reluctantly gave up his plan only when the king himself demanded he do so.)

• Despite Churchill's love of battles, most of the military actions that he directly initiated were failures, resulting in routs and slaughters of his own men. As secretary of the navy in World War I, he thought that an attack against a Turkish base at Dardanelles on the Gallipoli peninsula would be a brilliant stroke. Instead, Churchill's plan resulted in a bloody failure: Twenty thousand allied soldiers were slaughtered by machine-gun fire as they landed.

• Churchill worked most efficiently by not getting up from bed. He'd wake up, have a huge breakfast, and immediately begin dictating to his secretary from under bedspreads covered with documents and memoranda. Said a critic at the time, "He is ill-mannered, boastful, unprincipled, without any redeeming qualities except his amazing ability and industry."

• Churchill, part-American by birth, liked the United States and visited several times. It was there in 1900 that he was introduced by Mark Twain, improbably at the time, as "the future prime minister of England."

• Churchill never got used to U.S. traffic patterns. On a trip in 1931 he glanced right instead of left before crossing Fifth Avenue in New York and was promptly hit by a taxi. Just before passing out from injuries on the head and thighs, he announced grandly to doctors in the emergency room, "I am Winston Churchill, a British statesman."

• Churchill had many friends killed in World War I. He wrote to Hozier in 1914, "What would happen, I wonder, if the armies suddenly & simultaneously went on strike and said some other method must be found of settling the dispute?"

• Any pacifist sentiment on his part had completely disappeared by World War II. On objections to using poisonous gas on Germany, he said, "It is absurd to consider morality on this topic, when everybody used it in the last war without a word of complaint from the moralists or the church. On the other hand, in the last war the bombing of open cities was regarded as forbidden.

Now everybody does it as a matter of course. It is simply a question of fashion changing, as she does between long and short skirts for women."

• Churchill was plagued by politically embarrassing relatives. His cousin Clare Sheridan traveled to Russia in 1920, just a year or two after Churchill had tried to get Britain and its allies to declare war on the new Communist leaders. An artist, she charmed Lenin into posing for a portrait bust. Trotsky was next, not only sitting for the bust, but lying in her bed that night, in a whirlwind affair that left Churchill fuming.

• In 1933 Unity Mitford, a niece on his wife's side of the family, became a dedicated British Fascist. She traveled to Germany to be near "the darling führer," and (it was widely rumored) became his lover for a while, provoking the jealousy of Eva Braun. When war broke out between Germany and Britain, she botched a suicide attempt; brain damaged and depressed, she was returned to Britain via Switzerland. Her sister Diana, one of Churchill's favorite nieces but also a Fascist, was thrown into jail for the duration of the war. (Churchill intervened only to insure that she, as a female member of the upper class, would be given the privilege of a daily bath.) Meanwhile, a third sister, novelist Jessica Mitford, became a dedicated Communist.

• Churchill's wedding eve advice to oldest son Randolph was "All you need to be married are champagne, a box of cigars, and a double bed."

• Seven weeks after the Allies defeated the Germans, Churchill was voted out of office by a grateful nation. By custom, he immediately had to vacate 10 Downing Street. A friend visited the Churchills at the hotel where they had taken refuge and admired the amenities of their upper-story room. Churchill pointed to the balcony and replied, "I don't like sleeping near a precipice like that. I've no desire to quit the world, but thoughts, desperate thoughts, come into the head." Churchill was reelected prime minister a decade later.

• In 1946, in a speech in Fulton, Missouri, Churchill coined the phrase "Iron Curtain."

• In retirement, Churchill often painted in oil, mostly traditional landscapes. He had no love for modern art, remarking to a friend, "If I saw Picasso walking down the street ahead of us, do you know what I would do? I'd kick him up the ass." His wife believed in similar direct action: Twice she put her foot through unflattering portraits of her husband.

• Near the end of his life Churchill was wooed by tireless social climber Aristotle Onassis, who took Churchill out on his yachts and made sure he won all card games onboard. When they cruised the Mediterranean, Onassis timed it so that they passed the Dardanelles in the dead of night so Churchill wouldn't be reminded of the disastrous defeat at Gallipoli.

• "Under the mighty oak, the acorns cannot grow," Randolph used to say, explaining his family's troubles. Of Churchill's four children, only daughter Mary had a relatively happy life. Randolph was a lifelong, antagonistic drunk. Sarah, though less antagonistic, was even more heavily addicted to alcohol, getting herself arrested for public drunkenness over and over again. Churchill's other daughter, Diana, killed herself.

• In 1950 he had told a friend, "Today is the twenty-fourth of January. It is the day my father died. It is the day that I shall die, too." Fifteen years later, on January 15, 1965, Churchill had a major stroke. Before he went into a coma, his last words were "I'm so bored with it all." On January 24, just as he predicted, he died.

George Bernard Shaw

Of the Irish writer George Bernard Shaw, one of the literary giants of the twentieth century, another wit of the period, Oscar Wilde, said, "He hasn't an enemy in the world, though none of his friends like him."

• Born July 26, 1856, in Dublin, George Bernard Shaw was the third child and only son of Irish Protestant parents.

• While Shaw was a young working man, a couple of American evangelists came through Dublin. Shaw attended one of their services and came away unimpressed. He wrote a letter to the local paper saying if that was religion, he was definitely an atheist. The attention he received from writing something that shocked the townspeople may have convinced him that writing was the career path for him.

• Shaw arrived in London from Dublin in 1876 at the age of twenty. Shaw didn't have much success at first in getting published. In his first nine years as a writer, according to Shaw, he made only six pounds.

• Shaw was painfully shy. When invited to someone's home, he would sometimes pace the street in front of it for twenty minutes before getting up the nerve to approach the front door.

• Shaw declared that Karl Marx "made a man of him." Shaw was the major figure in the socialist Fabian Society for twenty-seven years. For the first twelve of those years he made several public speeches a week in public halls and on street corners, from which he gained confidence and a command of his language—so much so that it became a social liability at times. Shaw's play *Major Barbara* contains a telling exchange: Lady Britomart urges Undershaft, "Stop making speeches, Andrew! This is not the place for them!" to which he replies, "My dear! I have no other way of conveying my ideas!"

• No one could accuse Shaw of being too brief. In fact, G. K. Chesterton said Shaw was "a man who would write a very long preface to a very short play . . . he is indeed a very prefatory sort of person." For example, Shaw's preface to the collection of his and actress Ellen Terry's love letters, published in 1931, ran ten thousand words. In *The Intelligent Woman's Guide to Socialism and Capitalism*, the eighty-four chapter headings alone total more than fourteen thousand words, containing so much information that a reader need not read the rest of the book.

• Shaw apparently consummated his first affair at the age of twenty-nine with a widow fifteen years his senior. She remained his mistress for eight years and became the model for many of his women characters.

• Shaw claimed that he only got married because he believed he was dying. He had injured a foot and it wouldn't heal. Charlotte Payne-Townshend, Irish millionairess and Fabian comrade, visited him at his mother's house. She was so appalled at the squalor there that she whisked him off to a house of her own. He insisted they marry if she was going to live with and take care of him, so marry they did in June 1898. (She bought the license and the ring.) Much to Shaw's surprise, he did not die after all, and the Shaws remained married for forty-five years.

• During his long life Shaw conducted many passionate romances by mail. His letter-writing love affair with Ellen Terry, almost nine years his senior, lasted twenty-six years, during which time they met only twice. "I really do love Ellen," he wrote, and "let those who may complain that it was all on paper, remember that only on paper has humanity yet achieved glory, beauty, truth, knowledge, virtue, and abiding love."

● He read to his wife many of his love letters to other women. "I must now go and read this to Charlotte," Shaw wrote at the end of one of his letters to another famous actress, who went by the name Mrs. Patrick Campbell. "My love affairs are her unfailing amusement: all their tenderness finally recoils on herself."

● Charlotte may have had other ideas about that. She and T. E. Lawrence ("Lawrence of Arabia") conducted their own correspondence—six hundred letters in thirteen years. Shaw had edited Lawrence's *The Seven Pillars of Wisdom*, and his wife had proofread it. When she died in 1943 at age eighty-six, Shaw read her diaries and copies of her letters. He concluded, "Of all the women I have known (and I have known many), I knew Charlotte least of all."

● Shaw was, among other things, a vegetarian. Shaw biographer G. K. Chesterton reported, "Of the many sincere things Mr. Shaw has said, he never said a more sincere one than when he stated he was a vegetarian, not because eating meat was bad morality, but because it was bad taste."

● Chesterton called Shaw the "least social of all Socialists." In the ideal socialist state, Shaw wrote, everyone would be given the same income. He specifically exempted playwrights from these financial constraints however, "because the pleasure we give is delightful and widespread."

● When Shaw was asked to attend the Stratford Tercentenary, he wrote, "I do not keep my own birthday, and I cannot see why I should keep Shakespeare's." Socialist Shaw applied his unkindest cut of all, "Shakespeare was a capitalist! If the fellow had not been a great poet, his rubbish would have been forgotten long ago!"

• One of Shaw's early biographers, Archibald Henderson, planned in 1905 to write a brief study of the man and his plays, so he sent some questions to Shaw. The playwright inundated him with over 180,000 written words. The project that Henderson had intended to finish in six months took six years to complete.

• Shaw was an early proponent and defender of the Norwegian playwright Henrik Ibsen. Shaw felt that the role of the playwright should be the same as Cromwell's had been, namely, to give the people "not what they want, but what is good for them," which he thought Ibsen did admirably well.

• In 1923 Shaw was offered a knighthood and an earldom but refused them because of his socialist beliefs. In 1925 he was awarded the Nobel Prize in literature "for his work which is marked by both idealism and humanity, its stimulating satire often being infused with a singular poetic beauty."

• In June 1912 Shaw, then fifty-six, read his new play *Pygmalion* to Mrs. Campbell, whom he wanted to play Eliza Doolittle, even though she was forty-seven at the time and too old for the part. The actress invited Shaw to her house to discuss business. Shaw suspected that she was going to use her feminine wiles on him during the business negotiations. He was undaunted, however, believing he could handle "a dozen such Dalilahs." But when the actress took his hand and touched her breast, "I fell head over heels in love with her—violently and exquisitely in love—before I knew that I was thinking about anything but business."

• Once she got the part, though, Mrs. Campbell spurned Shaw's amorous advances. Shaw took the rejection hard. He was adamant in his instructions to directors and his translators that there was to be "no sentimental nonsense" about Eliza Doolittle and Henry Higgins being lovers. Instead, Shaw insisted that Eliza marry Freddy Eynsford-Hill, who was being played by George Cornwallis-West, whom Mrs. Campbell married just as *Pygmalion* was about to open. (Cornwallis-West had just divorced his previous wife, Winston Churchill's mother; see page 235.)

• Years later, when *Pygmalion* was adapted for the screen as *My Fair Lady*, the producers were finally able to convince Shaw that the Doolittle-Higgins matchup as an ending made better commercial sense.

• Shaw made a curtain call following the production in London of one of his plays. There was thunderous, sustained applause for Shaw, but as the clapping died down in anticipation of a few words from the author, there came a single, loud "Booooo!" from the upper balcony. Shaw stepped forward to the edge of the stage, raised an eyebrow, and said, "I quite agree, my dear fellow, but what are we two against so many?"

• When Charlotte Shaw died in 1943, she was cremated. When Shaw died seven years later, his ashes were mixed with hers and then both sets of ashes were scattered together.

Marlene Dietrich

Marlene Dietrich, a German sex bomb in Hollywood, starred in movies like The Blue Angel.

- Marlene Dietrich was born Marie Magdalene von Losch in Berlin on December 27, 1901 (or if you prefer her math, 1904). At age thirteen she invented the name "Marlene" by taking the beginning of Marie and the ending of Magdalene. Her family nicknames were Lena and Pussy Cat.

- The von Losch family ate dinner in strictest silence, as chatter was considered a hindrance to proper digestion.

- Lena's father, Louis, was killed in World War I. When her mother remarried, Lena wore black.

- In her teens Dietrich developed a crush on a succession of girls and women. She wrote in her diary about an aunt, "Last night I kissed her a lot but still feel something is missing—the one kiss she gives me is not enough. I am so happy when she gives me a kiss."

- In 1917 she wrote that she was starting to love a girl from her sister's class. "I would like to hold her hand and kiss it wildly until I die. She thinks I only like her a lot. But this time it's really passion, deep, deep love."

● She became infatuated with movie star Henny Porten. After Dietrich went to see her movie *The Captive Soul*, she wrote, "She takes her robe off to go bathing—naked. You see only to her shoulders, but on the sides, you can see more."

● Dietrich learned how to played the piano, violin, and mando-lin. (Later, as an adult, she learned the musical saw as well.) Lena's violin teacher found the urge to touch his stunningly pretty pupil so overwhelming that he kept his hands in his pockets dur-ing their lessons. However, teacher and student eventually suc-cumbed and Dietrich gave her virginity to him at age sixteen. She found the experience disappointing. "He groaned, heaved, panted," she wrote. "Didn't even take his trousers off. I just lay there on that old settee, the red plush scratching my behind, my skirts over my head. The whole thing was very uncomfortable. Now it's all over. The whole thing didn't mean a thing to him. And I let myself go and showed him how much I liked him."

● Dietrich started getting minor parts on the stage in Berlin. She once went to an "extra" casting call wearing a pirate's hat with a pheasant's tail feather stuck through its crown, a velvet coat with dangling red fox, and her father's monacle. She got the part.

● Dietrich married Rudolf Sieber on May 17, 1923. She was twenty-one, and he was twenty-seven. When she became preg-nant a year later, she told her husband that there would be no more sex because it could harm the child. She managed to elim-inate sex from their marriage entirely (but not from her life), but they remained married for over fifty years.

● When Dietrich was offered the lead part in *Naughty Lola*, she asked her husband if he could see her playing a cheap whore. "Yes," he responded. They had often frequented transvestite bars and cabarets, the clientele of which served as inspiration in plan-ning her wardrobe: "We have to go drive around the streets and look for whores! Remember the one who always wore a garter belt with a white satin top hat? We have to find him—I want his panties!"

- Dietrich had a prudish side, too. She found the popular 1920s song "Makin' Whoopee" to be "just too vulgar for words."

- When Dietrich was told that Sigmund Freud had died of cancer, she said, "Good! All he did was talk about sex and got people all mixed up." When the Kinsey Report came out, she said, "Sex, sex, sex! What is it with people? Put it in, pull it out—this they have to study?"

- In April 1929 a Berlin tabloid reported that Dietrich was romantically involved with Greta Garbo.

- Sieber collected human organs. Around their house, in jars of formaldehyde, he proudly displayed a heart, a liver, a piece of brain, and half a kidney.

- She had a phobia about strange bathrooms. No matter where she went, she carried a bottle of surgical alcohol to make sure that "the filth that men have and then leave on toilet seats" was annihilated.

- While filming, Dietrich had her own personal full-length mirror positioned so that she could see whatever the camera saw.

- As a publicity stunt, the Paramount movie studio once insured her legs for $1 million.

- On April 26, 1932, Paramount announced that Dietrich had been put on suspension for refusing to obey contractual conditions and would be replaced in *Blonde Venus* by Tallulah Bankhead. Tallulah was quoted as saying, "I always did want to get into Dietrich's pants." Eventually the conflict was settled and Dietrich made the movie.

- According to her daughter, Dietrich bought Heinz white vinegar by the case, believing that a vinegar and ice-water douche regimen kept her invigorated and pregnancy free. Another thing that helped on the latter point was that Dietrich strongly preferred fellatio to intercourse.

• When she was sixty-four years old, Dietrich called her daughter, Maria, and asked her what a condom was. When Maria explained it to her, Dietrich replied, "Oh! *That* thing. That, I never let them use! So stupid, they have to fuss around in the dark with it. Anyway, it makes them nice and so grateful when you tell them they don't have to wear it."

• Dietrich believed that her hands and feet were unattractive. She went to great lengths to hide and camouflage them, and demanded that publicity photos be retouched to lengthen and smooth her fingers.

• When Maurice Chevalier died in 1972, Dietrich immediately took to drinking huge quantities of Contrexeville, a diuretic mineral water, saying, "He couldn't pee—that's why he died! I'm not going to die of that!"

• She owned a collection of exotic animal pelts that would be a conservationist's nightmare: leopard, tiger, cheetah, red fox, silver fox, gray fox, white fox, red-blond fox, beaver, nutria, seal, ermine, broadtail, chinchilla, zebra, snow leopard, mink, and silver-tipped sable.

• Dietrich and Ernest Hemingway were friends. She called him "Papa," and he called her "The Kraut."

• In one film she thought that she would look better if her eyes were dark, so she got drops from the eye doctor to dilate them. However, with her eyes dilated, she couldn't see her marks, or much of anything else.

• To get her look of high, well-defined cheekbones and narrow cheeks, Dietrich had all of her molars pulled out.

• Dietrich bought a farm in Austria as a European retreat from Hollywood. One year a cow was having a hard time giving birth. She ran into the house and grabbed a big bottle of Elizabeth Arden's blue grass facial oil and poured it into the heaving cow's behind. She and the caretaker took hold of the calf's front legs and pulled. Out plopped a very nice-smelling calf. Afterward, Dietrich ordered a case of the oil sent from New York for all future birthings.

● Immediately after World War II Dietrich flew to Germany to search through mounds of corpses at the Bergen-Belsen concentration camp, looking for her sister, whom she believed to be there. Her sister was found alive.

● When daughter Maria was going overseas to entertain the troups, Dietrich looked through her luggage and rushed her to the gynecologist's office. An hour later Maria was the owner of a half-dozen diaphragms. Asked her mom, "How did you imagine you could go overseas to entertain soldiers without one?"

● During the filming of *Golden Earrings*, Ray Milland was feeling queasy and desperately trying not to get sick to his stomach. Dietrich plunged her hand into a pot on the fire, pulled out a big juicy fish head, and sucked out its bulging eyes, sending Milland running for the bathroom.

● Dietrich and Yul Brynner had an affair for four years. For the affair Dietrich rented a hideaway on Park Avenue, furnished it in Siam silk and gold, and had her son-in-law install strip lights under the base of her king-size bed. Brynner couldn't take Dietrich's possessiveness and eventually walked out. Thirty-four years later, Dietrich sent her daughter a newspaper clipping of Brynner in a wheelchair, emerging from a cancer clinic. Across his haggard face she had written in a big silver marker, "Goody-goody—he has cancer! Serves him right!"

● Another of her men was Edward R. Murrow. She was annoyed that he smoked even while they were making love.

● She also reportedly had affairs with Harry Cohn, Michael Wilding, Adlai Stevenson, Sam Spiegel, Fritz Lang, Charles De Gaulle, Harold Arlen, Edith Piaf, and, she claimed, John F. Kennedy. But John Wayne turned her down, saying that he never wanted to be part of anybody's stable.

- Over the years she swallowed enormous amounts of cortisone as well as Butazolidin, phenobarbital, codeine, belladonna, Nembutal, Seconal, Librium, and Darvon. One of her doctors gave her "vitamin B shots," which made her feel so good that Dietrich convinced other family members to have the shots also. When her son-in-law had one of the shots, it took him three days to calm down. This doctor was later arrested for trafficking in amphetamines.

- In France she got dependent on a potent sleep suppository. Because the medication put her to sleep so quickly, she christened it with the name of the actor she considered the most boring man in Hollywood, Fernando Lamas.

- Sieber died in June 1976. Dietrich did not go to her husband's funeral, telling her friends that her daughter would not let her go.

- As her lovers and pals died, she would hang their framed pictures on her "death wall."

- Dietrich, knowing that the end was near, started making plans. She decided she wanted to be buried in a raincoat so that worms couldn't get through and devour her. And she asked that carnations be provided for her mourners—red for those who had slept with her, and white for those who claimed that they had slept with her but never had.

- When she died of cancer in 1992 she had so few tangible assets that her will was a one-page document.

Vincent van Gogh

Postimpressionist painter Vincent van Gogh did not become an artist until ten years before his death. He is today considered one of the founding fathers of modern painting.

- Vincent Willem van Gogh was born in the Netherlands on March 30, 1853, to Pastor Theodorus van Gogh and his wife, Anna Cornelia, the eldest of six surviving children. Exactly a year earlier to the day, his mother had given birth to a stillborn son who also had been given the name Vincent Willem. The baby was buried in a grave right next to the church door; going to church each Sunday, the future painter had to walk past a tiny tombstone with his own name and birthday on it. Vincent was an unusual child, solitary and unsociable, difficult and moody.

- There were several Vincent van Goghs in his family—besides his deceased older brother, he also had an uncle and eventually a nephew with that name.

- Vincent's namesake uncle, known to family members as "Uncle Cent," was a partner in Goupil & Cie, a French-based chain of art galleries. When Vincent was sixteen and old enough to work, Uncle Cent found him a job as a clerk at the company's gallery in The Hague. An excellent worker, Vincent transferred to the London branch four years later. That is where the trouble began.

• Van Gogh fell hopelessly in love with his new landlady's daughter, Ursula. After a year of mooning around, he told her of his love. Ursula turned him down, telling him she was already engaged. Van Gogh's already moody and temperamental nature grew significantly more so, and his performance on the job suffered. He obsessively began studying the Bible.

• Hoping a change would do some good, Uncle Cent had Vincent transferred to Goupil's Paris gallery. It didn't do much good. Vincent, displaying increasingly erratic behavior, was fired in April 1876, ending six years of training as an art dealer. Vincent wrote to Theo van Gogh, his brother and best friend, "When the apple is ripe, a soft breeze makes it fall from the tree; such was the case here. . . ."

• Van Gogh saw an ad for a teaching position at a school in the London slums that catered to the poor. He was accepted as the German and French master, even though he had no significant experience in either language and no training as a teacher. As part of his duties he collected tuition, which required that he visit some of the most desolate corners of London. Appalled by the conditions there, van Gogh decided to enter the ministry.

• He tried theological school, but couldn't see the point in learning subjects like Latin and Greek, when all he wanted to do was help the poor and suffering. He failed to win a post as a lay minister, so he went as an unsponsored volunteer to the rough coal-mining district of southern Belgium.

• Unfortunately, van Gogh was unsuited for even an unpaid position. He was a very poor public speaker, and his sermons— centered on the idea that sadness and suffering were more valuable than joy and happiness—failed to comfort his flock. He gave up washing and began wearing rough shirts made from packing sacks. In July 1879 the local church mission board, tired of his fanatic asceticism, asked him to leave. Van Gogh walked many miles to Brussels to talk with a pastor who encouraged him, with or without church support, to return to the mining district.

• The pastor wrote to van Gogh's family, "Vincent strikes me as somebody who stands in his own light." The family, in turn, sent Theo to convince Vincent to try shining his light in some other line of business. Instead, Vincent cut off contact with his family and friends for nine months, during which time he apparently went through some unexplained but terrible emotional crisis. Afterward, in a long letter to Theo, he wrote, "What molting time is for birds, so adversity or misfortune is the difficult time for us human beings. One can stay in it . . . one can also emerge renewed, but it must not be done in public and it is not at all amusing; therefore, the only thing to do is to hide oneself."

• Having gone into his crisis as a religious fanatic, van Gogh emerged from it full of anger against organized religion. He gave up his preaching and decided to become an artist. In August 1880, at age twenty-seven, he began to draw.

• Van Gogh's first "studio" was a small, cramped bedroom in a miner's cottage in Borinage, Belgium, which he shared with the miner's children.

• For the first four years of his brief, ten-year career, he concentrated on drawing. One reason was that he thought he wanted to be an illustrator. Another was that charcoal was much less expensive than paint. He was just scraping by, completely dependent on Theo's financial support.

• Eventually, van Gogh moved back in with his parents in the Netherlands. He continued his dreadful luck with women by falling in love with his widowed cousin Kee Vos. Her response to his romantic entreaties was, "No, at no time, never." He pursued her to Amsterdam. She refused to speak with him further; he held his hand in the flame of a lamp, insisting to her parents that he be allowed to speak to Vos for just the short time that he could stand the pain. They blew out the lamp and found van Gogh lodgings for the night.

• Thwarted in love, van Gogh moved in with a prostitute, Sien Hoomik, and her five children. He was diagnosed as having gonorrhea. (He would also come down with syphilis later in life.) At Theo's urging, he eventually moved out, leaving Hoomik with the only gift he had to offer: some painter's canvas from which she could make clothes for her children.

• From March 1886 through February 1888 Vincent lived with Theo in Paris. Vincent had a way of turning any place into a wreck, and he was not easy to get along with. Still, when their sister Wilhelmina suggested that he kick Vincent out, Theo (who had also been trained as an art dealer thanks to Uncle Cent) wrote back, "If he only had another profession, I would long ago have done what you advise me . . . but I think . . . I must continue in the same way. He is certainly an artist, and if what he makes now is not always beautiful, it will certainly be of use to him later; then his work will perhaps be sublime."

• Van Gogh was mostly self-taught, though he did try to take lessons occasionally. Because of style or temperament, neither his lessons nor his teachers ever lasted very long.

• At age thirty-one van Gogh joined a painting class at L'Académie d'Anvers. He painted quickly, applying so much color that paint slid off the canvas and splashed on the polished wooden floor. Instead of a regular palette, he used the top of a wooden sugar case. The academy director was horrified and sent van Gogh away from the class, saying, "I do not correct these rotten dogs. . . . Go as fast as you can to the drawing class!"

• Referring to what has become part of the unique, "signature" style of his painting—the thick impasto applied directly from the tube and then modeled with the brush—he wrote to Theo, "In a certain way I am glad that I have not learned painting, because then I might have learned to pass by such effects as this."

• To gain a deeper understanding of tones and color values, he took piano lessons from an old organist. Van Gogh believed that music was like painting, with notes expressing colors. He insisted on comparing the tones on the piano with specific colors so often that the teacher discontinued his lessons, fearing that he was dealing with a madman.

● Van Gogh also compared other things to musical tones, referring to the sun in Arles as a "high yellow note" and to the cypress trees in Provençal as "black notes."

● While Vincent was in Paris, Theo helped him meet other artists. One was the diminutive Henri de Toulouse-Lautrec, who later challenged to a duel someone who had insulted Vincent. Lautrec, like van Gogh, died at age thirty-seven after a short but brilliant career. Another artist friend was the impressionist Pissarro, whose understanding and compassion for Vincent was second only to saintlike Theo's. Years later, Pissarro said he'd known Vincent "would either go mad or leave all of us far behind. I didn't know then that he would do both."

● In 1888 van Gogh decided to head south for new surroundings. Before leaving his brother's house, he decorated the walls of his room with Japanese prints, and he left one of his unfinished paintings on an easel so that Theo would have the feeling he might return at any moment. Although his life was now much less complicated, Theo wrote Wilhelmina, "It seems strange to be without him. He meant so much to me."

● Van Gogh's plan had been to go to Marseilles, but he ended up at the little town of Arles instead. During the spring and summer of 1888 he developed a distinctive calligraphic drawing style using reed pens. The influence of Japanese art on his work was evident. With exquisite detail, he used pen strokes—hatched lines, dots, sinuous curlicues—in exactly the same way he later used color and brush strokes to define spaces and textures.

● Despite his skill at drawing, van Gogh stopped making preliminary under sketches on his canvas for paintings. He simply worked with colors. As infantry lieutenant P. Milliet (who took drawing lessons from van Gogh and modeled for one of his paintings) said later, "This fellow who had a great taste and talent for drawing became abnormal as soon as he touched a brush. . . . He painted too broadly, paid no attention to details, did not draw first. . . . He replaced drawing by colors."

● In Arles, van Gogh worked like a madman. Between his arrival in February and a mental collapse the following December, he made at least ninety drawings and one hundred paintings, including some of his most famous works, such as *Sunflowers, Starry Night on the Rhône*, and *Fishing Boats on the Beach at Saintes-Maries*.

● He loved to paint the stars and would often paint at night, putting candles in his hat for light to paint by.

● Van Gogh wanted to establish a colony of artists in Arles. He figured such a colony needed a strong leader, and he chose Paul Gauguin. After much reluctance on the elder painter's part, van Gogh persuaded Gauguin to move into his own little yellow house in Arles. The two men were temperamentally and stylistically unsuited to one another, and it didn't take long for Gauguin to announce that he was moving out.

● The famous night of the bloody ear actually occurred early in the morning of Christmas Eve 1888. Van Gogh caught up with Gauguin in the street and seemed about to do something violent to him with a razor. Gauguin stared him down. Van Gogh abruptly turned and rushed back to the house that he and Gauguin still shared uneasily.

● It was there that he cut off his earlobe. Despite popular legend, it was not his whole ear. He took the lobe and wrapped it up, presenting it to "Rachel," a favorite prostitute of a brothel that he and Gauguin both frequented. According to a brief newspaper article in the local paper, he told her, "Guard this object carefully." Later he wrote to Theo, "Yesterday I went to see the girl I had gone to when I was out of my wits. They told me there that in this country things like that are not out of the ordinary. She had been upset by it and had fainted but had recovered her calm."

● When Gauguin returned to the house, he was stopped by police who, from reports of the earlier events, believed van Gogh was dead. Instead, van Gogh was lying motionless in a fetal position on his bed. Gauguin, afraid of a repeat of the previous evening's activities, left, telling the police superintendent, "Be kind enough, Monsieur, to awaken this man with great care, and if he asks for me, tell him that I have left for Paris. The sight of me might prove fatal to him." Van Gogh was taken from his room to a hospital. This was his first severe attack of madness.

● He had three such attacks over the next four months. During the second, the people of Arles taunted him in the streets and threw stones at his house. Finally, persecuted beyond endurance, he began screaming at his tormentors. People in Arles petitioned to have him put away. Van Gogh was sent to a prisonlike lunatic asylum where he was not allowed to have his paints.

● Now that he's safely dead, of course, Arles treats van Gogh much better. There are various van Gogh exhibits and festivals, and in and around Arles today there are square stones that mark the spots from which he did his paintings.

● Although his madness consumed his time for most of the period from that Christmas Eve to mid-April 1889, he continued to be productive. On May 2 van Gogh sent two crates of masterpieces to Theo.

● Van Gogh requested admission to the asylum of Saint-Rémy-de-Provence. Theo wrote a letter asking that they let his brother leave the grounds of the asylum to paint, something they were, at first, reluctant to do. Vincent stayed in Saint-Rémy for a year, finding some comfort in meeting others who shared some of his problems. He had two rooms—one for sleeping, one for painting—and he finished an average of two canvases per day.

- He was very prolific, especially considering that he was out of his head much of the time. Of 850 paintings, over two-thirds—the paintings upon which van Gogh's considerable reputation as a painter is based—were painted from 1888 to 1890.

- Vincent painted more than forty self-portraits. Among the greatest painters, only Rembrandt produced more.

- He had four attacks of madness while at the asylum at Saint-Rémy. During one he tried to swallow his poisonous paints. He finally decided the asylum was not helping him. He began consulting with a doctor friend of Pissarro's, Dr. Paul-Ferdinand Gachet in Auvers-sur-Oise, who knew something of mental illness.

- Early in 1890, before van Gogh left Saint-Rémy for Auvers-sur-Oise, he received his first published review. Art critic Albert Aurier wrote a highly favorable article about van Gogh's work in an avant-garde publication, *Mercure de France*. Van Gogh was embarrassed by the article, feeling that he didn't deserve such praise. He asked Theo to tell Aurier not to write any more articles about him.

- About the same time he was told that one of his paintings, *The Red Vineyard*, had sold at public exhibition in Brussels to the painter Anna Boch. It was one of only two sales in his lifetime; the other was a self-portrait that Theo sold to Sulley & Lori, art dealers in London. Vincent immediately had another attack of madness: "As soon as I heard that my work was having some success, and read the article in question, I feared at once that I should be punished for it; this is how things nearly always go in a painter's life: success is about the worst thing that can happen."

- There has been much speculation about what it was, exactly, that van Gogh suffered from. Some speculate it was the advanced stage of venereal disease, or an obscure hereditary disorder, but no accurate records were ever made of his illness, so no accurate diagnosis is possible. Dutch psychiatrist Dr. G. Kraus concluded, "He was an individual in his illness, as well as in his art."

• On July 27, 1890, van Gogh took a gun along with his easel when he walked out into the cornfields he so often painted. Not far from the inn where he was staying, he stepped into a farmyard and shot himself in the abdomen. He staggered back to the inn. When the doctor told him he might live, van Gogh said, "Then I will have to do it all over again."

• After the shootings, van Gogh refused to reveal his brother's home address. The doctor sent a note to Theo's work address. When Theo read it the following morning, he rushed to the scene. "Do not cry," said Vincent to Theo. "I did it for the good of everybody." His last words were "I wish I could go home now."

• Van Gogh did not shoot himself in a fit of madness as some suggest. He was, in fact, very lucid at the time. So why did he kill himself? He may finally have been overcome by the guilt he felt at his brother's continual support of him, especially since, by then, Theo had a wife and new baby and was talking about leaving Goupil & Cie and striking out on his own. Vincent also feared that "a more violent attack may destroy forever my ability to paint."

• The two brothers had corresponded extensively and were so close that Theo himself eventually went mad from grief and died six months after Vincent's death. Theo was originally buried in Holland, but his wife later had him moved to Auvers. The brothers now lie side by side, and visitors to the graves traditionally leave yellow flowers.

• Tragically, much of van Gogh's work disappeared or was destroyed. Some paintings were sold as scrap canvas for pennies a bundle. Some were given to a junkman to peddle. Some were given as prizes to beer guzzlers. One was used to repair a hole in a wall. One whole collection of early work, stored in Antwerp in 1886, disappeared and has never been found.

• Van Gogh left some canvases behind when he went to Auvers from Saint-Rémy. Later, the son of the director of the asylum at

Saint-Rémy found the canvases. He and a friend used them for target practice.

• On some of his painting expeditions near Paris, van Gogh would take a single large canvas and divide it up into small rectangles, in which he would paint small studies. All of those canvases, each "a little museum," as one friend called them, have vanished.

Howard Hughes

Heir to a tool fortune, Howard Hughes dabbled in airplanes and the aura of Hollywood. He eventually became the victim of his own wealth and power, a paranoid, phobic, secretive recluse.

- Howard Hughes's father invented an oil-drilling tool bit, which became the foundation for Howard's vast fortune. His mother was an unstable heiress from Dallas. Howard was born on September 24, 1905; years later, though, he began claiming it was Christmas Eve 1905.

- As a child Hughes was delicate, reclusive, and inventive. He was also afflicted with otosclerosis, a hereditary, progressive deafness. In school he showed a marked preference for playing with girls and didn't show much interest in athletic activities. At age ten he was shipped off to Camp Dan Beard Outdoor School at Lake Teedyuskung, Pennsylvania. It was there, he said, he shed his "sissiness" and became proficient at "outdoorsy" activities like whittling, crafts, woodlore, and building huts out of two-by-fours.

- Hughes's fifteenth year was a busy one. He contracted mumps (which almost rendered him sterile), invented an electric motorcycle, began a lifelong love affair with flying, moved to Los Angeles, and was seduced by his uncle Rupert Hughes, a married, successful playwright and novelist.

• Hughes was unhappy about his homosexual leanings. Later in life he overcompensated for this with a domineering, "manly" personality and a voracious pursuit of women, often several at the same time.

• His mother had acute anxiety over germs and disease, and Hughes inherited that from her. He started getting eccentric about food, too. He ate so little roughage that he suffered from constipation all his life, spending so much time on the toilet that he sometimes conducted business meetings in the bathroom.

• Hughes's mother died suddenly in March 1923. His father died the following January. Only eighteen years old, Howard decided that he wanted to personally run Hughes Tool Company. He had already inherited half the company, and bought out the relatives who owned the other half. There was one problem: He could not run the business until he was an adult. Under Texas law, that was age twenty-one—a nineteen-year-old, however, could petition the courts to be declared an adult. To demonstrate his steadiness and maturity to the judge, and to calm nervous customers and suppliers, Hughes decided to marry as soon as possible. He chose a childhood schoolmate named Ella Rice (of the family that founded Rice University) for what, from the honeymoon on, was a miserable relationship of convenience. The ploy worked, however; when he petitioned the court after his 19th birthday, the judge declared him an adult.

• Hughes was described as neglectful, judgmental, and dispassionate as a lover. He preferred oral sex, performed by either men or women, over any other kind. He also enjoyed climaxing while thrusting between a woman's breasts rather than during vaginal intercourse. He seemed incapable of having a close, sharing relationship with anyone, although he came close a few times, most notably with Cary Grant (with whom he conducted an on-again, off-again affair for twenty years) and Katharine Hepburn.

• Having extra money and enjoying the lures of Hollywood, Hughes decided in 1926 to become a movie producer. He started toying with the idea of a movie about flying, which eventually became the 1930 classic *Hell's Angels*, which to this day is noted for its breathtaking aerial sequences. (They used no phony special effects for this movie: in one plane-crash stunt, a plane mechanic died when he couldn't bail out in time.) Hughes learned to fly while filming the movie.

• In 1928 Rice left Hughes for good and moved back to Texas, filing for a divorce, which was granted in December 1929. In 1926, while still married, Hughes had begun an affair with a very young Carole Lombard. In 1929 he broke off that relationship when he became obsessed with the actress Billie Dove. He bought Dove's acting contract from Jack Warner for $250,000 and a divorce from her husband for $325,000—astronomical amounts in those days.

• Hughes Tool's worth grew to $75 million by 1930, mostly due to the efforts of his right-hand man, Noah Dietrich, who convinced all the Arab countries and even the USSR to use the Hughes drill bit. Hughes was mostly interested in "planes, sex, and partying."

• During the mid-1930s Hughes decided to go adventuring in a different way. He hopped a freight train with one hundred dollars in his pocket and roamed all over America, traveling with the hobos. In Houston he was briefly detained for vagrancy. He enlisted as a baggage handler for American Airways under the name of Charles Howard, and went on to become a part-time pilot until he was found out and fired. He also advertised himself as Wayne R. Rector, successfully establishing himself as a society and child photographer, a ruse that he used on and off for years to meet and bed young mothers and others.

• Hughes began a longtime romance with Cary Grant, picking him up on the rebound from an affair with actor Randolph Scott. Scott had long before been one of Hughes's lovers; he abandoned Grant to marry Marian Du Pont, fabulously wealthy heiress to the Du Pont fortune.

- While visiting Grant on a movie set in 1935, Hughes met and became romantically involved with Katharine Hepburn. He liked the fact that she was angular and athletic, like him, and from an aristocratic background.

- In August 1937 Hepburn moved into Hughes's home in Los Angeles. While living with Hepburn, and having simultaneous affairs with Grant and Ginger Rogers, he conducted a short fling with Bette Davis. When Davis's hubby caught them in bed in February 1938, he insisted on a seventy thousand dollar payoff to keep his mouth shut. Hughes complied then and there, but Davis insisted on paying him back. The relationship with Hepburn eventually ended because she got exasperated with his odd behavior and got tired of shouting due to his deafness, but mostly because she "got very bored."

- Later that year, on September 12, 1935, Hughes broke the world airspeed record in Santa Ana, California, with his H-1 Hughes Racer. He was clocked at 352.46 mph.

- On January 13, 1936, Hughes took off from Los Angeles in a Northrop Gamma plane to break the transcontinental flying record of a little over ten hours. His radio antenna broke at takeoff, wiping out all air-to-ground contact, and his compass was damaged in turbulence over Wichita, forcing him to fly by maps and landmarks in the dark for the last twelve hundred miles. Still, he made it, breaking the record by flying coast to coast in nine hours and twenty-seven minutes.

- In June of the same year, he struck and killed a pedestrian with his car. He was charged with manslaughter but the case never went to court.

- On July 10, 1938, Hughes and a crew of five took off in an overloaded Lockheed 14 to try to beat the record time for a trip around the world. When he successfully landed in Moscow he was greeted by Russian aviators. To make him feel at home, they solemnly presented him with a box of Kellogg's Corn Flakes.

Hughes landed in New York again after only three days, nineteen hours, and eight minutes, beating the old record handily. The thousands of cheering fans waiting to greet him scared Hughes so much that he only managed to croak out five sentences in his soft nasal Texan voice before fleeing the airfield.

• While attending a subsequent party in his honor, he met and quickly became involved with the actress Fay Wray, who was married to Hughes's former stepcousin, John Monk Saunders. The affair so upset Saunders that he killed himself. Hughes quickly dropped Wray and pursued Olivia de Havilland. He also became involved with de Havilland's sister, Joan Fontaine, who went out with Hughes and then reported everything back to de Havilland. Both dumped him.

• Next, while carrying on with actress Gene Tierney and actor Tyrone Power, Hughes started wooing Lana Turner. However, Turner didn't like his idea of lovemaking, nor did she care for his near-total lack of personal hygiene.

• In 1940 Hughes had the idea of making a movie about Billy the Kid. This turned into *The Outlaw*, which took three years to get a theatrical release because of its off-color story line, bisexual undertones, and the raunchiness acted out by the luscious Jane Russell and her handsome costar Jack Buetel. Hughes never made a play for Russell, possibly because she was too over-powering and he knew he didn't have a chance; however, he happily bedded Buetel. *The Outlaw* was mainly a self-indulgent project for Hughes. He'd watch the day's rushes over and over throughout the night in his private screening room and during the day he'd insist on more close-up shots of the naughty portions of the stars' anatomy. He even went into his shop and invented a seamless bra for Russell, but it was too uncomfortable, so she just fixed one of her own and Hughes was never the wiser.

• A few people did resist Hughes, including Ava Gardner and Errol Flynn. He had more success with Linda Darnell, whom he chased and caught repeatedly from 1940 to 1946, even after her

1943 marriage. And although he didn't bed Gardner, they did maintain a platonic friendship for many years, and, when he thought she was having an affair, he jealously had her followed by his "Mormon bodyguards." (He hired Mormons because they didn't smoke or drink and they kept their mouths shut.)

● In 1945 he hooked up with Yvonne De Carlo, TV's future Lily Munster.

● Hughes bought TWA and treated it as his own private airline. He always kept seats available in case one of his friends had to go somewhere. Powerful movie gossips Hedda Hopper and Louella Parsons always flew for free.

● In 1948 Hughes bought a controlling interest in RKO Pictures. He was seeing actresses Jean Peters and Rita Hayworth. His fear of germs became more pronounced. He started using Kleenexes to handle anything that might be "contaminated." He also got very possessive. Hughes had Peters chaperoned everywhere, and had other women try on clothes for her so she wouldn't have to leave him to go shopping.

● Howard also managed to get Rita Hayworth pregnant. Unfortunately, Hayworth was just coming out of a rocky marriage to Orson Welles and was on pretty shaky mental ground. She let her studio boss, Harry Cohn, and Hughes (who loathed children) talk her into an abortion. She went to Paris and never saw Hughes again.

● Hughes, however, was already on the scent of fresh game with eighteen-year-old actress Terry Moore. A practicing Mormon, Moore managed to hang on to her virginity until Hughes arranged an offshore marriage by his yacht captain, Carl Flynn. Unbeknownst to Moore, however, was that Hughes had the yacht sail into international waters "so the marriage wouldn't be legal."

● In the early 1950s Hughes continued his active prowling. He was named as a co-respondent in a divorce case filed by a woman against her husband. Evidently, hubby was a mild-mannered businessman by day, but by night he dressed up and performed at Finocchio's, a drag nightclub in San Francisco, where he met Hughes and began an affair. The wife eventually accepted a settlement from Hughes to change her story.

• By 1952 his new company, Hughes Aircraft, was thriving. During World War II, it had been awarded $40 million from War Department contracts to develop and build Hercules flying boats and fast-flying XF-11 reconnaissance planes. The company made quite a bit of money, even though neither project was anywhere near completion by war's end.

• Hughes kept working on both despite the end of the war. He himself flew the prototype XF-11 on its maiden run over Los Angeles in 1948. It malfunctioned and he crashed into the side of a house in Beverly Hills. He was pulled out of the burning wreckage, nearly dead. In the hospital while recovering, he demanded higher and higher doses of morphine and codeine, beginning an addiction that would last the rest of his life.

• The Hercules was the huge wooden airplane dubbed the "Spruce Goose" by critics. In 1949 Hughes brought it out to Long Beach Harbor, where he taxied it on the water. It lifted off, flying for a mile at an altitude of seventy-five feet before Hughes set it back down again. It was the first and last time the Hercules flew. The plane disappeared into a warehouse and wasn't seen in public again until three decades later, after Hughes's death.

• A Congressional committee looked into the contracts that had been awarded Hughes Aircraft and decided that influence peddling and other irregularities had given Hughes an unfair advantage in getting them. If so, the corruption offered its own punishment—Hughes Aircraft had lost more than $7 million on the deal.

• Hughes was still seeing Terry Moore, Jean Peters, and another actress, Barbara Payton, but he also found the time to pursue Jean Simmons and Elizabeth Taylor, both young, beautiful, and busty. He bought Simmons's movie contract and used it as leverage against her, even though she was married to actor Stewart Granger at the time. Meanwhile, he tried to break up Elizabeth Taylor and her fiancé, Michael Wilding, by having Hedda Hopper attack Taylor for considering marriage to a gay man, which was ironic considering Hughes's proclivities. Actually, Wilding did have a relationship with playwright Noel Coward. Still, he had forsworn gay sex for years, and Taylor went ahead and married him anyway. Simmons, however, weakened under Hughes's onslaught and began meeting secretly with Hughes, yet wasn't physically unfaithful to Granger.

• In 1952 Moore became pregnant and delivered a premature baby after several miserable months of pregnancy. The baby girl only lived twelve hours. Hughes was secretly relieved because he still had no use for children.

• By 1954 Peters got fed up with Hughes and married Stuart Cramer III, a CIA operative. Hughes continued to dog her heels, in addition to "proposing" to Susan Hayward and lusting after Ava Gardner.

• In 1955 Hughes sold RKO. Moore became pregnant again and he agreed to "remarry" her. At this time Hughes was living in Las Vegas as a tax dodge. Moore's other lover, Nicky Hilton, tried to break up the couple by pointing out all the other women Hughes was dating there, including Mitzi Gaynor, Debra Paget, and Peters (her marriage to Cramer over by now). It worked, and Moore left with Hilton; she miscarried at three months. (Some years later Moore married Cramer.)

• Hughes finally convinced Peters that his miserable, lost soul needed her. Softhearted Peters married him on January 12, 1957, in Nevada. It wasn't until some time after the ceremony that Peters, who dreamed of having his babies, found out that Hughes had gotten a vasectomy in 1955 and hadn't bothered to tell her.

● Hughes and Peters moved into separate bungalows at the Beverly Hills Hotel. Hughes sank much more deeply into an abyss of paranoia and hypochondria. Even years earlier, while living with Hepburn, Hughes had guests use inexpensive plates and glasses, which he then had broken and discarded so as to not be exposed to their germs. Hughes became obsessive over, among other things, flies. He hired three Mormons to work in shifts around the clock, doing nothing but catching flies. (They weren't allowed to use swatters for fear of stirring up airborne germs.) Hughes stopped wearing clothes because they had germs and constricted him; he sat for hours at a time in his room wearing only a diaper of Kleenexes.

● In the fall of 1957 Vice President Richard Nixon reached out through contacts to Hughes for a "loan" for his financially troubled brother, Donald. The amount was $205,000 and Hughes approved it himself. In return, the Howard Hughes Medical Institute, a money-laundering and tax-avoidance scheme, was given tax-exempt status. Donald went broke anyway, and the whole episode got dredged up in 1960 during the Nixon-Kennedy race for the presidency, aiding in Nixon's defeat.

● Meanwhile back at Bungalow 4, Hughes grew even more strange. One example was the arrival of his magazines. His men would buy three copies of each issue and deliver them on a cart. Hughes would carefully remove the middle issue without touching the other two which were burned.

● Hughes began sleeping on a bed covered with Kleenexes. When Hughes had his bedsheets changed, which was rarely, they were burned instead of washed.

● Hughes refused to touch doorknobs. Instead, he would kick the door as a signal and his staff would open it.

● The bungalow stunk with human debris of every kind. He refused to let anyone use the toilet. At first, he would pee on the floor and then fling some Kleenexes down to soak up the urine.

Then he started to preserve his urine in mason jars, taking his collection with him whenever he traveled.

● During the 1950s and into the 1960s and 1970s, Hughes became closely associated with the CIA. He got huge contracts for supplying various espionage weapons and even leased an island in the Bahamas to the CIA for use in secret operations against Cuba.

● By the mid 1960s Hughes bought and settled into the Desert Inn in Las Vegas. He had sold TWA, and with the proceeds had decided to buy up as much of Las Vegas as possible. In 1967 he bought the Sands Hotel, in part because he wanted the property, and in part to lord it over Frank Sinatra, of whom he was jealous because of Sinatra's relationship with Ava Gardner. Hughes ended up owning a large chunk of Las Vegas, including a CBS affiliate TV station, which he bought in part to make sure they programmed plenty of old movies to watch all night long.

● Hughes's food habits continued to become more odd. He liked Campbell's chicken noodle soup but carefully inspected the contents of each can, rejecting any that had a hint of dark meat.

● He became obsessed with banana nut ice cream from Baskin-Robbins. However, banana nut became a discontinued flavor. Hughes had an assistant contact the ice cream company, and ordered three hundred gallons, the minimum required for a special order. Oddly, when the precious cargo got to Hughes at the Desert Inn, he'd lost interest. The ice cream was given out as a bonus to the employees.

● In 1968 a new fear overcame Hughes—nuclear testing. Fifteen years earlier he'd produced a movie, *The Conqueror*. Parts of it had been filmed at a location where testing had been conducted. Since then, several crew members and stars were stricken with cancer, including John Wayne, Susan Hayward, and Agnes Moorehead. Nuclear testing was scheduled to resume in Nevada, and Hughes literally feared for his life.

● The 1968 presidential election was fast approaching and Hughes wanted to back a candidate who'd stop the testing. It definitely was not Richard Nixon who otherwise would have been his natural choice. Hughes opted to support Hubert Humphrey, sending him a contribution of one hundred thousand dollars, well over the five thousand dollar legal limit. Nixon got wind of this and became incensed that he didn't get the same amount. Hughes complied, asking Governor Paul Laxalt of Nevada to make the drop-off, and demanding a receipt.

● In 1970 Peters, fed up with Hughes's odd behavior, announced her intention to divorce him. Because of his drug addictions, his kidneys were beginning to fail. Hughes continued storing his urine to prevent the possibility of anyone analyzing it and learning something was wrong.

● In October 1970 Hughes embarked on a series of joint ventures with the CIA. One, Operation Jennifer, was a plan to have the Glomar II (a Hughes vessel) explore the ocean floor a couple hundred miles southwest of Hawaii, supposedly looking for gold. In actuality its purpose was to investigate a sunken Russian nuclear submarine that contained cipher machines. These machines could translate a vast collection of intercepted transmissions that the CIA had stored.

● Appropriately, Hughes died aboard an airplane, en route to a medical facility in Houston on April 5, 1976. He had been in a coma for two days and died without ever coming out of it. The cause of death was reported as acute kidney failure, combined with dehydration. Cancer was found in the prostate gland and in the scalp but never reported.

● AIDS was not well understood or diagnosed at the time, but it's believed by experts and close Hughes associates that he might have died from it. At the end of his life, he became blind, was delusional and lucid by turns, and withered down to ninety-three pounds even though he consumed two thousand calories a day.

He also had recurring bouts of pneumonia, tumors, and loss of muscle tone.

● His estate was worth $650 million and thirty separate wills were filed, all staking claim to the vast fortune. Claimants ranged from a man who said he lived in a flying saucer and alleged he was Hughes's illegitimate son to a man who supposedly had a chance encounter with Hughes on a deserted stretch of highway in Nevada in 1968.

● Hughes Aircraft was bought by General Motors, and the Hughes Tool Company was renamed the Summa Corporation in 1972. In 1980 the estate was divided between Hughes's aunt Annette Lummis, her son William, and a host of eighteen cousins and lesser relatives.

Selected References

A History of England, by Goldwin Smith. New York: Charles Scribner's Sons, 1966.

Abbie Hoffman—American Rebel, by Marty Jezer. New Brunswick: Rutgers University Press, 1992.

Agatha Christie: The Woman and Her Mysteries, by Gillian Gill. Macmillan Inc., 1990.

Albert Einstein: A Photographic Biography, by Kenjii Sugimoto, translated by Barbara Harshaw. New York: Schocken Books, 1989.

Albert Einstein: The Human Side, edited by Helen Dukas & Banesh Hoffman. Princeton: Princeton University Press, 1979.

An Autobiography, by Agatha Christie. Dodd Mead and Co., 1977.

Around the World on Hot Air and Two Wheels, by Malcolm S. Forbes. New York: Simon & Schuster, 1985.

Behind the Candelabra—My Life with Liberace, by Scott Thorson with Alex Thorleifson. New York: E. P. Dutton, 1988.

Bernard Shaw, by Michael Holroyd. 4 Vols. New York: Random House, 1988–93.

Bernard Shaw, by Pat M. Carr. Frederick Ungar Publishing Co., 1976.

Buried Alive, by Myra Friedman. New York: William Morrow, 1973.

Churchill, A Life, by Martin Gilbert. New York: Henry Holt & Co., 1991.

Disney's World, by Leonard Mosley. Stein and Day Publishers, 1985.

Edison—A Biography, by Matthew Josephson. New York: Mc-Graw-Hill, 1959.

Einstein: Profile of the Man, by Peter Michelmore. Dodd, Mead & Co., 1962.

George Bernard Shaw, by G. K. Chesterton. New York: Hill and Wang, Inc., 1956.

Gertrude Stein on Picasso, edited by Edward Burns. Liveright Publishing, 1970.

Going Down With Janis, by Peggy Caserta as told to Dan Knapp. New York: Dell, 1973.

Henry Ford and Grass-Roots America, by Reynold M. Wik. Ann Arbor: The University of Michigan Press, 1972.

Hitch, by John Russell Taylor. New York: Pantheon Books, 1978.

Hitler: The Pictorial Documentary of His Life, by John Toland. New York: Ballantine Books, 1978.

Houdini: His Life and Art, by The Amazing Randi and Bert R. Sugar. New York: Grossett and Dunlap, 1976.

Houdini: The Man Who Walked Through Walls, by William L. Gresham. Austin: Holt, Rinehart and Winston, 1959.

Houdini: The Untold Story, by Milbourne Christopher. Thomas Y. Crowell Co., 1969.

Howard Hughes: The Secret Life, by Charles Higham. New York: Berkley Books, 1993.

How They Became the Beatles, by Gareth L. Pawlowski. New York: E. P. Dutton, 1989.

James Dean: Little Boy Lost, by Joe Hyams. New York: Warner Books, 1992.

J. Edgar Hoover: The Man and the Secrets, by Curt Gentry. New York: W. W. Norton & Co., 1991.

Joe and Marilyn—A Memory of Love, by Roger Kahn. New York: William Morrow & Company, Inc., 1986.

John Lennon, by Richard Wootton. New York: Random House, 1985.

Judy, by Gerold Frank. New York: Harper & Row, 1975.

Judy Garland: The Secret Life of an American Legend, by David Shipman. Hyperion, 1993.

Judy: The Films and Career of Judy Garland, by Joe Morella and Edward Epstein. The Citadel Press, 1969.

Legend of Henry Ford, by Keith Sward. Austin: Rinehart, 1948.

Life in the Third Reich, by Richard Bessel. New York: Oxford University Press, 1987.

Lindbergh: A Biography, by Leonard Mosley. New York: Doubleday, 1976.

Lindbergh: The Crime, by Noel Behn. New York: The Atlantic Monthly Press, 1994.

Madame Curie, by Eve Curie, translated by Vincent Sheean. New York: Doubleday, 1939.

Malcolm Forbes: The Man Who Had Everything, by Christopher Winans. New York: St. Martin's Press, 1990.

Man About Town: Frank Lloyd Wright in New York City, by Herbert Muschamp. Cambridge: The MIT Press, 1983.

Many Masks: A Life of Frank Lloyd Wright, by Brendan Gill. New York: G. P. Putnam and Sons, 1987.

Marie Curie: A Life, by Francoise Giroud, translated by Lydia Davis. Holmes & Meier, 1986.

Marie Curie, by Mollie Keller. New York: Franklin Watts, 1982.

Marilyn Monroe—The Biography, by Donald Spoto. New York: HarperCollins, 1993.

Marlene Dietrich, by Maria Riva. New York: Alfred A. Knopf, Inc., 1993.

Matchless Model A, by Dan R. Post. Post Motor Books, 1961.

Michael Jackson, by Gordon Matthews. New York: Wanderer Books, 1984.

Michael Jackson: The Magic and the Madness, by J. Randy Taraborrelli. New York: Ballantine Books, 1991.

Mr. G. B. Shaw: A Sketch (Strictly Unauthorised), by A. P. Crouch. Folcroft Library Editions, 1975.

Muhammad Ali—His Life and Times, by Thomas Hauser. New York: Simon & Schuster, 1991.

Official and Confidential: The Secret Life of J. Edgar Hoover, by Anthony Summers. New York: G. P. Putnam's Sons, 1993.

Oscar Wilde, by Katharine Worth. New York: Grove Press, 1984.

Oscar Wilde, by Frank Harris. New York: Dorset Press, 1989.

Oscar Wilde, by Richard Ellman. New York: Alfred A. Knopf, Inc., 1987.

Patton: Ordeal and Triumph, by Ladislas Farago. Ivan Obolensky, Inc., 1963.

Patton: The Man Behind the Legend, 1885–1945, by Martin Blumenson. 1985.

Paul McCartney: Behind the Myth, by Ross Benson. Victor Gollancz Ltd., 1992.

Pearl—The Obsessions and Passions of Janis Joplin, by Ellis Amburn. New York: Warner Books, 1992.

Picasso: His Life and Work, by Roland Penrose. Berkeley: University of California Press, 1981.

Queen Victoria, by Cecil Woodham-Smith. New York: Alfred A. Knopf, Inc., 1972.

Queen Victoria—Born to Succeed, by Elizabeth Longford. Harper and Row, 1964.

Richard Milhous Nixon: The Rise of an American Politician, by Roger Morris. New York: Henry Holt & Co., 1990.

Richard Nixon—The Shaping of His Character, by Fawn M. Brodie. New York: W. W. Norton & Co., 1981.

Secrecy and Power: The Life of J. Edgar Hoover, by Richard Grid Powers. New York: The Free Press, 1987.

Selected Letters of Oscar Wilde, by Rupert Hart-Davis. New York: Oxford University Press, 1979.

Shaw: George versus Bernard, by J. P. Hackett. Foxcroft Press, Inc., 1937.

Talk on the Wilde Side, by Ed Cohen. New York: Routledge, 1993.

The Alfred Hitchcock Album, by Michael Haley. Prentice-Hall, Inc., 1981.

The Art & Music of John Lennon, by John Robertson. New York: Birch Lane Press, 1990.

The Dark Side of Genius: The Life of Alfred Hitchcock, by Donald Spoto. New York: Ballantine Books, 1983.

The Death of James Dean, by Warren Beath. New York: Grove Press, 1986.

The Disney Version, by Richard Schickel. New York: Simon & Schuster, 1968.

The Drawings of van Gogh, by Nicholas Wadley. Paul Hamlyn, 1969.

The Importance of Being Constance, by Joyce Bentley. Beaufort Books, 1983.

The Intimate Sex Lives of Famous People, by Irving Wallace, Amy Wallace, David Wallechinsky, and Sylvia Wallace. New York: Delacorte Press, 1981.

The Life and Death of Adolf Hitler, by Robert Payne. Praeger Publishers, 1973.

The Master Builders, by Peter Blake. New York: Alfred A. Knopf, Inc., 1960.

The Mind of Adolf Hitler: The Secret Wartime Report, by Walter C. Langer. New York: Basic Books, 1972.

The Private Lives of Winston Churchill, by John Pearson. New York: Simon & Schuster, 1991.

The Rock Revolution, by Arnold Shaw. Crowell-Collier, 1969.

The World of Picasso, by Lael Wertenbaker and the editors of Time-Life Books. Time-Life Books, 1967.

The World of van Gogh, by Robert Wallace. New York: Time-Life Books, 1969.

They All Laughed, by Ira Flatow. New York: HarperCollins, 1992.

Trading with the Enemy, by Charles Higham. New York: Delacorte Press, 1980.

Understanding Picasso, by Domenico Porzio and Marco Valsecchi. New York: Newsweek Books, 1974.

Valentino—The Love God, by Noel Botham and Peter Donnelly. New York: Ace Books, 1976.

Victoria, by Stanley Weintraub. New York: E. P. Dutton, 1988.

Vincent van Gogh, by Marc Edo Tralbaut. New York: Viking, 1969.

Virginia Woolf, by James King. New York: W. W. Norton, 1995.

Virginia Woolf: A Biography, by Quentin Bell. New York: Harcourt Brace Jovanovich, 1972.

Virginia Woolf: The Impact of Childhood Sexual Abuse on Her and Work, by Louise DeSalvo. New York: Ballantine, 199

Walt Disney: An American Original, by Bob Thomas. New York: Simon & Schuster, 1976.

Walt Disney: Hollywood's Dark Prince, by Marc Eliot. New York: Carol Publishing Group, 1993.

W. C. Fields by Himself: His Intended Autobiography, by W. C. Fields, with commentary by Ronald J. Fields, 1973.

Winston S. Churchill, Vol. 1, Youth, 1874–1900, by Randolph Churchill. Boston: Houghton Mifflin Company, 1966.